THE ART OF PREACHING

The Art of Preaching

A Theological and Practical Primer

Daniel Cardó

Foreword by Timothy Gallagher, OMV

The Catholic University of America Press
Washington, D.C.

The paper used in this publication
meets the minimum requirements of
American National Standards for Information Science—
Permanence of Paper for Printed Library Materials, ANSI Z39.48-1984

Names: Cardó, Daniel, author
Title: The art of preaching: a theological and practical primer
Daniel Cardó; foreword by Timothy M. Gallagher, OMV

Description: Washington, D.C. : The Catholic University of America Press, [2021] | Includes
bibliographical references and index. | Summary: "The Art of Preaching: A Theological
and Practical Primer explores the theological understanding of the homily, lessons from
classical and contemporary rhetoric, the relevance of preaching for the life of the Church,
highlighting recent teachings of the Magisterium, and it presents the incarnation as the
foundation for preaching, understood as an essential aspect of the priestly life and mission. This primer offers a simple and effective method for the preparation and delivery
of homilies. The book also provides a selection of homilies from the great preachers of
the Church, organized chronologically, with brief introductions and commentaries that
highlight what those homilies teach us for preaching today" —Provided by publisher.

Identifiers: LCCN 2021023392 (print) | LCCN 2021023393 (ebook)
ISBN 9780813234731 (paperback) | ISBN 9780813234748 (ebook)

Subjects: LCSH: Catholic preaching. | Catholic Church–Sermons

Classification: LCC BX1795.P72 C364 2021 (print) | LCC BX1795.P72 (ebook
DDC 251/.01—dc23 LC record available at https://lccn.loc.gov/2021023392
LC ebook record available at https://lccn.loc.gov/2021023393

Printed in the United States

Book design by Burt&Burt
Interior set with Minion Pro and Meta Pro

To my parishioners
at Holy Name Parish

and

to my students
at
Saint John Vianney Seminary

For if I preach the Gospel,
that gives me no ground for boasting.
For necessity is laid upon me.
Woe to me if I do not preach the Gospel!
(1 Cor 9:16)

But where does your delight spring from?
Surely from a night that has
become radiant with light
because Christ the Lord
is preached to us?
(St. Augustine of Hippo)

Contents

Foreword

Early in my priesthood, I met a Redemptorist priest who was professor of homiletics at a major seminary. I wanted to learn from him and asked to accompany him on a parish mission he was scheduled to give.

I had never seen anything like it. The church was packed, nave, vestibule, and choir loft. Chairs were even placed in the central aisle to accommodate as many as possible. For the same reason, children were invited to sit on the floor near the pulpit. His message was simple, clear, and Christ-centered, interspersed with warm humor, anecdotes, and quotations. We were willing to listen as long as this priest would speak, wanting him to continue.

One day during the mission, he showed me how he prepared. He had with him files of material gathered from books, newspapers, journals, and films. References to works of art, classic texts, lives of saints and their writings, figures of history, and similar were also included, all of this sorted alphabetically by topic. He told me that daily, as he observed, listened, and read, he added to these files. When he preached, abundant material of a kind impossible to improvise was at hand to illustrate his points.

As a seminarian and later as a priest, I listened repeatedly to the talks of Venerable Fulton Sheen. Like so many, I found his preaching fascinating. As I listened, I asked myself: Why is this so attractive? Why is this so engaging? Why do I want to listen? From him, I learned much about winning interest from the first sentence, establishing contact with the listeners, and the use of stories and quotations. Above all, I understood that good preaching requires serious preparation.

In 1989, I watched on television as St. John Paul II preached during the concluding Mass of World Youth Day. 600,000 young people listened as the pope spoke. In that homily, he cited the words of Jesus that formed the theme of the event: "I am the way and the truth and the life" (Jn 14:6). With that rich, deep, and powerful voice that characterized his preaching, and from his heart, he pronounced Jesus's words, "I am the way!" Spontaneously, a prolonged applause arose from his 600,000 listeners. "And the truth!" Again, prolonged applause. "And the life!" Once again, applause.

Like these young people, I was deeply moved. Later, I thought about this and asked myself why. Like his listeners, I had heard these words many times. But these familiar words, said by this man and in this way, acquired power, meaning, and a thrill of freshness. They inspired the heart. They awakened new energy. I understood that we cannot speak in this way unless our words are born of prayer, communion with and love for Jesus. I knew that in John Paul II such prayer and such love were a living reality.

If you are reading this, you are most likely a seminarian preparing to preach or a priest who does preach. You want to preach well and with fruit. You want to be effective as a preacher.

You have before you a book that will help you attain this end. You will find it impossible to read this book and settle for mediocrity in preaching. It will reveal afresh to you the nature and importance of preaching. In it, you will learn from classic sources, the best of a long tradition, what helps to foster good preaching. You will hear, as the author expresses it, "from the pews" what people desire when you preach. You will deepen your grasp of how to prepare for your homily—no small thing. You will encounter wise counsel on how to deliver your homily—mistakes to avoid and approaches that assist.

Read the foundational Part I attentively. It is not long. It is well written. The author's competence is evident in every page. It covers the key issues well.

A thoughtful and, if possible, shared reading and discussion of Part II—fourteen examples of effective homilies by great figures in the Church's tradition—will enflesh the content of Part I. As Father Cardó writes, "Familiarity with the best makes us better." Attentive and prayerful reading of these homilies and reflection on the questions provided will consolidate the teaching of the first part. You will feel yourself equipped to preach well.

A woman once told me of a priest, the pastor of her parish, whose preaching blessed her life. She said, "When he says Mass and preaches, I feel as though he opens for me the way to Jesus. I feel that Jesus is present to me and that I can meet him." May the same be said of your preaching. This book will help you reach that goal.

Timothy M. Gallagher, OMV

Author of *The Discernment of Spirits: An Ignatian Guide for Everyday Living* (Crossroad 2005); St. Ignatius Chair for Spiritual Formation at Saint John Vianney Theological Seminary (Denver); Faculty of Institute for Priestly Formation, Omaha, Nebraska

Acknowledgments

I would like to say a word of gratitude to all those who have been part of the creation of this book. To the many preachers who have inspired me and who might never read these pages: I offer you my grateful prayers. To my parishioners at Holy Name, who have patiently heard my homilies for more than eleven years: your kindness and openness have moved me to care more and more about preaching. And to my students at Saint John Vianney Seminary in Denver: our many conversations about homiletics have given me more insights than any book.

I also thank those who have helped me in the preparation and editing of this work: Angie Woods, Geraldine Kelley, and especially Kathleen Blum. Your generosity and intelligence have made this book so much better. I give thanks to the Lord for having blessed me with talented and kind friends.

I am grateful as well to Fr. Sergio Tapia and Fr. Eric Zegeer for their suggestions, and to Fr. Daniel Leonard, rector of Saint John Vianney Seminary, for his constant support for my research. Finally, I express my gratitude to John Martino at CUA Press, for his interest for and commitment to this project. I trust and pray that the generosity of so many people will be rewarded a hundredfold.

The Art of Preaching

Introduction: Why Preach?

We live in increasingly difficult times. In the context of global crises of unprecedented impact and growing distrust of tradition, institutions, and one another, the confusion and polarization within the Church weigh heavily on the shoulders of good people who just want to know how to follow Jesus Christ today. The scandals that have rocked the barque of Peter in recent years bring further disorientation along with an understandable disappointment at what appears as a lack of leadership. An aggressive secularism continues to penetrate the institutions of our society and the minds of the new generations, insinuating that what was sacred a few years ago is purely a matter of personal preference today. We witness the failure of many of our ecclesial methods and comfortable systems; the status quo is collapsing. When we realize that less than ten percent of millennials raised in the Catholic Church still practice their faith, the likely bleakness of the next decades fills us with real uncertainty. What can we do?

There is no program that can fix the problem. These are times to go to the roots of our faith and cling to Jesus Christ, "the Way, the Truth, and the Life" (Jn 14:16), who says to his weary followers, "come to me, and I will give you rest" (Mt 11:16). Here we come to a decisive point: most Catholics do not know how to "do" this. The majority of baptized Catholics do not necessarily experience communion with Christ as a personal reality—that is, one that is embraced in the integrity of their humanity as friendship with and discipleship to a divine person. Most Catholics have learned things about God; many try to live according to his teaching; few have learned to know him.

Wonderful ministries and movements designed to help people know God better are bearing real fruit in the Church. But still, most Catholics do not and probably will not attend events, talks, bible studies, or prayer groups. Very few will read books about the faith. Most will not even make use of some of the cutting-edge technological resources that offer creative and necessary contributions to the Church today. While we must promote these outstanding initiatives, we should also realize that most Catholics who practice their faith will attend one "event," and one event only: Sunday Mass.

This is, indeed, the crucial thing. The sacred liturgy, with the Eucharist at its core, is the source and summit of the life and mission of the Church.[1] There we find the life, strength, hope, and grace we need to persevere amid difficulties, to know and love God, to love and serve our neighbor, and to proclaim the good news in a renewed way in today's world. There we become disciples and, thus, apostles of Jesus Christ.

The renewal of the liturgy is at the core of the renewal of the Church. The renewal of the liturgy in each parish is at the core of the renewal of each parish. There is nothing more important and more urgent from a theological standpoint; but it is also important from a practical perspective, as most Catholics will experience the life of the Church only at Mass. This means that though they may not read the books or watch the programs, they will hear every week, with at least some openness and benevolence, a preacher delivering a homily.

In fact, for better or for worse, few things are expected with greater interest at any given Sunday Mass than the homily. While this may signal an inadequate understanding of the richness of the mysteries being celebrated, it is certainly a reflection of the importance of the homily as a privileged means of sacred communication. There is a growing awareness of its importance at the level of the simple faith of believers, at a more "technical-theological" level, and also—as we will see—at the level of the Magisterium of the Church.

We must therefore consider the potential force and reach of the homily. A practical reflection will be helpful here. On a typical Sunday, there will be around fifteen million Catholics going to Mass in the United States.[2] On any given weekend there are some seventy thousand homilies preached in this country. It is hard to imagine any other institution offering so many live

---

[1] See *Sacrosanctum Concilium*, 10; and *Lumen Gentium*, 11, in Marianne Lorraine Trouve, ed., *The Sixteen Documents of Vatican II* (Boston: Pauline Books & Media, 1999).

[2] On the decline of Mass attendance see Stephen Bullivant, *Mass Exodus: Catholic Disaffiliation in Britain and America since Vatican II* (Oxford: Oxford University Press, 2019), 223–52.

speeches on the same topic every week in front of so many people. Humanly speaking, the opportunity is optimal. What happens in those thousands of homilies? What do those more than fifteen million Catholics hear? How moved are they by those words?

A few years ago, in the face of the importance of voting down a law that would promote some specific actions contrary to the teachings of Christ, a bishop asked his priests to preach on the topic for three consecutive Sundays. The resources offered to the preachers to prepare their homilies were clear about avoiding politics, and instead talking about the issue at stake in light of God's Word. More committed parishioners did not find the issue a complicated one: anyone familiar with basic Catholic teaching about life and family would know what to do, or so they thought. Probably most priests held a similar view. In most of the parishes throughout this diocese the petition of the bishop was observed: preachers addressed the topic over one thousand times in front of audiences of hundreds of people. What other institution has that kind of reach, that amazing possibility of speaking directly, face to face, about real-life issues? Surely the law would not pass.

That law passed by more than 70 per cent. Statistically, most Catholics probably voted in favor.[3] The more than one thousand homilies did not cause any significant change in the general trend. We failed. Of course, there were many complicated reasons for this, but it is safe—and honest—to say that those homilies were not effective. It was not just a missed opportunity; it was a sign of a deeper problem. How could God's people come, week in and week out, and hear their priests preach, but not heed their call to action on a specific matter dear to the Church's social concern? Perhaps because they had developed a habit of listening that St. Augustine described centuries ago: "An audience can be taught and delighted, and still not give their full assent to the speaker. And what use will those two be if this third thing is lacking?"[4] In this modern-day case, the bishop and priests of that diocese were able to see how unaccustomed most Catholics are to giving their assent to what is preached.

Of course, every Catholic is free to accept or resist God's Word, and when the credibility of the Church overall is in question, it is more difficult

---

3 On the differing views of most Catholics in regard to faith and morals, see important data in Michele Dillon, *Postsecular Catholicism: Relevance and Renewal* (Oxford: Oxford University Press, 2018), 23.

4 Augustine, *Teaching Christianity: De Doctrina Christiana*, trans. Edmund Hill, OP (Hyde Park, N.Y.: New City Press, 1996), IV.12.28.

to call upon her authority. But those of us who give homilies can still examine ourselves: How do we preach? How powerful is our word? Does anything change in the minds and hearts of the millions of weekly listeners? We read in the Acts of the Apostles that after Peter's preaching at Pentecost some three thousand people "received his word and were baptized" (Acts 2:41). Even if we tried to scrutinize this number and be more conservative, we can at least say that a very large number of people changed their lives after hearing the words of the apostle. Should we not try to make our own homilies similarly effective?

We should. Our people need preachers who do what Peter did. They need the preaching of bishops, priests, and deacons to be courageous, faithful, spiritual, engaging, deep, moving, serious, and not dumbed down for the supposedly incapable average listener. The example of Peter, an unschooled fisherman, should give us hope that extraordinary personal talent is not the key, but rather a knowledge of the Lord's ways through the history of salvation and in our own lives, both of which center on Christ. Peter did not aim at getting his listeners to try a little better to be nice to people—he aimed at conversion of hearts. What might not a couple of decades of Christ-centered preaching achieve? Might it not foment a true revolution that would change the reality not only of the Church but also of society? Catholics would know more about their faith but especially would know Jesus more personally and, bearing fruits, become his disciples more and more (see Jn 15:8).

Holiness is fostered by a good word said at the right time, in the right way; a moving word matured in daily prayer and study, in the joys and sorrows of pastoral life; in patient meditation, purified and improved by countless conversations and visits to parishioners, illuminated by the many psalms recited every day, confronted by the pains shared with those who suffer, formed by the words of the liturgy. Holiness is encouraged by priests who, though imperfect themselves, want to be saints, and who honestly, vulnerably, freely, and passionately share that desire in their homilies.

The first task of the priest seeking to reach God's people is thus to foster his own holiness, to know the Lord and his mercy himself, for "out of the abundance of the heart the mouth speaks," (Mt 12:34) and "apart from me you can do nothing" (Jn 15:5). Yet the preparation of a homily itself is also a vehicle for spiritual growth for the priest, in striving for effectiveness and spiritual insight. We can always be considering ways to improve the preparation and delivery of those homilies, seeking for better resources and tools, and searching for better words and greater eloquence, so that, with flexible faithfulness, the truth of the Gospel and the honest longings for goodness can be communicated afresh in the best possible way, according to the many different kinds of people, situations, and contexts.

It can seem that the people of God are drifting further from our Lord every day, and indeed the statistics say so. In this context, we must resist the temptations of impatience and of seeking success in numbers. Rather, as then-Cardinal Ratzinger said, the courage needed today for the new evangelization "means to dare again with the humility of the small grain, leaving up to God the when and how it will grow (Mk 4:26–29) ... the new evangelization must submit to the mystery of the grain of mustard seed."[5] Preaching in this time of new evangelization means the same: humility, trust, and courage. The fruits, as always, are in God's hands. And while we cannot foresee the details of tomorrow, we know that for those who love God and are called according to his purpose (Rom 8:28) the future is still promising, full of hope.

This new spring for the Church does not start with megaplans, expensive studies, big staffs, or the latest creative programs. This revolution comes from who we are as the Church of Christ. The source and summit of our life is the sacred liturgy, with the Eucharist at its heart. And there, in that river of grace, the words of good homilies will make a difference. Catholics will know Jesus Christ more deeply; more Mass attenders will be disciples; more disciples will be apostles. And this will change the world.

This revolution is realistic and simple. The springtime that we need will come from an unpretentious movement: to love Christ, and to know how to speak about him. This book hopes to offer a contribution for that future.

CONTRIBUTION

My aim has not been to write a scholarly manual for the academic discussion of the discipline of homiletics, but rather a book for anyone who wants to learn more about the art of preaching.[6] In particular, this book can be helpful for the teaching of homiletics in seminaries, as a tool for professors

---

5 Joseph Cardinal Ratzinger, *Address to Catechists and Religion Teachers Jubilee of Catechists*, December 12, 2000. Original Italian version found in: https://www.vatican.va/roman_curia/congregations/cfaith/documents/rc_con_cfaith_doc_20001210_jubilcatechists-ratzinger_it.html (my translation).

6 Two examples of the former kind of handbook are *A Handbook for Catholic Preaching*, ed. Edward Foley (Collegeville, Minn.: Liturgical Press, 2016), and *The New Interpreter's Handbook of Preaching*, ed. Paul Scott Wilson (Nashville, Tenn.: Abingdon Press, 2008).

and students alike, who will find in these pages reflections on the *what* and *how* of preaching.

For a few years I have grown in the awareness of the need for a simple yet profound resource written for the classroom. Starting from the experience of preaching and teaching how to preach (and, I must add, of hearing homilies) I have spent some years thinking, studying, praying, and talking with people about the kind of contribution that can be more beneficial for the Church here and now. This book is the fruit of this time of reflection and work. It is presented as a primer—that is to say, a place from which to start—that combines in one volume the necessary theological and academic foundations for preaching with practical indications and suggestions for those learning to preach—and, hopefully, also for those who would like to find renewal in their own preaching ministry. Therefore, some chapters will contain theological reflections; others, summaries of foundational teachings about homiletics; others, spiritual insights into the challenges of preaching; and others, finally, very practical advice and tools for the preparation and delivery of the homily. While much more could be said about any of these topics, and the preacher can always be looking for new resources with different emphases, I think it is important to hold together these different aspects of the art of preaching.

HOW TO USE THIS BOOK

This primer can be used in a number of ways. I have had in mind particularly the possibility of having it as a resource throughout one or two semesters of homiletics, depending on the needs and circumstances of each group of students.

The first chapter explores the challenges and opportunities of preaching in our present context, and then provides a synthesis of what the Church teaches about the homily. Assuming that we agree on the importance of good preaching, the second chapter offers an overview of the best insights of the art of public speaking, reviewing key elements of classical and contemporary rhetoric. The third chapter goes from the human wisdom of public speaking to the necessary foundations of a theology of preaching. The fourth chapter continues this exploration by reflecting on the Incarnation as a key—both theoretical and practical—for preaching. Based on the importance of being always "incarnate" in our preaching, in the fifth chapter we pay attention to

INTRODUCTION: WHY PREACH?

the words of advice of some people who do not preach but listen to and care for our homilies.

The sixth chapter enters into the practical question of the preparation of the homily: Should we prepare? If so, how? After reviewing a simple but effective method to prepare the homily, the seventh chapter will address aspects of its delivery: how, when, from where, and so on. Then, trying to visualize how all of what we have learned so far can become real, chapter eight will present to us the example of one of the most brilliant and pastorally sensitive preachers of our tradition: St. Augustine. Finally, chapter nine will remind us that preaching can become the source of unity for our busy lives, as we exercise our theology as preachers.

The second section of this primer is a homiletics reader. In any art, achieving some degree of mastery demands knowing those who have taken it to its best expressions. While few of us will be able to aspire to the precision or learning of the greatest Christian preachers, it nevertheless improves our abilities simply to spend time in their company and perceive in their homilies the fruit of their love for God and their flocks. Reading a selection of great homilies, chronologically organized and with brief introductions and commentaries, can thus be an excellent way to learn the true art of preaching.

I would like to recommend using both sections of this primer, either by reviewing first the chapters and then the homilies of the reader, or by alternating their use. Finally, when we learn the art of preaching, we have to practice. These three elements—the topics developed in the chapters, the exemplary homilies of the reader, and the practice of preaching—can determine how the study of the art of preaching can be organized.

When I began working on this book, I had no idea that the last stages of this project would take place in such a challenging time for the world and for the Church. Writing about preaching during 2020 felt more urgent than ever. That our people need to hear words of hope, that our homilies must offer clarity amid so much confusion, and that our preaching will play a decisive role in the life of the Church in the challenging times ahead of us sound like understatements. My hope is that this book can offer some contribution for our beautiful and decisive call to preach the good news of Jesus Christ.

Part I

Foundations of Preaching

1

Homiletics:
The Challenge and
the Opportunity

A CHALLENGING CONTEXT

Preaching the good news is, in itself, a challenging mission that requires continuing growth in personal holiness. The specific circumstances of our time also pose certain challenges that preachers need to recognize in order to fulfill their mission faithfully.

We see how the aggressive progress of secularism affects the minds and hearts of believers and unbelievers alike. A common ground of moral convictions about family, life, and human identity is a thing of the past, a past from which some think themselves to be happily liberated. The prevalence of disbelief or uncertainty about God's existence and of indifference to it means that vast numbers of people espouse the philosophy of relativism and effectively exclude God from daily life, from their real decisions and actions. Those who try to make moral choices often do so based on false principles or mere personal preferences. In this climate, even Christians can be tempted to relegate their faith to the realm of the private in the belief that it is not appropriate to tell other people what is right or wrong. And the Church, suffering from the poor testimony of some of her members and leaders, finds herself widely mistrusted by the secular world and even by believers.

What is it like to preach in this context? Two stories illustrate some of the problems facing preachers today. In his 1968 classic *Introduction to Christianity*, Joseph Ratzinger shared the "irritating image" of a clown whose touring circus caught on fire.[1] The clown sped to the neighboring village to warn the people of the danger to their homes. But the villagers thought that he was playing a clown's trick to gain attention and convince them to go to the circus. As the clown's desperation at being disbelieved grew, the people laughed more. Finally, the flames came and consumed the village. Ratzinger saw here an image of the theologian; we can apply the story to the preacher and ask ourselves: Are we credible? What can we do to be taken seriously? Do we understand and convey to others the urgency of our life-or-death message? Can we convince our people that there is something truly important and serious in what we say?

Another illustrative story was told at a conference by British scripture scholar N. T. Wright. While he was travelling abroad, England's cricket team won a decisive championship. To Wright, a good son of England, this was very good news, so good, indeed, that he could not possibly stay in his hotel room alone. He went down to the lobby to find someone with whom he could share the joy. The person he found and told about the victory did not know what cricket was. Being polite, he congratulated Wright in a generic way, but without really understanding. There was no way of sharing the joy of the moment. At best, the person thought, "That's what the British like; good for him."

Is that what polite people think of preachers—"Good for you, if that's what you like"? Do they think that faith in Christ is a personal preference, like following cricket, or baseball, or soccer? We know that our faith is true, compelling, universal, and that its call is urgent. We must think about how best to preach it to a world that is not disposed to appreciate what we say.

AN AMAZING OPPORTUNITY

Opposition to the truth of Christ is of course not new in human history. It is important to recall that whatever the false theories he proposes or the bad principles he convinces himself he holds, every human person has a heart that is restless until it finds its rest in God, as Augustine famously said. It still longs for the truth, for a love that is stronger than death, for joy and peace. "For what does the soul desire more strongly than the truth?"[2] The human

1 See Joseph Ratzinger, *Introduction to Christianity*, trans. J.R. Foster and Michael J. Miller (San Francisco: Ignatius Press, 2004), 39–41.

2 Augustine, *Tractates on the Gospel of John*, trans. John W. Rettig, 5 vols. (Washington, D.C.: The Catholic University of America Press, 1988–1995), 25.5.

heart will always need the good news of Christ. It is the momentous task of contemporary preachers to find the right way of proclaiming the good news here and now.

When most people accept or at least respect the Gospel, there is certainly an opportunity for making progress in formation and actual Christian life. But, at the same time, there lurk the risks of a comfortable and at times lukewarm discipleship, and of a commonplace and irrelevant preaching. On the other hand, ignorance and even rejection of the Gospel can become, mysteriously, an occasion for a renewed way of preaching the good news. The challenging context in which we live, marked by apathy and even antipathy towards the Christian message, is a sharp wake-up call and an opportunity for renewal. And the renewal does not begin with mere human eloquence.

On the way to his martyrdom, St. Ignatius of Antioch wrote to the Church in Rome words that sound very timely for us: "When Christianity is hated by the world, the work is not a matter of persuasion, but of greatness."[3] If the Church responds with renewed greatness, with honest zeal for God and the salvation of humanity, with courage and integrity, with fidelity and creativity, with a fresh desire for holiness and for bringing hope to the world, then that greatness will be the beginning of a new persuasion, one that arises from actions and continues with words.

The personal effort of living a life according to the good news is the ever-necessary first step in the art of preaching. This is what St. Gregory the Great described in his *Pastoral Rule*:

> It is obviously necessary that they who give utterance to words of holy preaching, should first be awake in the earnest practice of good deeds, lest, being themselves slack in performing them, they stir up others by words only. Let them first rouse themselves up by lofty deeds, and then make others solicitous to live good lives…. Let them carefully examine themselves and discover in what respects they are idling and lagging, and make amends by severe penance. Then, and only then, let them set in order the lives of other by their words.[4]

While we should discuss a number of important topics in regard to the preparation and delivery of the kinds of homilies that can "set in order the lives of others," one thing is clear: we cannot afford any kind of uneventful

---

3 Ignatius of Antioch, *Letter to the Romans,* trans. Bart D. Ehrman (Cambridge, Mass.: Harvard University Press, 2003), 3.3.

4 Gregory I, *Pastoral Care*, trans. Henry Davis, SJ (Westminster, Md: Newman Press, 1950), III.40.

preaching. The word *uneventful* is key; a generic, self-centered, comfortable style that does not touch the human heart is simply sterile. Preaching must be *eventful*. Something *happens* when the good news is proclaimed again with love and faith; it is a true event, a mysterious occurrence. It was the conviction of Paul and the apostles that what happened in the death and Resurrection of Jesus happened in some way in the hearts of those who received their proclamation of the good news, that message of the utmost importance which the apostles themselves received and then preached with all their energy. This has to be, still today, the conviction of anyone entrusted with the responsibility of preaching the good news, particularly the liturgical homily: there is an energy at work that makes those words "living and effec-tive" (Heb 4:12). As Jean Corbon said, when the Gospel is proclaimed in the liturgy, through the Holy Spirit, "the words of Jesus are more than a form of teaching; they become an event."[5] It is the duty of the preacher to speak in such a way that the event becomes clearly recognizable for his people.

WHAT THE CHURCH TEACHES ABOUT THE HOMILY

The word homily (*homilia*) means "to converse" (Lk 24:14; Acts 24:26), to have communion with another person, and so to join in company.[6] The Greeks used it to describe the personal instruction given by the philosopher to his pupils. Very early, the word was used in the sense that we use it today, as sacred instruction. The Acts of the Apostles describes the instruction given by St. Paul in the context of the breaking of the bread, saying that Paul "talked a long time" (Acts 20:11). St. Ignatius of Antioch would ask St. Polycarp to deliver a "homily" and offer some sacred teaching in order to instruct the people.[7] St. Justin Martyr, in the earliest full description of the eucharistic celebration, tells that "when the reader has ceased, the president of the assembly verbally admonishes and invites all to imitate such examples of virtue."[8] It was in the third century that the word *homily* was clearly under-

---

5 Jean Corbon, *The Wellspring of Worship* (San Francisco: Ignatius Press, 2005), 149.

6 Needless to say, we are not entering here into any technical discussion about the use of the term *homilia* and its progression in the Church's tradition. For a scholarly review of this problem before Origen, see Alistair Stewart-Sykes, *From Prophecy to Preaching: A Search for the Origins of the Christian Homily* (Leiden: Brill, 2001). For a thorough historical approach to the homily see O.C. Edwards Jr., *A History of Preaching* (Nashville, Tenn.: Abingdon Press, 2004).

7 Ignatius of Antioch, *Letter to Polycarp*, 5.

8 Justin Martyr, *First Apology*, trans. Thomas B. Falls (New York: Christian Heritage, 1948), 67.

stood in the way we use it today.[9] With variations in theology and practice, from that point until today the homily has remained a key element of the liturgical life of the Church.[10]

The recent Magisterium of the Church has paid increasing attention to the centrality of liturgical preaching, emphasizing the fact that the homily is an integral part of the liturgical action. Here we will review some of the most relevant magisterial teaching points in regard to the homily.[11]

The homily "forms part of the liturgy itself."[12] As such, it is "an act of worship" oriented, like the sacred liturgy, to the sanctification of the people and to the glorification of God.[13] This emphasis on the "liturgical context" of the homily is significant because it highlights not only the fact that the homily is so important during the offering of the Eucharist that it should only be omitted for *serious* reasons, but also that its nature is liturgical; in fact, that it is a "quasi-sacramental" action.[14] The Magisterium emphasizes the intrinsic bond between the liturgy of the word and the liturgy of the Eucharist in the eucharistic celebration.[15] This will be discussed further when we review a theology of preaching.

Based on these foundations we can understand the nature of the homily as defined by the Church.[16] The *General Instruction of the Roman Missal* indicates that the homily "should be an exposition of some aspect of the readings from Sacred Scripture or of another text from the Ordinary or from the Proper of the Mass of the day and should take into account both the mystery being celebrated and the particular needs of the listeners."[17] In

---

9 See Alden Bass, "Preaching in the Early Church," in *A Handbook for Catholic Preaching*, 52.

10 For a useful broad historical review of the evolution of preaching through the ages see Foley, *A Handbook for Catholic Preaching*, 41–101.

11 For a review of the evolution of the recent magisterial documents on the homily see Stephen Vincent DeLeers, *Written Text Becomes Living Word: The Vision and Practice of Sunday Preaching* (Collegeville, Minn.: Liturgical Press, 2004), 13–44.

12 *Sacrosanctum Concilium*, 52; see also *General Instruction of the Roman Missal*, 65.

13 Congregation for Divine Worship and the Discipline of the Sacraments, *Homiletic Directory* (Washington, D.C.: USCCB, 2015), 4.

14 *Homiletic Directory*, 11; see also *Code of Canon Law*, 767; see *Sacrosanctum Concilium*, 52; Francis, Apostolic Exhortation *Evangelii Gaudium* (November 24, 2013), 142.

15 See Benedict XVI, Apostolic Exhortation *Sacramentum Caritatis* (February 22, 2007), 44.

16 Generally speaking, there is a certain recent distinction between homily and sermon: the former is typically understood as a commentary on the actual liturgical celebration while the latter might address other spiritual topics. We should not be very strict about this distinction. About this see Robert P. Waznak, SS, *An Introduction to the Homily* (Collegeville, Minn.: Liturgical Press, 1998), 1–2.

the recent *Homiletic Directory* we read: "The homily is a discourse about the mysteries of faith and the standards of Christian life in a way suited to the particular needs of the listeners."[18] And the *Catechism of the Catholic Church* says that the homily "is an exhortation to accept this Word as what it truly is, the Word of God, and to put it into practice."[19] Let us unfold the main elements of these definitions:

- The homily is described as an exposition and a discourse: it is an oral means of communication.
- Its content is the mysteries of faith and the standards of Christian life.
- Its goal is to help the people accept the Word of God and put it into practice.
- It should also take into account the particular needs of the listeners.
- A homily ought to be directly connected with the specific mystery celebrated by the liturgical celebration.[20]
- The sources of a homily depend on the mystery being celebrated: the readings from Scripture, the Ordinary, or the Propers of the Mass. It is important to note that the homily should be about "some aspect" of these texts, and not about *every* aspect of *all* sources.
  - Another source for liturgical preaching is the rite itself. Along with the biblical and liturgical texts, the homily can also explore the meaning of some of the liturgical rites.[21]

Therefore, according to this understanding of a homily, it appears clear that by nature a homily is not:[22]

- A sermon on an abstract topic
- An exercise in biblical exegesis
- A catechetical instruction

17 International Committee on English in the Liturgy, *General Instruction of the Roman Missal* (Washington, D.C.: USCCB, 2003), 65.

18 Congregation for Divine Worship, *Homiletic Directory*, 11.

19 *Catechism of the Catholic Church*, 1349.

20 This is a reference to the practice of preaching different series of sermon topics (e.g., the patriarchs, the Ten Commandments) which often had little or no connection with the specific mystery being celebrated. This emphasis of the Magisterium is not in contradiction with the possibility of a series of thematic homilies, as long as there is a connection with the liturgical celebration.

21 See Congregation for Divine Worship and the Discipline of the Sacraments, Instruction *Redemptionis Sacramentum* (Washington, D.C.: USCCB, 2004), 67.

22 See Congregation for Divine Worship, *Homiletic Directory*, 6.

• The preacher's personal witness

These elements—theological topics, biblical exegesis, doctrinal instruction, and personal witness—have a specific place in liturgical preaching, but do not define or take the place of a homily as a whole.

Recent magisterial teaching on preaching also emphasizes the preacher's responsibility for preparing the homily. Ordained ministers should prepare their homilies carefully, avoiding what Pope Benedict called "generic and abstract" preaching.[23] Indeed, preparation for preaching has to be held as a central priority in the life of a priest. To act differently would be, in the words of Pope Francis, "dishonest and irresponsible."[24]

In the end, the preparation of the homily is an outgrowth of the preacher's love for God and his people. It is that love that makes the difference. God will certainly help his ministers, but he counts on our cooperation. As St. John Paul II said, "the greater or lesser degree of holiness of the minister has a real effect on the proclamation of the word."[25] Whatever may be the challenges of our time, our personal prayer, study and efforts for growing in holiness are, in the end, the more decisive ways of being faithful to the ministry of preaching God's Word.

AN EXAMINATION ON PREACHING

The state of preaching today is far from what it ought to be. Benedict XVI put it simply: "The quality of homilies needs to be improved."[26] Recently, Pope Francis addressed concerns expressed about the ministry of preaching, going so far as to say, "We know that both they [the faithful] and their ordained ministers suffer because of homilies: the laity from having to listen to them and the clergy from having to preach them! It is sad that this is the case."[27] The unfortunately common situation of poor preaching is a source

---

23 See Benedict XVI, *Sacramentum Caritatis*, 46. Instead, he writes, "I ask these ministers to preach in such a way that the homily closely relates the proclamation of the word of God to the sacramental celebration (*Sacrosanctum Concilium*, 52) and the life of the community, so that the word of God truly becomes the Church's vital nourishment and support (*Dei Verbum*, 21)."

24 Francis, *Evangelii Gaudium*, 145. The importance of the preparation of the homily will be further developed in chapter 6.

25 John Paul II, Apostolic Exhortation *Pastores Dabo Vobis* (March 15, 1992), 25.

26 Benedict XVI, *Sacramentum Caritatis*, 46; Apostolic Exhortation *Verbum Domini* (September 30, 2010), 59.

of discouragement for many in the pews, while for many preachers the nega-
tivity they perceive from their congregations brings dejection and fatigue.[28]
Further, Pope Francis has called for "serious consideration by pastors" in
regard to the homily.[29] In light of this, we will survey some of the common
distortions seen today in preaching.[30]

Common Distortions

Following the Holy Father's call to seriously consider our homilies, and in
order to have a clear picture of the context in which we are called to preach,
we will review now some of today's common traps in preaching. This is done
without any generalization, in the effort to grow in humility and be aware of
what can be improved, hoping to better respond to our call. As preachers, we
all probably have, at one point or another, fallen into one or more of these
distortions. Trying to imitate the honesty of Pope Gregory the Great when
he offered his own charitable challenge to preachers—"Someone may think
I am speaking unjustly, and so I accuse myself equally"—let me propose a
list of common traps.[31]

Unpreparedness

This of all distortions is perhaps the first. Inadequate preparation for preaching often shows itself in homilies with a stream-of-consciousness quality,
absence of connection between the ideas, lack of substance, unnecessary
length, and endless endings. These homilies are normally uninspiring and

---

27 Francis, *Evangelii Gaudium*, 135.

28 See United States Conference of Catholic Bishops, *Preaching the Mystery of the Faith: The
Sunday Homily* (Washington, D.C.: USCCB, 2012), 2; see also Karla J. Bellinger, *Connecting Pulpit
and Pew: Breaking Open the Conversation about Catholic Preaching* (Collegeville, Minn.: Liturgical Press, 2014), 21. Augustine wrote of some possible causes for discouragement while teaching
the faith; see *Instructing Beginners in Faith*, trans. Raymond Canning (New York: New City Press,
2006), I.10.14.

29 Francis, *Evangelii Gaudium*, 135.

30 On the crisis in preaching, see Joshua J. Whitfield, *The Crisis of Bad Preaching: Redeeming the Heart and Way of the Catholic Preacher* (Notre Dame, Ind.: Ave Maria Press, 2019), xi,
2–3. On different emphases in preaching among Christian confessions, including content
and length, find relevant current information in: https://www.pewforum.org/2019/12/16/
the-digital-pulpit-a-nationwide-analysis-of-online-sermons/

31 Gregory I, *Forty Gospel Homilies*, trans. Dom David Hurst (Kalamazoo, Mich.: Cistercian Publications, 1990), 17.14.

irrelevant; parishioners become accustomed to daydreaming, reading the bulletin, or quietly dozing off until the preacher is finished.

Moralism

Homilies should not focus exclusively or mainly on precepts and prohibitions, on doing and not doing. Needless to say, homilies can and must address practical aspects of Christian life, but in a way that flows from the patient formation given in weekly spiritual preaching. A tone of negative judgment can make a homily particularly sterile, while even rousing calls to action can lead to forms of Pelagianism in a parish if they are not rooted in words that lead to God's love and truth as the reason for our works.

Questionable sources

Hoping to connect with our congregations, we may rely excessively on unnecessary references to pop culture: TV shows, movies, music. Surely, some people might enjoy those familiar references, but such light fare might also trivialize the sacredness and gravitas of our mission. This is not to mention that if we try too hard to be "cool" or relevant, the result is oftentimes the opposite. Better to be in touch with the "joys and the hopes, the griefs and the anxieties of the men of this age"[32] than what people are binge-watching or surfing on the Internet.

Niceness and humor

Sometimes we can try too hard to be nice, accepted, and liked by affecting sympathies, exaggerating human kindness, and telling the seemingly necessary jokes and stories that have been the trademark of homilies for some decades. In the good effort to go to where the people are, at times we end up remaining there rather than taking them to a higher place. Of course, when done well and naturally, occasional wit and playfulness that might elicit some laughter can be a delightful addition to a homily.

Gospel of cheap grace

Homilies sometimes seem to bring the good news of prosperity and therapeutic religion rather than the call to greatness and holiness inherent in the Gospel. This is not to say the Gospel is not therapeutic and healing, but

32 *Gaudium et Spes*, 1.

sociologists have argued that many young (and not-so-young) Americans approach God through the lens of "moral therapeutic deism," for whom the emphasis is what God can do for me.[33] It can be easy, especially in affluent settings, to settle for this comfortable preaching.

Disconnected speech

We can get so excited about the last book we have read, or some new nuance of ancient Greek we have found, that our homilies can resemble academic papers or exegetical commentaries, the language of which is a theological jargon that is incomprehensible to most people. Of course, we should aim to meet the needs of our most intellectual listeners as well as the less educated if we can, but it does not hurt to ask some honest and typical parishioners if what we are saying is losing them. It is easy to forget, after years of academic immersion in seminaries, what regular people do and do not know.

Unauthoritative counseling

If we lack faith in the authority bestowed upon us in ordination, our courage and gravitas will falter, and we might sound like a kind of public counselor who gives generic advice more akin to self-help programs than to the radical demands of the one whose first recorded words are "convert and believe in the Gospel" (Mk 1:15). For, as C. S. Lewis wrote, "mere improvement is not redemption, though redemption always improves people."[34] What really "helps" human beings is the word of transformative love spoken by the Word of God to all people, of which we are the unworthy stewards who nevertheless are charged to proclaim it.

New theories

We can also be too keen to proclaim from the ambo the thought-provoking new ideas about the faith recently read in the works of edgy authors. Though there may be a proper place for sharing these theories, doing it during the

---

33 Pope Benedict wrote in his first *Jesus of Nazareth* book, "Healing is an essential dimension of the apostolic mission and of Christian faith in general. It can even be said that Christianity is a 'therapeutic religion, a religion of healing.'" Pope Benedict XVI, *Jesus of Nazareth: From the Baptism in the Jordan to the Transfiguration* (New York: Doubleday, 2007), 175–76. On the term "moral therapeutic deism," see Christian Smith and Melinda Lundquist, *Soul Searching: The Religious and Spiritual Lives of American Teenagers* (Oxford: Oxford University Press, 2011). The authors contrast this with "a religion of repentance from sin, of keeping the Sabbath, of living as a servant of a sovereign divine, of steadfastly saying one's prayers, of faithfully observing high holy days, of building character through suffering" (163–64).

34 C. S. Lewis, *Mere Christianity* (New York: HarperOne, 2000), 216.

homily is a disservice to the people of God. What G. K. Chesterton said about education might have some analogy here, especially considering that the ages and formation levels of our parishioners usually vary: "Obviously, it ought to be the oldest things that are taught to the youngest people; the assured and experienced truths that are first put to the baby . . . . But in a school today the baby has to submit to a system [of thought] that is younger than himself."[35] True creativity and newness stem from fidelity to the perennial truth, that Truth whose beauty is "always ancient and always new," as Augustine said.

Self-centeredness

We sometimes occupy too prominent a place in our homilies. While being personal and personable is important, that does not mean that homilies should always include personal stories, opinions, and testimonies. These can diminish the fruitfulness of the ascetic disposition which knows that the preacher is the voice, and not the Word. Certainly, there is a place for our personal testimony (see 1 Cor 11:1), but we need to be always attentive to the temptation of subtly becoming the center.

Questions for Reflection and Conversation

- *Why is the current situation such a challenging and amazing opportunity for preaching?*
- *What does it mean that preaching has to be eventful?*
- *What is a homily?*
- *In your experience, what are the most common distortions for preaching today?*

---

35 G. K. Chesterton, *What's Wrong with the World* (San Francisco: Ignatius Press, 1994), 143.

2

Homiletics and Public Speaking

I t is important to situate our study of the art of preaching in the broader context of public speaking. For the homily, as anything willed by God for his Church, is a place in which divine grace perfects nature. And we ought to be grateful for the many things we can learn from those who have cultivated the technical aspects of oratory, even when their achievements were accomplished only at a human level. In the end, all of that human wisdom comes from the mysterious wisdom of God, "from whom all good things come."[1] We can say, as St. Justin said about the philosophical feats of the Greeks, "the truths which men in all lands have rightly spoken belong to us Christians."[2]

The word is at the core of what being a human is. The ability to speak, tell stories, and share wisdom marks the dawn of what can be truly called "history." The wonder of language and the capacity to communicate it distinguish us from any other living being. The use of words allowed humanity to progress, to live longer, to keep traditions, to explore, to discover, to share good news.

Many wise words eventually were written down in order to preserve them and pass them on effectively. However, humanity has

---

[1] Collect for the Tenth Sunday in Ordinary Time. The whole prayer could be fruitfully said by anyone trying to learn and discern the art of preaching: "O God, from whom all good things come, grant that we, who call on you in our need, may at your prompting discern what is right, and by your guidance do it."

[2] Justin Martyr, *Second Apology*, translated by Thomas B. Falls (New York: Christian Heritage, 1948), 13.4.

never lost its fascination for the unique character of the spoken word. How different it is to read one of Shakespeare's plays than to hear the words flow in a live performance! How different to hear the warm voice of a mother telling a story before bed than to read those same words! How different for a bride to read a poem than to hear it from her beloved! Why is it that today, with all our hitherto-unimaginable means of communication, we still watch and hear important speeches live? The information conveyed at a State of the Union address or an inaugural homily does not change if the words are read later in print, but the experience is different. Data could be communicated more precisely if university professors simply emailed lectures to their students, but we would lose the wonder of learning from someone, not only of hearing the information, but of being formed by acquired wisdom, of being moved by personal experience. There is something irreplaceable about the spoken word.

The importance of public speaking has not diminished, even in our technological and information-saturated age. Quite the opposite: we are witnessing the increasing appeal of talks, amplified by the recent capability of sharing that same speech millions of times on the Internet. This is true as well for the Church: homilies, talks, interviews, and video blogs about a myriad of topics are shared online every day, and the impact of and fascination with public speaking increases.

The ancient and centuries-long study of rhetoric offers important lessons for those learning how to preach to a world that is still enamored of the spoken word. St. Augustine would say that it is good to be wise as we speak—and indeed this is what matters most—but if a preacher can speak not only wisely but also eloquently, he is more useful to the Church.[3] For a preacher, eloquence is not only a matter of aesthetics, of cosmetic improvements, but a matter of salvation. Striving to preach well is about being able to persuade as many as possible to know and love God and to actually follow his truth; it is a necessary duty of love at the service of the serious task of cooperating with God's grace for the salvation of souls.

Of course, there are evident differences between secular public speaking and liturgical preaching that need to be taken into account.

---

3 See Augustine, *Teaching Christianity*, IV.5.8.

It would be wrong to simply try to apply all the rules of rhetoric in any given homily. The nature of liturgical preaching demands a spiritual disposition that leads to greater sobriety and calls for pastoral flexibility to adapt rhetorical theories for the good of the people of God. Unquestionably, there has to be discernment in the manner of learning and applying the wisdom of oratorical principles; but it is still undeniable that such stores of wisdom, including non-Christian sources, are well-stocked and available for us to browse, take, and use. The fathers of the Church, many of them deeply trained in the best of classical rhetoric, are wonderful models of discernment both in learning and putting into practice secular wisdom in order to be effective preachers, all out of love for their people.[4]

What we will do in this chapter is to learn just a little from the wisdom of good rhetoric that can be more clearly and fruitfully used in the practice of preachers. Because of this, the following pages are an intentionally brief and curated synthesis of rhetorical wisdom ancient and modern.[5] We will first review some noteworthy elements of classical rhetoric, and then some useful contemporary perspectives. In both cases, we want to learn some lessons from the theory and "best practices" of successful speakers, in order to find in them what can enrich and equip our preaching today.

ADVICE FROM CLASSICAL RHETORIC

Rhetoric is, broadly speaking, "the art of speaking well,"[6] *ars bene dicendi*, according to Quintilian (ca. 40–95 AD), one of the most important ancient

---

[4] Augustine writes about the importance of using the best of pagan wisdom, not rejecting altogether all that is not Christian, just as the Israelites, in fleeing Egypt and their idols, were smart in taking the best of their vessels and ornaments for "their own, and indeed better, use." *Teaching Christianity*, II.40.60. About the prudence of the Fathers in using classical rhetoric in their preaching, see Carol Harrison, *The Art of Listening in the Early Church* (Oxford: Oxford University Press, 2013), 58–59.

[5] Far from being a discipline from the past, rhetoric is still a relevant area of research. For those interested in reviewing recent volumes on the topic, see Patricia Bizzell, Bruce Herzberg, Robin Reames, *The Rhetorical Tradition: Readings from Classical Times to the Present* (Boston: Bedford Books, 2020); Dennis Glover, *The Art of Great Speeches and Why We Remember Them* (Cambridge: Cambridge University Press, 2011); George Kennedy, *A New History of Classical Rhetoric* (Princeton, N.J.: Princeton University Press, 1994); Thomas M. Conley, *Rhetoric in the European Tradition* (Chicago: University of Chicago Press, 1990); Ryan N. S. Topping, *The Elements of Rhetoric: How to Write and Speak Clearly & Persuasively—A Guide for Students, Teachers, Politicians & Preachers* (Kettering, Ohio: Angelico Press, 2016).

[6] Quintilian, *Institutio Oratoria,* trans. Harold E. Butler, vol. 1 (Cambridge, Mass.: Harvard University Press, 1953), II.17.37.

writers on the topic along with Aristotle (384–322 BC) and Cicero (106–43 BC).[7] It is the art of persuasion.[8] More recently it has been said that "rhetoric is language at play—language plus."[9] Three elements of rhetoric are particularly relevant for the study of homiletics: the modes of persuasion, the goals of a speech, and the making of a speech.[10]

Logos, Ethos, Pathos

Aristotle wrote of three main modes of persuasion through which the speaker causes *pistis* (trust) to become a state of mind in his audience. These are *logos, ethos* and *pathos*. Let us review briefly them.[11]

Logos is the argument itself, the substance of a speech, the words and their inner logic, the content of what is said. Thus, a good *logos* is built upon a use of language that is clear and concise, and upon prior reflection on what will be said. *Logos* also demands that the speech be effectively structured. The Spanish philosopher Ortega y Gasset simply defined structure as "elements + order," which in our case means ideas well-organized, with a direction and flow that come from the (obvious) awareness that a speech (a homily) is always addressed to someone.

The speaker should aim to engage the audience in his reasoning. Aristotle argues that the most effective way to advance an argument is to be able to bring the hearers to reach the conclusion by themselves. The use of analogy, syllogisms, and other tools can be helpful for effectively communicating *logos*.

Ethos is the trust in the speaker that induces the audience to give him a fair hearing. We could say that ethos is about the authority of the orator, his "credentials." In a secular environment these might be his academic degrees or special accomplishments. In general, *ethos* should mean confidence in

---

7 See Heinrich Lausberg, et al. *Handbook of Literary Rhetoric: A Foundation for Literary Study* (Leiden: Brill, 1998), 17. This handbook is a valuable resource for the learning of classical rhetoric.

8 On the teachings of Quintilian and Cicero see Duane Liftin, *St. Paul's Theology of Proclamation: 1 Corinthians 1–4 and Greco-Roman Rhetoric* (Cambridge: Cambridge University Press, 1994), 87–108.

9 Sam Leith, *Words Like Loaded Pistols: Rhetoric from Aristotle to Obama* (New York: Basic Books, 2012), 6.

10 For a very useful and simple glossary of key concepts of rhetoric see Leith, *Words Like Loaded Pistols*, 281–97.

11 What follows is largely (and loosely) based on Alberto Gil, *Cómo Convencer Eficazmente: Hacia una Retórica Anclada en la Personalidad y en los Valores* (Madrid: Palabra, 2014); a few things are based on Leith's *Words Like Loaded Pistols*, and Augustine's *Teaching Christianity*.

the honesty of the speaker, whom we trust will be fair in his words. For a homilist, *ethos* should not depend on human achievements, but rather on the sacramental grace that sustains his efforts. Of course, the authority of a word well-said and supported by a coherent life will be more powerful than any technique. For an effective *ethos* to exist in a homily, the flock must know its shepherd in a real, human way, and the shepherd must know his flock; it requires a common bond that creates an ordinary connection of trust and respect. This is advanced by self-mastery, balance, sobriety, and a joyful demeanor from the preacher.

Pathos is the use of emotion in order to connect not only with the intellect but with the whole person, and so be effectively persuasive. A good use of *pathos* is based on respect, appreciation, and affection; it also comes from truly knowing one's audience. For a homily, *pathos* is the fruit of pastoral love and knowledge that enables a preacher not only to say the right thing, but to do it in the right way, moving the hearts of his people to respond to what the Lord shows them.

Pathos cannot be confused with a cold manipulation of emotions for Machiavellian ends. *Pathos* is the honest and vulnerable emotional appeal that moves the hearts of the listeners towards something good. For a homily, it is allowing the Gospel to touch the heart, whether that causes joy, repentance, longing, or consolation. The difference from a merely human appeal to *pathos* is that we trust that Jesus himself is *the Logos*, and he will know how to touch the hearts of his disciples. A preacher has only to be the instrument of that process.

The Goals of a Speech: Teach, Delight, Sway

Another important teaching that any preacher should learn from classical rhetoric is about the goals of a speech. According to Cicero and Quintilian, a good speech has three objectives: to teach, to delight, and to move.[12] Augustine communicates this idea thus: "An eloquent man [Cicero] once said, you see, and what he said was true, that to be eloquent you speak 'so as to teach, to delight, to sway.' Then he added, 'Teaching your audience is a matter of necessity, delighting them a matter of being agreeable, swaying them a matter of victory.'"[13]

---

12 Cicero, *Brutus*, trans. George L. Hendrickson (Cambridge, Mass.: Harvard University Press, 1952),185; Quintilian, *Institutio Oratoria*, XII.10.50.

13 Augustine, *Teaching Christianity*, IV.12.27.

Therefore, a homily has to:

• Teach about the mystery celebrated
• Touch the heart
• Move to conversion

Augustine clarified that teaching is about *what* the preacher says, while the other two goals are found in *the way* in which he preaches, so that he can be fruitfully heard with understanding, with enjoyment, and with obedience. It is not enough to aspire merely to repeat some teachings without expecting a more profound experience in the audience, without hoping for actual growth. Because of this, "it is the duty, therefore, of the eloquent churchman, when he is trying to persuade the people about something that has to be done, not only to teach, in order to instruct them; not only to delight, in order to hold them; but also to sway, in order to conquer and win them."[14]

This *duty* is not an arbitrary theoretical imposition on the homilist. Rather, it comes from human nature and the structure of our faith. We might find here a connection with three dimensions of the act of believing: the assent given by the *mind* to what is revealed, the adhesion of the *heart* to what has been heard, and the commitment of the *will* to what has been received.

Similarly, we encounter here a link with the very structure of being: we are made for what is true, beautiful, and good. Although some might appear distracted and not always show interest in what we say, every human being desires the truth, every person longs for beauty, every heart wants what is good. Our duty, our sacred duty as ministers of the Word, is to give them what they need through homilies that actually teach the truth with depth and courage, that delight the heart with beautiful words, that move them to good lives.

A first step toward this is to make sure we elicit some interest in what we say. There is nothing worse for a homily than to carry that sort of "white-noise-church-lingo" that causes the impression of the same thing being said in the same way. How are we going to get the attention of our people? This is, to be sure, not an invitation to be showy or condescending, as if we were to assume that homilies needed to be watered down or adorned with childish tricks. People need what is authentic; people need what is true, beautiful, and good. We must reverence the dignity and greatness of the human

---

14 Augustine, *Teaching Christianity*, IV.13.29.

hearts expecting this from us. Questions, pauses, the right quotation, the appropriate story, the example to follow—these are some ways in which we can gain the attention of our people. And, while Cicero taught that our speeches ought to assume a specific tone according to its theme—calm to teach, moderate to delight, grand to sway—we believe with Augustine that a good homily must freely combine those elements, because when we preach "everything we say is a great matter."[15]

The Making of a Speech

The third element of classical rhetoric that we must consider is what has been called the "canons of rhetoric." Quintilian put it succinctly: "the art of oratory, as taught by most authorities, and those the best, consists of five parts:—*invention, arrangement, expression, memory,* and *delivery* or *action.*"[16] Let us briefly review each part.

Invention (*inventio*)

The first step of invention is a discovery: the search for what is worth saying. This intellection (*intellectio*) begins with observation (*spectare*) and wonder (*mirari*). Invention is the contrary to "inventing" as in "making something up." Rather, it is the process of exploring, uncovering, finding out what to say in a specific circumstance. The truth is always ancient, but always new, as Augustine famously said. Hence, it is always beautiful; there is forever something new to be said. Invention's second step is one of discrimination: deciding which information to use and not to use. This means selecting evidence, developing the topic, and choosing which means and tools to employ.

Calm, peace, reflection, prayer, and reverence are essential for any good homily and make the time dedicated to the invention fruitful. We will explore this in more detail when we develop a method for preaching.

Arrangement (*dispositio*)

Having found what to say, the speaker must determine how best to say it, particularly in regard to the distribution of the ideas—that is, the structure of the speech. Every speech, and as such every homily, ought to be well organized, no matter how brief it is or how small its audience. A good speaker

15 Augustine, *Teaching Christianity*, IV.18.35.
16 Quintilian, *Institutio Oratoria*, III.3.1.

will know how to begin, how to develop the core of his message, and how to bring it to a satisfactory end. We will review four parts of a good speech:

- **Introduction** *(exordium):*
  This is the starting point, the intriguing entrance hall of a castle to be explored. There is much to do here. These words will *present a problem* to the audience with a question offered in a *personalized* way so as to be relevant for them and will at the same time inspire in the hearers that benevolence based on trust (*ethos*) that is necessary for an effective speech.

- **Narration** *(narratio):*
  The speaker "sets the stage" with clarity and brevity, offering the right context for the argument. It makes clear the who, what, when, where, and how of the talk.

- **Argumentation** *(argumentatio or probatio):*
  This is the central part of the arrangement of a speech, and therefore, the most important use of *logos*. Argumentation proves the point through persuasion. *Probatio* consists of the positive, plausible, and convincing arguments used to prove a point, and *refutatio* of the negative arguments refuting the opposing views.

- **Conclusion** *(peroratio):*
  The key moment for the *pathos* appeal, this is the time to highlight the decisive points already exposed and reach the conclusion that is the convincing answer to the question posed in the introduction. It can be a memorable experience for listeners when done well.

Style (*elocutio*)

Once the speaker has discovered the idea to be said, and the order of exposition, it is important to consider style. What kind of language is appropriate? How simple or grandiose should the words be? These are not just vain and useless questions; the choice of language itself has a powerful capacity to communicate.

Three points ought to be considered. First is purity (*puritas*), which in the art of rhetoric means that the language is grammatically correct. Purity in language is important not only for the obvious reason of clarity, for avoiding the distraction of errors and unnecessary words such as "like," or "you know," but also for adhering to the conventions of a specific linguistic community. Words and phrases have different meanings in different places, and the speaker must be aware of that. Second is clarity (*perspicuitas*): a speech has to be intelligible to an audience. Words can offer not only logical arguments but also images, so that the hearers can interiorly *see* what they are hearing. Third is ornamentation (*ornatus*): if what is said is true, then it is good and beautiful. The use of lovely words and certain turns of phrase can fittingly express what is meant interiorly.

Memory (*memoria*)

A good speech is never a reading session. Certainly, there might be times when that is necessary, but it is easy to agree on the superiority of words spoken directly from the mind of a speaker to the minds of his hearers as he looks in their eyes, sees their reactions, and elicits communion.

This requires the work of memorization. But this faculty of the mind is underused today: in a kind of process of decay, we are losing the ability to remember things. Memory is not just a thing from the past, from those distant days when paper (or smartphones) had not been invented. Memory is the ground in which we build ideas, "the stuff we think with," and the condition for ultimate effectiveness in a speech.[17]

A common objection to memorization of the homily originates in the ideas of an educational system that has undervalued the importance of memorizing for generations. It goes like this: if I memorize my speech, I will be more rigid and less spontaneous. In homiletics jargon: can I be open to the Holy Spirit if I memorize what I have previously prepared?

There is absolutely no contradiction between preparing and memorizing, and being open to the inspiration of the Holy Spirit. Rather, the fact that a speech has been carefully considered, organized, prepared, and practiced (yes, memorized) is what allows any truly good adaptation of the material. It is because there is a real command of the topic deposited in our memory that we can look at who is in front of us and choose from what is available in that storage room (using the image of St. Augustine) in the best possible way. There will be times when what we have prepared will be exactly the right thing to say; there will be times when we will need to change much and adapt. But the truth is that neither one can be done with excellence if our memory is not well-stocked with what has been previously stored and matured with diligence and skill.

---

17 Leith, *Words Like Loaded Pistols*, 149.

Delivery (*actio*)

Everything we have seen so far about the canons of rhetoric refers to the preparation of the speech; only this last point makes us think about its actual delivery. This action is, needless to say, decisive for the success of any speech. It requires thinking about the external aspects, the use of voice and gestures.

Modulation of the voice is important. Of course, some people have more beautiful voices than others. What matters here is that voice is strong enough, pleasant, and clear. What make the difference are the rhythm, the pauses, the pace, the variation of tone and volume, and the use of a conversational style at some times and of a more solemn way of speaking at other times.[18] The voice can communicate passion, calm, warmth, or serenity, according to what is being said. Any speaker who really wants to use his voice to the best effect has to spend time practicing his speech out loud. There is no way of finding the right way of using our voice except by actually using our voice.

We need to pay attention to our gestures as well. And though it is not properly a gesture, eye contact with the audience is of great importance here. A speech is always said to someone! A good degree of eye contact guarantees the necessary personal character of oral communication. Then we consider the appropriate position and posture of the body, particularly the hands. A sober movement of hand and arm can be expressive, as long as it is done naturally. We need to avoid fake gestures and mannerisms. In these areas, as in those discussed before, there is but one way of improving: practice.

A CONTEMPORARY APPROACH

After having reviewed some useful and proven wisdom from classical rhetoric, let us briefly turn our attention to a specific way of applying it to a contemporary setting. The incredible success of the TED Talks series led its head and curator Chris Anderson to write a TED guide for public speaking, which contains some insights that will prove valuable for homilists.[19]

TED can offer insights relevant to homiletics for two reasons. First, after years of success, Anderson and his team have reflected on what works and

---

18 On the conversational style of a homily see Michael E. Connors, CSC, "To What Effect? Qualities of Effective Catholic Preaching," in *Effective Preaching: Bringing People into an Encounter With God,* ed. Michael E. Connors, CSC (Chicago: Liturgy Training Publications, 2018), 27.

19 Chris Anderson, *TED Talks: The Official TED Guide to Public Speaking* (Boston: Mariner Books, 2016).

what does not with particular attention to a contemporary audience and have put that in writing. Second, there are compelling similarities between a TED talk and a homily: both are a short speech (never more than 18 minutes for a TED talk, often shorter than that) with one chance to persuade an audience, and both are on one topic, one idea that is "worth sharing." Is there anything more worth sharing than the good news that revolutionized the world? Should we not see those weekly 10 minutes as a precious chance for which we prepare with love, using all the resources and insight available to us? In this section I will present some reflections and advice from the TED team's experience that can be useful for the preparation and delivery of homilies.

Foundations

The mission of any speaker is to take something that deeply matters to him (or her) and "rebuild it inside the minds of [his or her] listeners."[20] The question then is, "do you have ideas that deserve a wider audience?"[21] If there is, indeed, something worth saying—and for preachers there certainly is—we need to find the way of doing it well.

This leads us to consider the marvel of language: how amazing it is that our ideas can be shared by others! This happens through a clear and effective use of language. Thus, a speaker has to use the linguistic tools that the audience has access to and refrain from sophisticated but unintelligible words and phrases.[22]

A good talk is a journey through which the speaker, as a tour guide, takes his audience.[23] As such, a speaker must begin where the audience is and never leave them behind by making confusing conceptual leaps or strange changes of direction. While the journey begins where the hearers are, it never remains there. Any talk has a destination, a place where they all should arrive together, something new to see. How important is this for preaching! Too often homilies take hearers on a strange journey with too many stops, an unclear route, and no exciting destination.

20 Anderson, *TED Talks*, 12.

21 Anderson, *TED Talks*, 13.

22 Anderson, *TED Talks*, 19.

23 Anderson, *TED Talks*, 20.

A speaker needs to know the destination or goal, and to be well-prepared for the journey. He must avoid some "common traps" along the way.[24] The first trap is a "greedy approach" that gives the impression that the speaker has something to gain. Another is pride in unpreparedness; this may be expressed as a claim to be too busy to prepare. A homilist in particular may excuse his lack of preparation by claiming that this makes him open to and reliant on the Holy Spirit. But lack of preparation, expressed in excessive rambling, shows lack of respect and is evident to any attentive hearer.[25] Third, a talk ought to avoid any intra-organization language which will mystify outsiders; this may be theological lingo or quotations that fascinate no more than one percent of the audience. Finally, it is crucial to avoid a fake inspiration that will use tricks to amuse or, even worse, manipulate the audience. Inspiration cannot be performed; it comes only from authenticity and honest work; for a preacher, it comes from God through a perseverant life of prayer as well.

One very practical and healthy practice of speech writers is to have a "throughline," a connecting theme, a "cord" that keeps all the parts of the speech together, so that the talk can be truly meaningful.[26] A simple exercise is to write a throughline of no more than fifteen words that encapsulates the "journey" of a talk. Anderson proposes the questions, "What is the precise idea you want to build inside your listeners' minds? What is their takeaway?"[27] I am convinced that if this one practice were implemented by all preachers, we would witness a quick and significant improvement in the quality and timing of homilies. Anderson insists on a certain unexpectedness that allows the throughline to be effective. True, we all know the end of the story of the Gospel, but are there not infinitely new and intriguing ways of unpacking the *kerygma*? Which way are we going to use for this one journey of this one homily? What will the people in the pews take away with them?

Once the throughline has traced the path for the journey, we need to avoid the temptation to include everything that we could say about a topic,

---

24 Anderson, *TED Talks*, 22–29.

25 As the Unitarian preacher Jenkin Lloyd Jones said, "A speech is a solemn responsibility. The man who makes a bad thirty-minute speech to two hundred people wastes only a half hour of his own time. But he wastes one hundred hours of the audience's time—more than four days—which should be a hanging offense." Quoted in Leith, *Words Like Loaded Pistols*, 189.

26 Anderson, *TED Talks*, 30–35.

27 Anderson, *TED Talks*, 31.

since "overstuffed equals underexplained."[28] How true is this, and how common in homilies! An effective talk is the fruit of believing that "less can be more," and that some ideas, quotes, or stories dear to us might not be helpful to our hearers, at least not now. The goal is to cover only as much ground as we can actually dive into with the right amount of depth to be compelling.[29]

Acknowledging that homilies are different from TED talks, we can nevertheless learn from them:

- A homily without personal connection is not much more than a talk on abstract theology (when not on personal opinion).

- A preacher who conveys egocentrism and "tries too hard" to be funny and liked will be effective neither in sharing the Gospel nor in being truly loved for who he is.

- A homily with powerful stories helps the assembly to relate to what is said (and, by the way, not only is the Gospel full of stories, but it is itself the greatest story ever told).

- A homilist who does not elicit interest and curiosity in his hearers will find it more difficult to explain the mysteries of the faith.

- A preacher who cannot persuade his assembly about an important topic or necessary action is not fulfilling his mission.

- A church should be filled with awe and enthusiasm after hearing the good news preached anew.

Questions for Reflection and Conversation

- *Why is it important for preaching to know the foundations of rhetoric?*
- *Why is the homily (as any speech) a journey?*
- *What aspects of the TED guidelines for public speaking are most appealing to you?*

---

28 Anderson, *TED Talks*, 35.

29 Anderson, *TED Talks*, 39.

3

A Theology of Preaching

In the previous chapter we reviewed some foundational aspects of public speaking; now we transition into the theological foundations of preaching. What does it mean to preach? In a nutshell, preaching is "proclaiming with authority the Word of God."[1] A preeminent ministry in the Church, it consists in the spoken communication of God's revelation, and it is the fundamental means of instruction in the faith.[2] Ultimately, "preaching the Gospel is simply a continuation of the divine mission of Christ."[3]

Preaching has always been part of the life and mission of the Church, as the New Testament attests.[4] The disciples knew that the great commission (see Mt 28:16–20; Mk 16:14–18) was not only about a functional task parallel to many of their other duties, but something that deeply and integrally marked their being: they *were sent*; their existence *was mission*. Like Jesus, the one sent by the Father (see Jn 17:3), they became apostles—that is, the ones sent by him to the world.[5] With words and deeds, they lived and died to proclaim the good news: Jesus Christ, crucified and risen (see 1 Cor 1:23).

---

1 Louis Bouyer, *Dictionary of Theology* (New York: Desclee, 1966), 359.

2 See Peter M. J. Stravinskas, *Our Sunday Visitor's Catholic Encyclopedia*, rev. ed. (Huntington, Ind.: Our Sunday Visitor, 1991), 802.

3 John Eudes, *The Priest: His Dignity and Obligations*, trans. W. Leo Murphy (Fitzwilliam, N.H.: Loreto Publications, 2008), 81.

4 See Edwards, *A History of Preaching*, 3–8.

5 In the New Testament, *apostle* "always denotes a man who is sent, and sent with full authority." Karl Heinrich Rengstorf, s.v. Ἀποστέλλω (πέμπω), Ἐξαποστέλλω, Ἀπόστολος, Ψευδαπόστολος, Ἀποστολή," ed. Gerhard Kittel, Geoffrey W. Bromiley, and Gerhard Friedrich, *Theological Dictionary of the New Testament* (Grand Rapids, Mich.: Eerdmans, 1964–1976).

Because they were called and sent, they knew their mission was to proclaim through a special commission, to herald with persuasion the authoritative message of God.[6]

Their proclamation of the Gospel was done in more than one way, as we can see in the testimony of apostolic preaching. Right after his baptism, Paul went to the synagogue to proclaim something quite simple yet revolutionary: Jesus was the Son of God (see Acts 9:20). This he certainly did without the theological understanding we find later in his letters, the fruit of years of prayer and study. At that point, Paul had one thing to say to those who had never heard it: Jesus was the Messiah.

Another kind of preaching is exemplified by the speech given by Peter to the Christian leaders gathered in Jerusalem (see Acts 15:7–11). In his exposition of God's work, he powerfully proclaimed to believers how God's salvation comes to both Jews and Gentiles.

A third way of preaching occurs in a liturgical context, as we can see in the references made by Paul to the Corinthian church to his own testimony of preaching with the wisdom of the Cross or to the regulation of liturgical assemblies (see 1 Cor 2:1–5; 14:29–31).[7] In Acts of the Apostles, we read of the long speech given by Paul in the context of the breaking of the bread, so long that it almost cost young Eutychus his life when he fell asleep (see Acts 20:7–12)!

Thus, from the earliest days of the Church preaching has taken different forms. Today, we hear about the preaching of retreats, of missions, of homilies; preaching takes place in churches, auditoriums, halls, houses, public squares, and schools. It only makes sense: every place and every occasion can be the setting for sharing the good news of Jesus Christ. Generally speaking, oral proclamation of the good news is for one of three purposes: "to produce faith, to know faith, to live faith," which correspond to evangelization, catechesis, and homily.[8] The homily, as liturgical preaching, is our focus here. Who preaches the homily? Where does preaching take place? What is the content of liturgical preaching? In the next pages we will reflect on these questions.

---

6 Such is the meaning of "proclaim"—κηρύσσομεν. See Horst Balz and Gerhard Schneider, eds., *Exegetical Dictionary of the New Testament*, vol. 2 (Grand Rapids, Mich.: Eerdmans Publishing, 1990), 288.

7 For a scholarly review of the earliest evidence of liturgical preaching see Stewart-Sykes, *From Prophecy to Preaching*, 6–23.

8 Domenico Grasso, SJ, *Proclaiming God's Message: A Study in the Theology of Preaching* (Notre Dame, Ind.: University of Notre Dame Press, 1965), 223.

WHO? THE PRIEST AS PREACHER

As with John the Baptist, a preacher is a voice for the Word, according to St. Augustine's image.[9] Augustine's meditation on John as the voice of the Word illuminates the identity of the preacher. He is not the center, not the content, not the protagonist, but a servant, one that lends his voice so that the Word can resonate in the right way and at the right time.

As a voice, a preacher is an instrument of the grace given by God, who is always the principal subject of preaching.[10] Thus it is that, while there are many important tasks surrounding the mission of preaching, the most fundamental one is to know God. A preacher is not called simply to convey information about God, but to listen to him and share from that personal knowledge. Preaching is a privileged way of being a witness. Indeed, a preacher is a herald, a teacher, an interpreter, and a witness.[11]

Just as Jesus called his disciples "friends" because he told them all he had heard from his Father (see Jn 15:15), so the disciples could not refrain from speaking of what they had heard and seen (see Acts 4:20). The Gospel tells us clearly that the Lord called the twelve to be with him and sent them forth to preach (see Mk 3:14). The order is relevant: the first mission of an apostle is to be with Christ, to accompany him, to know him, to love him, to follow him. Only out of that real and personal knowledge can anyone meaningfully fulfill the mission of preaching.

This truth is particularly important for understanding liturgical preaching. The specific closeness to Christ required for the mission of a homilist is not the one shared by all believers, but one rooted in the sacramental life of the Church in general, and in the sacrament of holy orders in particular, as the homily can only be given by ordained ministers.[12] A man receives the sacrament of holy orders not because of his own personal merits but because of God's mercy, and when he is ordained, he is ordained to preach—that is, his life is ordered to the proclamation of Christ. He exists now in order to proclaim the good news. This was the turning point in the life of the twelve apostles: after Jesus went about preaching the good news in all cities, he saw the crowds and was deeply moved with compassion for them. He asked his disciples to pray for more laborers for the abundant harvest. Then, and only

---

9 See Augustine, *Sermons* 293.3; 293A.5; 293C.1.

10 On the understanding of God's causality in preaching, see Grasso, *Proclaiming God's Message*, 23–46.

11 See Waznak, *An Introduction to the Homily*, 31–67.

12 See *Code of Canon Law*, 767 § 1.

then, out of his merciful and compassionate heart, and after praying, Jesus called the twelve and sent them to proclaim that the kingdom was at hand (see Mt 9:35–38; 10:1–7). The task of preaching comes from the merciful and prayerful heart of Jesus, and it is entrusted to those consecrated by him.

We can hardly insist too much on this point. Preaching is not an accessory element in the life of a priest. This mission arises from the particular sacramental character of his conformation to Christ the Head. Preaching is not simply one among other possible priestly missions, such as being a chaplain, or a parochial vicar, or a professor. Those missions are related to the particular call of each particular priest, but *all* priests have been ordained to preach the Gospel. Preaching is not an extrinsic assignment but rather an essential and permanent vocation imprinted by the indelible character of sacramental ordination.

This is a truth evident in the rite of ordination itself. The first question the bishop asks after an ordination candidate has accepted the office of priesthood as a presbyter is about preaching: "Do you resolve to exercise the ministry of the word worthily and wisely, preaching the Gospel and teaching the Catholic faith?" Similar is the first question answered by a priest to be ordained a bishop, after he accepts the episcopal office: "Do you resolve to preach the Gospel with constancy and fidelity?" And then, in the prayer of priestly ordination, the bishop intercedes for the priest with these words: "May he be a worthy co-worker with our Order, so that by his preaching and though the grace of the Holy Spirit the words of the Gospel may bear fruit in human hearts and reach even the ends of the earth." All priests, as co-workers with the order of bishops, are ordained to preach.[13]

We can understand thus why the Second Vatican Council teaches that among the many important duties of a bishop preaching occupies "an eminent place"; this echoes the Council of Trent, which describes preaching as "the principal duty of Bishops."[14] Priests, as cooperators with the order of

---

[13] The rite of ordination for deacons insists on the call to minister—that is, to serve—according to the essence of their vocation as seen in the New Testament, when the apostles "appointed seven men of good repute to assist them in the daily ministry, that they might devote themselves more fully to prayer and preaching of the word" (Prayer of Ordination for Deacons). Called to be "heralds of the Gospel," as they hear when they receive the book of the Gospels, deacons receive the imposition of hands "not unto the priesthood, but unto a ministry of service." The call to liturgical preaching for deacons does not seem to have the essential place it has for the other degrees of holy orders, and it should be always understood in the logic of service and exercised "occasionally, according to circumstances," (*General Instruction of the Roman Missal*, 66) as assistance to the ministry of bishops and priests.

[14] *Lumen Gentium*, 25; Council of Trent, Session 5, 2, in *The Canons and Decrees of the Council of Trent*, trans. Theodore Alois Buckley (London: George Routledge and Co., 1851), 26.

bishops, take part in this primary mission: "Dependent on the bishops in the exercise of their power, nevertheless [priests] are united with the bishops in sacerdotal dignity. By the power of the sacrament of Orders, in the image of Christ the eternal high Priest, they are consecrated to preach the Gospel and shepherd the faithful and to celebrate divine worship, so that they are true priests of the New Testament."[15] Earlier, the council fathers affirm, "Through their [bishops' and priests'] excellent service He [Christ] is preaching the word of God to all nations and constantly administering the sacraments of faith to those who believe."[16]

The fact that the council says that Jesus Christ preaches the word through the service of bishops and priests leads us to consider again the sacramental reality of preaching. To be a priest means to partake in the priesthood of Jesus Christ and, therefore, in his sanctifying power exercised through the sacraments. Grasso explains this with clarity:

> The sacraments, however, cannot be effective without faith. Therefore, it is essential that he who has the power to sanctify should also possess the power to preach, because preaching is necessary to faith (Rom 10:17). Preaching and sacrament are, therefore, two realities intimately linked to each other. It is impossible to be a minister of the sacraments without also being a minister of the Word.[17]

We could say that the priest is the one who breaks the bread of God's Word and then breaks the bread of the Body of Christ at the altar.[18] Our understanding of these two aspects of the liturgical celebration has to be founded on their unity, for they are intrinsically connected: "Sacrament and word belong together and form the totality of worship which cannot exist without the effective spirituality of the word nor without the spiritual efficacy of the sacrament."[19] However, it might be good to go one step further and add that the unity of "consecration" and "proclamation" does not only consist in their being integral yet different parts of one action, but in the fact that both are liturgical and sacramental actions (sacramental understood here

---

15 *Lumen Gentium*, 28.

16 *Lumen Gentium*, 21.

17 Grasso, *Proclaiming God's Message*, 77.

18 This union between word and sacrament within the celebration of the Eucharist invites us to consider the preference of the main celebrant of the Mass being ordinarily the one who preaches the homily.

19 Söhngen, *Symbol und Wirklichkeit im Kultmysterium* (Bonn: Hanstein, 1937), quoted in Grasso, *Proclaiming God's Message*, 129.

in a broad sense). Augustine described the sacraments as "visible words."[20] The spoken words of the homily find their place within the celebration of the visible words of the liturgical action.[21] Preaching is not just a form of teaching within the liturgical celebrations, but a true liturgical action, or as Pope Francis said, it is a "quasi-sacramental action": not so much in the sense of being "almost sacramental" but as an action essentially rooted in the sacramental life of the Church. [22]

During the celebration of the Mass, the bread of God's Word is broken at the ambo before the eucharistic body of the Lord is broken at the altar. These two "breakings" are intrinsically connected, and one cannot exist without the other. In fact, as J. A. Jungmann said, "the only proper response to the εὐ-αγγέλιον [eu-angelion] is the εὐ-χαριστία [eu-charistia]."[23] The only proper way of responding to the proclamation of the good news is the Eucharist: to give thanks to the Lord, by offering the sacrifice of thanksgiving.[24]

The sacramental link between altar and ambo can prove helpful in clarifying a possible misunderstanding. Christ is present in his Word and in the sacrifice of the Mass, but not in an equal manner. The presence of Christ in the eucharistic species is real; this does not indicate that his presence in the Word is not real, but that only the eucharistic presence is substantial.[25] This distinction was already and strongly emphasized in the Council of Trent, as a response to the ideas of the Reformers, who identified the priesthood with, and thus reduced it to, preaching.[26] The answer is, as is often the case, one of synthesis and not of exclusion.

However, it might seem that in some cases a common view of the priesthood among Catholics has been somewhat forgetful—whether in theory

---

20 See Augustine, *Tractates on John*, 80.3. See also *Tractates*, 12.5 and 15.4.

21 See William Harmless, *Augustine and the Catechumenate* (Collegeville, Minn.: Liturgical Press, 2014), 418.

22 See about this Walter J. Burghardt, SJ, *Preaching: The Art & the Craft* (New York: Paulist Press, 1987), 108–18.

23 Joseph A. Jungmann, *The Mass of the Roman Rite: Its Origins and Development,* vol. 2 (Notre Dame, Ind.: Christian Classics, 2012), 115.

24 About the sacrifice of thanksgiving see Daniel Cardó, *The Cross and the Eucharist in Early Christianity: A Theological and Liturgical Investigation* (Cambridge: Cambridge University Press, 2019), 110.

25 See Paul VI, Encyclical Letter *Mysterium Fidei* (September 3, 1965), 39.

26 See Grasso, *Proclaiming God's Message*, 76.

or in practice—of the presence of Christ in his Word. In emphasizing the essential sacrificial and sacramental elements of Catholic theology, it appears as if in some cases the importance of the Word, and therefore of preaching, has not been sufficiently acknowledged. Furthermore, one wonders why it is that, as we have seen before, there is such discontent about preaching—why, to be candid, so many of us priests do not take seriously enough our task as preachers. While there are many reasons to explain such a complex reality, ultimately each of us needs to think about his identity as a priest, whether he has maintained a clear understanding of who he is as priest, as one ordained to preach and to offer sacrifice. When this self-understanding is not vividly clear, we will not be able to avoid the temptation of neglecting the paternal solicitude that ought to be a hallmark of any preacher, just as a father whose priority is his career (or something else) will not dedicate the time and energy to his children that the vocation to marriage and family life demands. And just as with a father who comes to the realization that his family has been neglected, so a priest who recognizes the centrality of this task will be motivated to overcome whatever obstacles—internal or external—stand in the way of his focus on preaching.

It is interesting, in this respect, to think about the self-understanding of ministers of some other Christian confessions. Bereft of the sacraments, their ministry is centered almost exclusively around the Word and its proclamation. Let us consider the powerful influence of understanding one's personal mission and identity as "a preacher" first and foremost. Would there be anything else more urgent or demanding than the preparation for a Sunday sermon? On this they judge themselves, and they know that on this they will be judged by their people. Again, our priestly vocation is wider. But in regard to being ministers of the Word, sealed by ordination to preach the Gospel, we should see ourselves, no less than any other minister, as preachers. In fact, the grave importance of preaching should be more keenly perceived by a Catholic priest, precisely because of preaching's liturgical and sacramental roots. If, therefore, we see ourselves as preachers, then hardly can we be satisfied with making excuses for not exercising this mission; we should start to strive today to fulfill this duty joyfully, generously, and responsibly. Once we have been ordained, we exist to sanctify God's people; consequently, we ought to live to offer sacrifice and preach the good news.

WHERE? THE CHURCH AS THE *PLACE* OF PREACHING

After reflecting on the identity of the priest as preacher, we move on to reflect on the *place* where preaching happens. The Church is the place of all preaching: both for the *ad extra* proclamation of God's love as an action directed towards "the peripheries," and for the *ad intra* proclamation to those gathered around the Lord, "*Ecclesia* is the point of reference of the proclamation."[27] The Church as *Ecclesia* (i.e., assembly) is not the goal and ultimate content of preaching, but its point of reference: she is the living community that is constantly fed by the breaking of God's Word and that cannot be content while many still have not heard the good news; she is the loving assembly that constantly needs to go deeper into the well of God's wisdom and the congregation never enclosed in itself but always generously committed to sharing the joy of the Gospel.

As such, the Church is not only the place of preaching, but also the acting subject of preaching.[28] This means that the Church is more than a useful organization of believers who share the same ideas; rather, it is the living assembly of God, the body of Christ. Therefore, liturgical preaching is not merely saying things about God, but God speaking to his people through the action of chosen men. The fact that only ordained ministers are entrusted with this ministry is a consequence of the ecclesial quality of salvation history: the Father sends his Son, who continues his work through his Church. Preaching is the action of the *totus Christus* (the complete Christ), Head and Body.

A consequence of this is the necessary and healthy tension between the universal and particular elements of preaching. A preacher does not speak on his own behalf, sharing his own personal views and preferences; nor does he speak only on behalf of a particular congregation or community. A preacher speaks on behalf of the Church; accordingly, there is always an essential universal quality to preaching. What is preached today is the same as what was said several centuries ago and what will be said in years to come. It is the proclamation of those words that "will not pass away" (Mt 25:25); it is the proclamation of the stable community of the Church as the unchanging Body of Christ. St. Irenaeus expressed this clearly in the third century: "Just

---

27 Joseph Ratzinger, *Dogma and Preaching: Applying Christian Doctrine to Christian Life*, trans. Michael J. Miller and Matthew J. O'Connell (San Francisco: Ignatius Press, 2011), 20.

28 Ratzinger, *Dogma and Preaching*, 21–22.

as God's creature, the sun, is one and the same the world over, so also does the Church's preaching shine everywhere to enlighten all men who want to come to a knowledge of the truth."[29] Indeed, the preaching of the Church is the same no matter the personal qualities of the preacher: "Neither will any of those who preside in the churches, though exceedingly eloquent, say anything else (*for no one is above the Master*); nor will a poor speaker subtract from the tradition. For, since the faith is one and the same, neither he who can discourse at length about it adds to it, nor he who can say only a little subtracts from it."[30]

However, that which is said by the one Church is said to a particular portion of the Church, gathered here and now. Therefore, the universal character of preaching has to encounter the specific demands of the concrete situation of those listening to the Church's message. Consequently, following the advice of St. John Henry Newman, a preacher must always keep in mind that what he says is not said "for the instruction of the whole world, but directly for the sake of those very persons who are before him."[31] Therefore, as Gregory the Great said, "every teacher, in order to edify all in the one virtue must touch the hearts of his hearers by using one and the same doctrine, but not by giving to all one and the same exhortation."[32]

The tension between the universal and particular aspects of preaching is a salutary reminder of the need to constantly discern how to proclaim the general aspects of revelation in a specific setting.[33] "In all the most important respects, indeed, all hearers are the same, and what is suitable for one audience is suitable for another."[34] However, "a preacher should be quite sure that he understands the persons he is addressing before he ventures to aim at what he considers to be their ethical condition; for, if he mistakes, he

---

29 Irenaeus of Lyon, *Against the Heresies*, trans. Dominic J. Unger, OFM.Cap. (New York: Paulist Press, 1992), I.10.2.

30 Irenaeus, *Against the Heresies*, I.10.2.

31 John Henry Newman, *The Idea of a University* (Notre Dame, Ind.: University of Notre Dame Press, 1982), 311.

32 Gregory I, *Pastoral Care*, trans. Henry Davis, SJ (Westminster, Md.: Newman Press, 1950), III.1. Gregory identifies thirty-six pairs of kinds of hearers (e.g., men and women, young and old, taciturn and loquacious, humble and haughty, etc.) and gives homiletic advice for each pairing. See this remarkable section in *Pastoral Care*, III.1–35.

33 This topic will be developed in a more detailed manner in the next chapter, "An Incarnational Approach."

34 Newman, *Idea of a University*, 311.

will probably be doing harm rather than good."[35] Truly, as Pope Francis has recently taught, "the homily is the touchstone for judging a pastor's closeness and ability to communicate to his people."[36]

Fidelity to the universal character of Christian preaching and to the particular needs of the different assemblies arises from and produces earnestness: "Earnestness creates earnestness in others by sympathy; and the more a preacher loses and is lost to himself, the more does he gain his brethren."[37] Communion in the eternal truths of the Gospel, shared according to the needs of the particular assembly, goes much deeper than the passing moments of successful human niceness. This authentic communion comes from the supernatural presence of Christ in his Church and strengthens the bond of love among his people.

WHAT? THE CONTENT OF PREACHING

The ordained minister of the Church does not preach himself: "For we do not proclaim ourselves; we proclaim Jesus Christ as Lord and ourselves as your slaves for Jesus' sake" (2 Cor 4:5). What does it mean to "proclaim Jesus Christ"?

It means, first and foremost, to share what we learn from God—not just *about* God, but *from* God. Origen describes thus the double demands of a priest: "Either learn from God by reading the divine Scriptures and by meditating often on them, or teach the people. But let him teach those things that he has learned from the Lord, not 'from his own heart,' or from human understanding, but what the Spirit teaches."[38] And we learn from God the good news, the unthinkable revelation: God became man. We learn from him what we never could have imagined and can receive only by faith: Jesus is God incarnate; he came to save us; he continues his work of salvation through the Church. In other words, we learn from God what we ourselves ought to proclaim: the kerygma, "the good news as it came forth from God's mouth," "the proclamation by the Church, as sent by Christ of the salvation-event that finds its accomplishment in Him."[39]

---

35 Newman, *Idea of a University*, 313.

36 Francis, *Evangelii Gaudium*, 135.

37 Newman, *Idea of a University*, 305.

38 Origen, *Homilies on Leviticus*, trans. Gary Wayne Barkley (Washington, D.C.: The Catholic University of America Press, 1990), 6.6.

39 Hugo Rahner, SJ, *A Theology of Proclamation* (New York: Herder and Herder, 1968), 13; Bouyer, *Dictionary of Theology*, 260.

What we preach is simple: Jesus is Lord. Of course, simple does not mean shallow or repetitive. The depths of the simplicity of God are infinite. For the preacher, this means "to preach with the words and the simplicity of holy Scripture, with the childlike depth of the teaching Church, with the most valued possessions of theology just as they were received into preaching from the beginning," just as we see (or hear) in the homilies of the greatest preachers of our history.[40] Their styles vary, and yet their voices form a wonderful, polyphonic song to the Lord, magnificently blended by the harmony of love. Is it a coincidence that the most memorable homilies of our tradition were preached by saints?

There are many topics to be developed in our preaching, and we will address this point later. But this cannot be done unless we believe that what we ought to preach is Jesus Christ and what he has revealed, and this is something that we must learn not only from books, but primarily from prayer and adoration.

It is lamentable that too many homilies today reduce the content of preaching to human concerns of social improvements or mere sympathies. When a priest does not speak about the mystery revealed and entrusted to us, he becomes, at best, one who can occasionally offer good advice and some help. But we have to preach eternal truths, as Cardinal Cantalamessa has recently reminded us. In the context of so much instability and fragility we must, more than ever, remind our people of three essential truths: "first, that we are mortal and 'we have no stable dwelling on earth' (Heb 13:14); secondly, that life does not end with death, because eternal life awaits us; thirdly, that we do not face the waves alone on the small boat of our planet because 'the Word became flesh and made his dwelling among us.' (Jn 1:14)."[41] Only the light of faith can illumine our life and our death, and only because of it do we preach. Hugo Rahner says:

> We should speak much more frequently to the faithful about revelation. They must know and become aware of the fact that the priest is concerned with deep mysteries, that he comes from out of the wilderness where he was burdened with the weight of his mission, to speak in God's name, to be a prophet. They must realize that Christianity is not just another religion which serves to help one to carry the miseries of life a little better

---

40 Rahner, *A Theology of Proclamation*, 14.

41 Raniero Cantalamessa, *First Sermon of Advent to the Roman Curia*, December 4, 2020, in http://www.cantalamessa.org/?p=3890&lang=en

and which also speaks occasionally of things hereafter. Revelation is the basic reason for our priestly mission and the justification of our claim to be heard. It is the Lord who bids us to speak.[42]

The revealed message we must communicate is the reason we speak. Their acceptance of our received commission to proclaim the kerygma is the reason our people hear. Anything else is beneath our dignity and mission.

Preaching is about revelation, or, as Domenico Grasso puts it, it is "revelation in transmission."[43] However, this does not mean only that we speak about revealed mysteries, but that there is a supernatural element present in liturgical preaching itself. Again, Pope Francis has said that the homily has a "quasi-sacramental" quality. Preaching a homily is more than human speech on theological ideas; it is an action that is conferred with an intrinsic "effectiveness," understood as a consequence of its connection with the sacramental activity of the Church.[44] Because of this, famed seventeenth-century preacher Jacques-Bénigne Bossuet could boldly say: "Before ascending his tribunal to condemn the guilty [Jesus Christ] speaks from the pulpit to call them back to the right way with charitable exhortations."[45]

Now, while the core of all preaching is simple (Jesus is Lord), there are many aspects of God's revelation that ought to be part of what we preach. The Church, wrote St. Irenaeus of Lyon, receives one preaching and one faith from the apostles and their disciples, and now preserves it carefully, "as if she dwelt in one house." This is it:

> The faith in one God the Father Almighty, the Creator of heaven and earth and the seas and all things that are in them; and in the one Jesus Christ, the Son of God, who was enfleshed for our salvation; and in the Holy Spirit, who through the prophets preached the Economies, the coming, the birth from a Virgin, the passion, the resurrection from the dead, and the bodily ascension into heaven of the beloved Son, Christ Jesus our Lord, and His coming from heaven in the glory of the Father to recapitulate all things, and to raise up all flesh of the whole human race, in order that to Christ Jesus, our Lord, Savior and King, according to the invisible Father's good

42 Rahner, *A Theology of Proclamation*, 19–20.

43 Grasso, *Proclaiming God's Message*, xxxiii.

44 About this, see the classic study of Otto Semmelroth, SJ, *The Preaching Word: On the Theology of Proclamation* (New York: Herder and Herder, 1965). See also Grasso, *Proclaiming God's Message*, 131–44.

45 Jacques-Bénigne Bossuet, *Ouevres complètes de Bossuet*, ed. *François* Lachat, vol. 9 (Paris: Vives, 1862), 40. Quoted in Grasso, 34.

pleasure, *every knee should bow [of those] in heaven and on earth and under the earth, and every tongue confess Him*, and that He would exercise just judgement toward all.[46]

The mystery of Christ is the key to knowing the other mysteries; it is "the mystery that has been hidden throughout the ages and generations but has now been revealed to his saints" (Col 1:26). Or rather, the one content of Christian preaching—Christ himself—is unfolded in several themes, already present in the preaching of the apostles: the Kingdom, the Word of God, the Gospel, the mystery.

Joseph Ratzinger and Hugo Rahner propose some of the major themes of preaching that come from God's revelation and that ought to be considered for our own preaching. Ratzinger organizes these major themes as follows:[47]

- God
- Christ
- Creation-Grace-World
- Church
- Eschatology

Hugo Rahner's list is more comprehensive:[48]

Spiritual and invisible themes:

- The Trinity
- Original Justice and Original Sin
- The Hypostatic Union
- Church, Grace, and Vision

Historically visible themes:

- The Life of Jesus
- The Visible Church
- The Visible Sacraments
- The Visible Priesthood

---

46 Irenaeus, *Against the Heresies*, I.10.1.

47 See Ratzinger, *Dogma and Preaching*, 77–271.

48 See Rahner, *A Theology of Proclamation*, 21–216.

Certainly, the liturgical homily is not a mere explanation of theological truths. The unifying factor in the exposition of these themes is Jesus himself. This means two things. First, preaching is Christocentric—Jesus is the fullness of revelation and the revealer.[49] He is the message and the messenger. He is the key to interpret the Scriptures, as becomes clear in his own exegesis of the Law and the Prophets to the disciples on the road to Emmaus (see Lk 24:13–35). He is "the whole exegesis" of Scripture, as Henri de Lubac said: "Jesus Christ brings about the unity of Scripture, because he is the endpoint and fullness of Scripture. Everything in it is related to him. In the end he is its sole object. Consequently, he is, so to speak, its whole exegesis."[50]

Jesus is also the center of history, its beginning and end, the key to read the drama of human history. In the end, "history has been *for him.*"[51] As such, he is also the key for our own personal history. He, and only he, as God and man, fulfills the otherwise impossible dream: to trust in a truth that is a person. For we need a truth to believe in and someone in whom we can trust. No one else can claim to be the truth, and our friend.

Second, the centrality of Christ in preaching refreshes the awareness of his continual action in his Church. Preaching finds its true meaning in the context of salvation history. What we say in our homilies is not mere teaching, but a humble and necessary participation in today's unfolding of the history of redemption. This is what we feel in Paul's words to the Corinthian church. He did not go there to teach valuable ideas; he went to preach Jesus Christ, knowing that Jesus Christ was working in him through the power of the Spirit. This is in no way a reality valid only for the nascent Church of the first centuries. This should still be the trademark of any homily preached in our parishes:

> When I came to you, brothers and sisters, I did not come proclaiming the mystery of God to you in lofty words or wisdom. For I decided to know nothing among you except Jesus Christ, and him crucified. And I came to you in weakness and in fear and in much trembling. My speech and my proclamation were not with plausible words of wisdom, but with a demonstration of the Spirit and of power, so that your faith might rest not on human wisdom but on the power of God. (1 Cor 2:1–5)

---

49 See *Dei Verbum*, 2.

50 Henri de Lubac, SJ, *Medieval Exegesis: The Four Senses of Scripture*, vol. 1 (Edinburgh: T&T Clark, 1998), 237.

51 Erasmo Leiva-Merikakis, *Fire of Mercy, Heart of the Word: Meditations on the Gospel According to St. Matthew*, vol. 1 (San Francisco: Ignatius Press, 1996), 59.

Questions for Reflection and Conversation

• *Why is it so important for a priest to understand himself as a preacher and not just as someone who sometimes has to preach?*

• *What does it mean to say that the Church is the place for preaching?*

• *What are the consequences of Christ's centrality in preaching?*

4

An Incarnational Approach

The mystery of the Incarnation of the Son of God is at the very core of the Christian creed, acting as a hinge or axis to the whole edifice of the faith. It communicates the simple yet absolutely revolutionary fact that God became man, the event that has divided history in two, the final revelation of God's love and fidelity. If human reason is capable of reaching a certain inkling of other mysteries, such as that of the Most Holy Trinity, the Incarnation of the Son of God completely surpasses any intuition or deduction—such a gift can only be known by revelation.[1]

Who could have dreamed that God loved the world so much that he sent his own Son to become one of us (see Jn 3:16)? The Incarnation of Christ, a mystery that has never ceased to fascinate the brightest minds and the simplest hearts, has radically changed our relationship with God: "In the person of Jesus and in the event of his Incarnation, we see that 'God' means: 'He who saves in the flesh out of love.'"[2] Christ, true God and true man, reveals the mysteries of God and of humanity. "Jesus translates God," and shows us what it means to be human.[3]

This revelation tells us that what was impossible is now a reality; the extremes are reconciled in Christ. "God is not simply infinite distance; he is also infinite nearness," because "by His Incarnation

---

1 Augustine suggests this in his work *On True Religion*: while other mysteries might be grasped or intuited by reason, the Incarnation can only be grasped by faith. See Henry Chadwick, *Augustine of Hippo: A Life* (Oxford: Oxford University Press, 2009), 117.

2 Leiva-Merikakis, *Fire of Mercy*, I:71.

3 Leiva-Merikakis, *Fire of Mercy,* I:70; See *Gaudium et Spes*, 22.

the Son of God has united Himself in some fashion with every man."[4] As true God and true man, Jesus becomes "more inward than my most inward part and higher than the highest element within me," *interior intimo meo et superior summo meo.*[5] In his human and divine heart we find the bridge to go to God and thus to our true humanity. We are not a mere enigma, a perpetually frustrated longing, a useless question; after the Incarnation we can reach our destination. Without Christ, says Augustine, we cannot travel to our "home country": "Of this we would be quite incapable, unless Wisdom herself [Christ] had seen fit to adapt herself even to such infirmity as ours, and had given us an example of how to live, in no other mode than the human one, because we too are human.... So since she herself [Wisdom] is our home, she also made herself for us into the way home."[6] Indeed, "clothing himself with flesh, he became the way."[7]

All of this has decisive consequences for preaching. For the Incarnation means that out of love the eternal Word assumed our human words, redeeming them and filling them with a new meaning. In *Dei Verbum* we find a key passage about this:

> In Sacred Scripture, therefore, while the truth and holiness of God always remains intact, the marvelous "condescension" of eternal wisdom is clearly shown, "that we may learn the gentle kindness of God, which words cannot express, and how far He has gone in adapting His language with thoughtful concern for our weak human nature." For the words of God, expressed in human language, have been made like human discourse, just as the word of the eternal Father, when He took to Himself the flesh of human weakness, was in every way made like men.[8]

When God, with infinite condescension [*synkatabasis*], speaks with a human voice in our own language, he makes our speech capable of saying good words about the Word. Speaking with human words, the eternal Wisdom becomes the way and the path for preachers, who, therefore, should

---

4 Ratzinger, *Dogma and Preaching,* 121; *Gaudium et Spes,* 22.

5 Augustine, *Confessions,* trans. Henry Chadwick (Oxford: Oxford University Press, 2008), III.6.11.

6 Augustine, *Teaching Christianity,* I.11.

7 Augustine, *Tractates on John,* 34.3.

8 *Dei Verbum,* 13. Includes note on quotation: "John Chrysostom, In Genesis 3, 8 (Homily 17, 1): PG 53, 134; *Attemperatio* [in English "Suitable adjustment"] in Greek *synkatabasis*."

not look first and foremost for the best *words* (whether that means words of precision, elegance, sympathy, or humor) but for *the Word* who has come to us, making this encounter possible: "Instead of climbing up to Heaven to find the eternal Word, you have to grasp that the eternal Word has come down from Heaven to find you."[9]

It is no exaggeration to say that communion with Christ the incarnate Word is the real foundation for good preaching, which in the end consists in accepting the Word in our lives, learning *from him* how to proclaim the good news, and learning to do so *with him*. Only in Christ are we truly capable of knowing God, *of whom we preach*; and of knowing our people, *to whom we preach*. Jesus "is always one speaker, one person … but he speaks for two worlds, two 'natures.'"[10] Analogously, he offers the same capacity to those whom he has consecrated by the sacrament of holy orders, as they are configured to Christ the Head and made capable of acting in him. A preacher ought to conform his life to the reality of the Incarnation in order to learn how to be with God and with his people, following the pattern opened by Christ in the Incarnation, beautifully described by St. Irenaeus: "He is the Word of God who dwelt in man and became the Son of Man, that He might accustom man to receive God, and God to dwell in man, according to the good pleasure of the Father."[11] Thus, in communion with Jesus, the preacher becomes capable of speaking of "two worlds," translating God to his people, and bringing his people to God.

We can try to better understand this reality by borrowing two patristic axioms. First is the *aproslepton, atherapeuton*, "that which was not assumed was not healed." Christ assumed our human voice and therefore redeemed it. This means that human language has been redeemed and filled with new meaning and power. This implies the importance of learning from the words of the incarnate Word. Jesus did not assume any kind of human speech, but only that which was truly human. In his words we can acquire the wisdom to speak well according to the circumstances and audience. Sometimes, the right word is a simple story, a parable, or a few words of forgiveness. At times the occasion requires a lengthy spiritual speech, while at other times hard words are necessary. Occasionally, our discourse should unveil a truth yet leave some mystery to unfold in time. We should speak to children in a

9 Rowan Williams, *On Augustine* (London: Bloomsbury, 2016), 132.

10 Williams, *On Augustine*, 134.

11 Irenaeus, *Against the Heresies*, trans. Dominic J. Unger, OFM.Cap. (Mahwah, N.J.: The Newman Press, 2012), III.20.2.

manner different from what we use with a small group of committed disciples, or with official authorities. A habit of prayerfully reading the Gospels and learning from Jesus himself how to speak well makes our human speech more redeemed and therefore more effective.

The second patristic "axiom" that we can apply to our homilies is the *admirabile commercium* (admirable exchange), "God became man so that man can become like God." This is a mystery of descent and ascent: God comes to our humanity not simply to stay here but to take us up with him. For preaching, this means that our homilies ought to come down to where our hearers are; like Christ and with him, we need to exercise the necessary "suitable adjustment" of our ideas so that they can be understood. However, even before thinking of this downwards movement, we need to be reminded of the necessary tension upwards. As Joseph Ratzinger wrote about the Incarnation, "anyone who wishes to understand descent, must first have grasped the mystery of the height."[12] In order to adjust our message, we must first have something higher that needs to be adjusted for its communication. In other words, if a preacher is not familiar with the mystery of the height of God, he will not bring what his people need to hear: the good news of God's love. A preacher who only wants to be at the level of his audience, without any words that speak of an otherworldly realm, without the surprises and challenges of the Gospel, would ultimately betray his mission. On the other hand, homilies that speak of lofty things using language that is incomprehensible to the audience will not fulfill their goal. The key, again, is the Incarnation, the admirable exchange: from the height of our sacramental and spiritual communion with God—that is, from what we learn from him—we go to our people with words and eloquence that they can understand, so that then we can bring them to the heights of Trinitarian love. The Incarnation as foundation of faithful preaching means constantly ascending God's mountain, coming down to share what has been seen, and leading everyone back up. We should, as Jesus said, "speak of what we know, and bear witness to what we have seen" (Jn 3:11).

In this sense, a preacher has to be an imitator of God himself: "Therefore be imitators of God, as beloved children. And walk in love, as Christ loved us and gave himself up for us" (Eph 5:1–2a). A homilist imitates God by Christ-

---

12 Joseph Ratzinger, *The God of Jesus Christ: Meditations on the Triune God* (San Francisco: Ignatius Press, 2008), 61. See also John 3:13: "No one has ascended into heaven but he who descended from heaven."

like sacrifice and humility. The mystery of Christ's *kenosis* (descent) requires us also to lose in order to gain.

We can understand this sacrificial descent or loss in two ways. First, a preacher who wants to imitate God will ceaselessly strive to preach better: "Christian teachers model the Incarnation by pouring their hearts into their hearers."[13] This demands a daily effort of spending time preparing the homily, a constant recourse to good resources for preaching, and a sincere commitment to let our heart be pierced by the Word. Second, *kenosis* in preaching means humility. In some real way, each preacher has to experience a "loss of his voice" if he is to truly "find his voice" renewed in Christ. This is a freeing process of truly having nothing to say if it is not said from Christ and with him. The personal *kenosis* of a preacher means becoming like little children—that is, *népios* (unlearned or without speech): "To be νήπιος [*népios*] in imitation of the eternal Son of the Father means having nothing of one's own to say independently of the Heart, Mind, and Being of God. It means to be *nothing but Word*, a glorious condition, because it is full of the being of the One who is loved."[14]

This is the glorious calling of the preacher: to become more and more like Christ in what he says and in the manner in which he speaks. Jesus, then, truly becomes the foundation and the way for the homilist. As Word made flesh (Jn 1:14), as eternal Wisdom assuming human speech, he himself becomes the "grammar" of our preaching, for only in Christ can we really come to know God and our people, and only in that way can we fulfill our mission, described by Pope Francis as "the wonderful but difficult task of joining loving hearts, the hearts of the Lord and his people."[15]

INCARNATIONAL PREACHING IN PRACTICE

From the knowledge of God and communion with him, a preacher has to come to his people, know them, love them, live with them. The Incarnation then becomes a living and practical principle based on which the one charged with the proclamation of God's Word constantly learns how to preach the good news here and now to the people he shepherds. There is no fixed formula

---

13 Michael Cameron, *Christ Meets Me Everywhere: Augustine's Early Figurative Exegesis* (Oxford: Oxford University Press, 2012), 243.

14 Leiva-Merikakis, *Fire of Mercy*, 1:695.

15 Francis, *Evangelii Gaudium*, 143.

for doing this; it is an exercise of love, a concrete expression of the fatherly solicitude of a priestly heart, a manifestation of pastoral charity. Incarnational preaching creates what Augustine wonderfully described as he explained how to teach the faith to his friend Deogratias: "For this feeling of compassion is so strong that, when our listeners are touched by us as we speak and we are touched by them as they learn, each of us comes to dwell in the other."[16] A preacher truly incarnate in the flesh of the flock entrusted to his care constantly discerns what to say and how to proclaim it, grasping the problems, questions, and possible objections to God's truth, and responding to them with *claritas* and *caritas*, just as a father reflects on what and how to teach his children. Indeed, teaching with a reverent and charitable fatherly care, while not always easy or immediately successful, will strengthen the trust necessary to learn and grow, and eventually will bear lasting fruit. A pastor who knows and loves his flock will find the openness of those who know and love him as they both—shepherd and flock—walk together through the dark valleys of history towards the green pastures of eternity.

While there is not one fixed set of rules for incarnational preaching, it is important to agree on certain attitudes that will allow the specific discernment of each preacher in any given situation. We will review some of these now, and then take a look at different occasions for preaching.

Listen to Your People

A good preacher is the one who learns from Christ his lesson of speaking with "comprehensive compassion."[17] This demands a constant and intentional effort to listen to the people of God. Pope Francis has reminded us that preaching occurs in an ecclesial context: the Church, as "a good mother, can recognize everything that God is bringing about in her children, she listens to their concerns and learns from them."[18]

We need to learn from our people. Needless to say, this does not mean that we can only preach of what they already like or know. What would we offer them if everything we said was plain and familiar? The common denominators of general culture and of theological, liturgical, and catechetical formation among our people cannot determine the level of our preach-

---

16 Augustine, *Instructing Beginners in Faith*, I.12.17.

17 Williams, *On Augustine*, 134.

18 Francis, *Evangelii Gaudium*, 139.

ing, for we have been called to guide them to the heights. To do this well, "the homilist must have empathy for human experience, observe it closely and sympathetically, and incorporate it into his preaching. The goal of the homily is to lead the hearer to the deep inner connection between God's word and the actual circumstances of one's everyday life."[19] Because of this, we must know our community, be aware of what is happening in their lives, take the pulse of their pilgrimage of faith. Indeed, "the true pastor and good shepherd knows his people's sorrows, their anxieties, their weaknesses, their capacity for love, their abiding joys, and their deepest longings."[20] In the words of Pope Francis, "the preacher also needs to keep his ear to the people and to discover what it is that the faithful need to hear. A preacher has to contemplate the word, but he also has to contemplate his people."[21] In the truest sense, we need to hear from our people and depend on their experience, support, and insight.[22]

There are a number of ways of listening to our people. Let us mention three:

- **Daily pastoral life**
  A preacher can most readily "contemplate his people" in daily life with them. Any pastor who tries to live his vocation will spend time with his flock and thus learn what they need, not by surveys but by personal interaction. How many occasions do we have for this! Home visits, sacramental calls, confession, dialogues, church events, coffee after Mass, et cetera. In sincere conversation and in joyful communion, we learn the names of the people given to us by the Good Shepherd, and read in their faces the work of God's grace, the struggles and joys of life.

- **Group meetings**
  A preacher who himself leads formation and prayer groups will be able to take the spiritual pulse of his community. This practice can be particularly fruitful if he can meditate on the Sunday liturgy with a group, listening to the manifold ways in which God moves their hearts.

19 United States Conference of Catholic Bishops, *Preaching the Mystery of the Faith: The Sunday Homily* (2012), 29.

20 USCCB, *Preaching the Mystery of the Faith*, 34.

21 Francis, *Evangelii Gaudium*, 154.

22 The next chapter will share the valuable advice of some brothers and sisters "from the pews."

· **Trusted advisors**
Every preacher should be able to find some friends and coworkers whom he can consult for feedback and ideas. The staff members of a parish or team members of other apostolates can become trustworthy and sincere counselors in the effort to discern what God wants us to say to his people.

One final idea about this point: in the midst of our busy lives it is not uncommon to miss some of the best lessons offered, directly or indirectly, by our people. It is imperative that we develop the habit of paying attention: listening and reflecting (perhaps even taking notes throughout the week) on the various experiences with our people, where we can always find valuable teachings that ought to be treasured, and from where we will be able to make a difference with our preaching. Indeed, "what our words can do is help people make connections between the realities of their lives and the realities of the Gospel … in order to do so, the preacher will have to be a listener before he is a speaker."[23]

Listen to What Happens in the World

Homilies that are incarnate in the reality of a community need to be fed also from constant attentiveness to what is happening in the world. The first words of *Gaudium et Spes* remind us of the reason for this: "The joys and the hopes, the griefs and the anxieties of the men of this age, especially those who are poor or in any way afflicted, these are the joys and hopes, the griefs and anxieties of the followers of Christ. Indeed, nothing genuinely human fails to raise an echo in their hearts."[24]

In order to preach with the effectiveness of love, we need to be informed about relevant world and local events, about the hopes and concerns of our people, about the real (and false) threats to their well-being and freedom. Certainly, in a time of an overload of information, we need to be prudent in how we attend to current events. But if we want to preach effectively, the need to remain well informed and therefore sensitive to what is taking place in the world is clear. The oft-cited saying of the Swiss Reformed theologian Karl Barth illustrates this attitude: "We must hold the Bible in one hand and the newspaper in the other." Of course, God's Word is more important than the

---

23 National Conference of Catholic Bishops, *Fulfilled in Your Hearing: The Homily in the Sunday Assembly* (Washington, D.C.: United States Catholic Conference, 1982), 29.

24 *Gaudium et Spes*, 1.

newspaper as it illuminates the news we read (perhaps on our smartphones), but it is also true that the newspaper helps us to incarnate the homily in a given *here* and *now*.

A Quick Word about Our Words

Another consequence of the Incarnation for preaching is the importance of finding the right words, words which—no matter the circumstance, topic, or style—should always be comprehensible: people must be able understand what we say. As a general rule, language should be simple, and phrases should be short. However, this does not mean falling into the trap of thinking that we need to dumb down our speech. Our words ought to be clear and down-to-earth but elevating. This does not rule out smart turns of phrase, beautiful expressions, and profound ideas, but it does give us a standard for their expression.

Synkatabasis is the key. We seek the right kind of adjustment of our message, the "going down together" with our people in order to bring them up to the heights; the simplicity of love, which is always deep and moving. The choice is not between simplistic and incomprehensible; the invitation is to train ourselves in choosing the best words for the occasion, and to learn to say them in a way that captivates our audience by the power of our testimony and the clarity of a speech that leads them to the mystery of God.

We do our people a great disservice when we water down the message and fill our homilies with jokes and stories because we assume they are incapable of paying attention and understanding anything truly deep. The widespread fascination with talks, both in person at venues filled with thousands of people or via Internet with millions of viewers, and the remarkable success of so many podcasts, shows that people can listen to talks more often and with greater attention than we sometimes believe. The real question is whether what they hear at church is said in a way that captures their interest. Believing the lay faithful to be incapable of following the arguments of a ten-minute speech or unable to appreciate the beauty of a moving discourse might be a sign of a paternalistic and condescending mindset on the part of a preacher. Simply put, even in the context of today's society, the lay faithful are capable of hearing and hungry for the truth of the Gospel. Our homilies should nourish them.

Occasions for Preaching

Just as the Word made flesh said different things and in diverse ways depending on the situation, so the awareness of the many different occasions in which we are called to preach is an indispensable element for the preparation and delivery of our homilies. Let us briefly survey now some of the most important occasions for preaching.

- **Sunday Mass**
  Most priests will be assigned to a parish or to a specific ministry in which normally, Sunday after Sunday, we will proclaim God's Word to the same community of believers. This opens up an amazing opportunity for a long journey in which priest and people will hear the Word and try to reflect on its meaning and import. We should keep this in mind as we plan our homilies (for an average parish assignment we can expect around three hundred Sunday homilies), knowing that we will have time to build, to develop some themes, to address important topics, and, ultimately, to pay attention to what the Lord speaks to a portion of his Church in a specific period of history. It could therefore be helpful to think and plan in advance the topics of our preaching, considering at times the convenience of a thematic series of homilies. Finally, the homilies of Sunday Mass are one of the best occasions for moving the hearts of the many faithful "Mass-goers" who perhaps still have not encountered the living Christ and are yet to become his disciples and apostles.

- **Daily Mass**
  Generally speaking, those who attend weekday Mass have an evident interest in matters of faith and are looking for a frequent encounter with Christ in the Sacrament. Therefore, they are more open to homilies that go the core of God's message for that day with little embellishment, expressed in preaching that is spiritual, direct, and brief.

- **Liturgical Seasons**
  The Church has reminded us lately—as we saw in the first chapter—that the homily should be a discourse that takes into account the mystery being celebrated. The liturgical season is the background against which a homily unfolds, and it ought to set the tone and the contents of our preaching.

- **Feast Days**
  The mysteries celebrated include the different solemnities, feasts, and memorials of our Lord, Holy Mary, and the saints. Because the liturgy reenacts and actualizes those mysteries, they cannot be ignored in our preaching.

- **Weddings and Funerals**
  A unique opportunity for preaching, both challenging and amazing, occurs at weddings and funerals. It might feel strange to bring these two quite different occasions into the same category, but there are two reasons for doing so. First, it is rather common for non-Catholics or nonpracticing Catholics to attend weddings and funerals of their Catholic relatives or friends. Their lack of familiarity with the Christian faith presents a challenge to the preacher and can be a spur to preaching the good news with renewed freshness. The second reason is that people celebrating love at a wedding Mass or mourning a death at a funeral are often more open to what really matters than they are during the routine of a distracted and busy life. The opportune word of a preacher, lovingly and reverently pronounced, can find fertile ground in hearts touched by these moving experiences.

- **Other sacraments and sacramentals**
  There are many other sacramental occasions in the life of a parish in which the preacher has to adapt his homily to the celebration. For example, the joy of a First Holy Communion should elicit a glad and simple homily; the new life of baptism ought to be explained in a brief and intimate manner; and a short homily during the blessing of a new home should be done in a familiar and grateful way.

- **Civic celebrations**
  It is also important to be aware of the significance of some days on which a country or community celebrates anniversaries or memorials in a manner that brings families and friends together and gives thanks for the gifts of life, freedom, and sacrifice, among others. While not being liturgical celebrations, these human festivities, if truly human, are always doors into the love and providence of the Heavenly Father.

Preaching about Sensitive Issues

There are times when a preacher has to speak about issues that are delicate and will probably cause division and tension in the audience. As we know, "the word of God is living and active, sharper than any two-edged sword, piercing to the division of soul and spirit, of joints and marrow, and discerning the thoughts and intentions of the heart" (Heb 4:12). As happened when the Lord Jesus himself preached, preaching his Word sometimes will bring division: "there was a division among the Jews because of these words" (Jn 10:19; see also Jn 7:43). One might even meet plain rejection: "Many of his disciples, when they heard it, said, 'This is a hard saying; who can listen to it?'… After this many of his disciples drew back and no longer walked with him" (Jn 6:60, 66).

In the fourth century, divisive topics might have included the Christological or Trinitarian controversies; in the eighth century, questions about images; in the sixteenth century, statements about the sacraments. Today the sensitive issues are almost always centered on moral problems.

How can we prepare for addressing these issues if there seems no way around causing offense to some while inspiring others? One first, general idea is that a sustained, long effort for good, faithful, courageous, and profound preaching will form a congregation step by step and lead it patiently and progressively to the truth of the Gospel. Isolated efforts to preach about sensitive issues are still important, but these will be much more fruitful if they are part of a continuous practice in which God's Word sheds real light upon the complicated situations we face in today's culture. Isolated instances of preaching that addresses moral issues might wrongly give the impression of a defensive strategy or a political campaign.

What follows is some practical advice for those Sundays on which we receive the commission to apply God's Word to a topic that will cause varied reactions in our people.

• Remember that the goal is not to show the preacher's courage but to win the people over to the truth of the Gospel. We have to prepare the content and the style of the homily according to the issue and to the characteristics of the congregation.

• Above all, we prepare by prayer. Any homily, but particularly one in which every word feels like a delicate statement, has to be truly built on the Word of God. This demands the trust that God's Word for that day will have the power and wisdom to illuminate our issues. We have to pray throughout the week for the grace and light to preach well, to discern what the Lord wants us to say to his people.

• Including ourselves in the reflections makes a difference; as a general rule, it is better to use the first person plural than the second person. This practice will not detract from the message and may forestall some negative reaction by making it clear that the topic is a challenging one, even for us. Along these lines, it is also prudent to show sympathy and not to be afraid of expressing our humanity and vulnerability, sharing how difficult it is to preach about certain topics. Showing compassion and understanding is an act of sincerity that creates an important bond of trust.

• We must avoid giving the impression of asserting that there is a simplistic division between "good" and "bad" Catholics, of insinuating the superiority of a certain "moral elite," or of wrongly reinforcing false stereotypes in a way that resembles political partisanship.

• The appeal to authority has to be used with great caution; it cannot be the only argument employed to explain an issue (e.g., "the Church teaches this" or "it is clearly stated in the Catechism"). In recent years, as we know, the institutional Church may have experienced a loss of credibility with some of the people in the pews.

• Data is objective and noncontroversial; stories are compelling. These two elements can increase the convincing power of a homily.

• There are plenty of available resources. We need to invest the necessary time to prepare and find the right sources.

• Finally, whether we feel confident or insecure about a certain topic to be addressed in a homily, we should never be reluctant to ask friends—priests and laity—for advice and feedback.

Questions for Reflection and Conversation

• *Which aspect of the Incarnation as theological foundation for preaching is more appealing to you? Why?*

• *What does "adaptation" or "condescension" mean in this context?*

• *Can you think of concrete ways to listen to your people and to the world as you prepare your preaching?*

5

Advice from the Pews

The incarnational approach to preaching must move us to pay attention to our people, to their hopes and fears, their needs and hungers. Needless to say, this does not simply mean to preach only about what they enjoy, but to really contemplate their lives and, based on that, to discern what we should say to them from the ambo.

Certainly, those in the pews appreciate our ministry and long for good homilies. In fact, we all have been there: we all have heard many homilies. Probably we all have thought at some point, "What a great homily!" Maybe we all have lamented some bad ones, as well.

How good it is when we hear, from the goodness of the heart, some good word of advice! How necessary it is to listen to what those sitting in the pews think about our preaching! We do run the risk of living in a closed circle of clerical life and not considering well enough the wisdom that comes from the Christian lives of our audience. Their experiences, their years—long or not—of listening to homilies, their expertise, family life, prayers, struggles, readings, work, and ministries can bring so much richness to our preaching. In this chapter we will hear the generous advice of twelve persons who do not preach but love preaching. They will share with us what they expect and do not expect from preachers.

I have asked individuals from different backgrounds, faithful from diverse parts of the country, of different ages and with varied areas of experience, to share their thoughts with us. Their advice is their own and, rather than endorsing every statement, I offer it here hoping that listening to their voices can help us to deepen our understanding and discernment of what our people really need.

MOTHER MARY ANGELA, PCC, AND COMMUNITY
(ROSWELL, NEW MEXICO)

Mother Mary Angela is the successor of the prolific Mother Mary Francis as abbess of the cloistered Poor Clares in Roswell. She told me that, since her entrance into the convent, she has probably heard sixteen thousand homilies. Their life of prayer and penance, faithful to the Rule of St. Clare, is a fertile soil for authentic preaching. The community spent one of their treasured recreations sharing ideas about preaching, and Mother Angela kindly gathered those thoughts in these words.

"What news from the King?" Thus did St. Clare question friars who visited the sisters at San Damiano. A homily will be "news from the King" insofar as the preacher himself is truly seeking God and his kingdom through deep reflection on his Word and generous fidelity to personal prayer. The foundation of all preaching is the preacher's personal relationship with Jesus Christ.

The hearts of listeners are captured by the holiness and zeal of the priest and by his evident loyalty to Christ and his Church. The priest's humble awareness that he is *alter Christus* will inform his words with dignity, authority, courage and charity. It is his *person* that makes the impression; his own virtue and integrity give his words credibility.

A homily will be "news from the King" when it is scripturally and theologically accurate and explains the Word of God for the day with simplicity. It will be thoughtful and well-prepared, both orthodox and creative, concise and memorable. The delivery matters much; a moderate pace and a clear, audible, well-modulated voice will contribute to peaceful receptivity in the congregation.

The homily ceases to be "news from the King" if it becomes overly subjective and focuses attention on the priest rather than on the One he represents. Chattiness and common language do not have a place in the homily and serve only to surprise and alienate listeners. An overly dramatic or emotionally charged homily will simply enervate or frustrate the congregation.

With his high expectations of the faithful, a good homilist challenges his listeners to recognize the nobility and dignity of their baptism, to assume the obligations of their royal priesthood, and to participate in the redemption of the world by offering their lives in union with Christ's sacrifice in the Mass. He must fulfill his role as teacher of the faith, applying the Gospel message to daily living and the needs of the congregation. Combating falsehoods perpetrated by the media and our secular, materialistic culture and addressing the particular sufferings or problems of his people, he will not fear to "speak the truth in love." He must seek to open the hearts of his listeners to the beauty of a virtuous life and educate them in the way of asceticism and prayer. His work is the formation of the human heart, fostering a longing for God and for heaven in his hearers.

MICHAEL FOLEY
(WACO, TEXAS)

Dr. Foley is associate professor of patristics at Baylor University and author of a number of books, among them a new translation with commentaries of the Cassiciacum dialogues of St. Augustine, and the celebrated Drinking with the Saints series. His perspective as a married man with four children, teaching at a Baptist university and promoting different aspects of Christian culture, will be valuable for preachers. Here is what he has to say.

Writing these words on Trinity Sunday, I cannot help but echo today's Gospel: "Teach them to observe all things whatsoever I have commanded you" (Mt 16:20). "All things" includes controversial topics: abortion and voting, homosexuality and transgenderism, artificial contraception, et cetera. The faithful desperately need instruction on these matters, for the culture in which they have been marinating is giving them a very different point of view.

On the other hand, since our faith is much more than a bullet list of politically incorrect moral positions, you must not give the appearance of moralism. Whatever practical admonition you give, subordinate it to an adoration of Father, Son, and Holy Spirit; whatever ethical stance you take, make sure that your audience sees how it flows from and leads back to the love of God and neighbor. Your job is to help them fall in love not with a policy but with a person.

Having addressed content, let me offer a few remarks on style.

First, write out your sermon or at least make an outline that you will follow strictly. In my experience, priests who preach extemporaneously tend to repeat themselves, go down rabbit holes, or take too long. It does not matter if you are not establishing constant eye contact with the congregation all the time. Sincerity, brevity, and coherence are more important than thespian or oratorical devices.

Second, as your words are meant to reflect the beauty of the Gospel, aspire to preach beautifully. Beautiful preaching avoids slang (although the occasional colloquialism can be quite effective), vulgar or overly graphic imagery (except, perhaps, the life of a martyr), and theatrics like pacing back and forth. And beautiful preaching need not be grandiloquent or sesquipedalian. St. Augustine, who knew a thing or two about rhetorical delivery, praises the eloquence of the prophet Amos even though his prophecies are "rustic" in comparison to St. Paul's Epistles. Amos was a simple shepherd, but this holy yokel achieved a marvelous "eloquence suited to [his] character and position" precisely because his goal was not to come across as a genius but to be the loyal messenger "of him who is the Author of all genius."

Third, preaching vis-à-vis "current events" can be a compelling way to instruct one's flock, but be careful. A Greek Orthodox deacon once told me that in seminary he was taught not to mention the proper names of anyone in a homily other than biblical figures or the saints. The reasoning is that if you say the name "Donald Trump" or "Nancy Pelosi," the listener immediately conjures up an image of that person in his mind (along with an emotional reaction) in a way that saying "the president" or "house speaker" does not (a remarkably Aristotelian insight for a Church that prefers Plato!). Since, however, sacred liturgy is a participation in the Heavenly Liturgy, the worshipper's imagination should only be filled with the supernal. Exceptions notwithstanding, this strikes me as a rather solid rule of thumb.

BRIANNA HELDT
(DENVER, COLORADO)

Brianna moved from California to Denver and then, through reading and reflection with her husband, found herself unexpectedly at the doors of the Catholic Church. After becoming Catholic, she and her family have been involved in the life of the Church in several ways, as their family continued to grow and meet the challenges of forming her kids, including some with disabilities. As a mother of a young family, she cares and hopes for good preaching.

When I first went searching for the Catholic Church's doctrines related to marriage and children—which would later joyously culminate in my husband and I being received into the fullness of the faith—it was ultimately *hope* and *truth* that I was seeking. I didn't want mere personal opinions or pithy remarks on the subject, subjective interpretations or sugarcoated sentiments. On the contrary, I longed to know what God wanted for my life, even if it might be difficult or challenging to hear. Initially, it was!

Similarly, a good preacher will openly share both hope and truth in his homily. People (myself included) are so very hungry for clarity, desperately hoping to discover who God created them to be in a world otherwise marked by confusion and chaos. Furthermore, I want my children, *particularly my teens*, to hear these truths, and to behold the hope and beauty that is Christ. The astounding thing about the truth is that even hard truths will, ultimately, result in *great hope*, as they reflect God's perfect plan for our lives. And if the faithful and the seeking don't hear it from the preacher, will they hear it at all?

The vocation to marriage and motherhood is a beautiful one, marked by self-giving and sacrifice. But many would like me to believe that my many small and hidden daily tasks are inconsequential, or somehow beneath me. All the more, then, a good preacher will courageously affirm not only the dignity but also the intrinsic *value and beauty* of the married vocation, particularly the vocation to motherhood. Mothers like me—in the trenches of raising babies and teens—need to be encouraged that God not only wants our humble "yes", but that we, like our mother Mary, are doing something *good and proper* not only for our Lord and our family, but also for the culture at large. We need preachers who will encourage parents to continue loving and striving for holiness, keeping in mind that we are fighting an uphill battle when we choose the simple things of this world in our mission of shaping the hearts, minds, and very souls of our children.

CHRISTINA LYNCH
(TUCSON, ARIZONA)

Dr. Lynch went from being vice president of Van Heusen to impacting the lives of many seminarians and priests through her wise counseling. She has spent many years serving the Church by developing programs of assessment, evaluation, and accompaniment for vocations to the priesthood. It is fair to say that, as a lay person, she understands well the heart of a priest and knows that we are called to be fruitful witnesses of the Lord through our preaching.

The most important information I, as a Catholic psychologist, desire to hear from my clients is how well do they know themselves in relation to others and to God. Knowing oneself involves understanding the context and influences that may have contributed to their development (humanly and spiritually). One's relationship experiences, if they lack love, can limit one's capacity to know how to intimately participate in any relationship. St. John Paul II describes this capacity: "He [man] remains a being that is incomprehensible to himself, his life is senseless, if love is not revealed to him, if he does not encounter love, if he does not experience it and make it his own, if he does not participate intimately in it."[1]

When I hear a homily, I want to be moved to learn how to have an intimate relationship with Jesus. I want to be drawn into the scriptures and into the real-life stories of those who walked before and with the Lord. I want to be motivated to act, to change and to be a better person. I want to be educated about the Church's teaching in relation to the word of God. I want to be inspired to serve and make a difference in the lives of others like the stories in the Gospels. I want a specific message from the scriptures to take away for the week and put into practice. Most importantly, I want to know God loves me yet be challenged by the homilist in directly addressing areas of sin that need God's merciful forgiveness and hear that there is hope by confessing my sins in the sacrament of penance. I want to be reminded that God is fully present in the Eucharist, that he suffered, died, and resurrected for me. I want to be confident that God is calling me to conversion. I want to grow in personal holiness and be conformed to the will of God. Jesus "thirsts" for our love while on the Cross, and today so many people are "thirsting" in their own suffering for an intimate relationship with Jesus, yet

1 John Paul II, Encyclical Letter *Redemptor Hominis* (March 4, 1979), 10. The full paragraph reads: "Man cannot live without love. He remains a being that is incomprehensible for himself, his life is senseless, if love is not revealed to him, if he does not encounter love, if he does not experience it and make it his own, if he does not participate intimately in it. This, as has already been said, is why Christ the Redeemer 'fully reveals man to himself.' If we may use the expression, this is the human dimension of the mystery of the Redemption. In this dimension man finds again the greatness, dignity and value that belong to his humanity. In the mystery of the Redemption man becomes newly 'expressed' and, in a way, is newly created. He is newly created! 'There is neither Jew nor Greek, there is neither slave nor free, there is neither male nor female; for you are all one in Christ Jesus' [Gal 3:28]. The man who wishes to understand himself thoroughly—and not just in accordance with immediate, partial, often superficial, and even illusory standards and measures of his being—he must with his unrest, uncertainty and even his weakness and sinfulness, with his life and death, draw near to Christ. He must, so to speak, enter into him with all his own self, he must 'appropriate' and assimilate the whole of the reality of the Incarnation and Redemption in order to find himself. If this profound process takes place within him, he then bears fruit not only of adoration of God but also of deep wonder at himself. How precious must man be in the eyes of the Creator, if he 'gained so great a Redeemer', and if God 'gave his only Son' in order that man 'should not perish but have eternal life' [Jn 3:16]."

uncertain of how to attain it. A prayerfully prepared homily preached with the zeal of the apostles can lead us to that love.

PAUL WHITE
(WASHINGTON, D.C.)

Dr. White is a surgeon who has served in the Army for 20 years and is a consultant to the Surgeon General. His background of service, often marked by complex demands, gives Dr. White a unique perspective into the need for homilies that truly feed God's people, beginning with his wife and children.

I need to hear the truth so I can deepen my relationship with him who is Truth. Since the Church has been entrusted with that truth, I need to hear what she says. The faithful vary significantly in their education and theological knowledge, but on almost any topic all of us need both instruction in the faith, and exhortations toward living the faith.

We need to hear about sin, original and actual. Preach on natural law. We need to hear about the harm sin does to our persons and to others. We need to hear that actions aren't evil because the Church forbids them, but that the Church forbids actions because they harm human persons and the common good. We need to hear the sins to which we're most prone and the specific harms they cause. Preach against contraception, pornography, materialism, pride, lack of charity, greed, gossip. The Cross only make senses in relation to sin and salvation from sin, so don't be afraid to preach about sin.

But we also need to hear about redemption and our Redeemer. Remind us that God loves us so much that he died to save us from our sins. We need to be taught about the beauty and fittingness of redemption, of salvation history. Preach on grace, and its effects upon our souls. We need to know that through grace God's goodness can be our goodness despite our sins.

We need help to respond to grace. Teach us how to pray and remind us to pray. Preach about the sacraments, especially the Eucharist and reconciliation. Exhort us to seek out and make them routine and constant, but important and solemn, parts of our lives. We need to be taught how to live faith, hope and charity in our daily lives, even when it's hard.

EVELYN, VERONICA, AND ANNA
(ENGLEWOOD, COLORADO)

These three teenagers have been best friends since before their first Holy Communion. They continue to be involved in youth groups and attend Mass every Sunday. They have grown in an environment in which faith is the center, and yet many of their friends come from a very different experience. They care about sharing their faith and love the Lord. Their voices as youths, discerning their next step in their lives, are worth our attention.

Preaching is the most common way to learn about the faith. As such, teens have some small expectations when they prepare to listen to a sermon. One is for the Word to be applied to real-world applications, with clear guidelines. Teenagers often find themselves in the gray when solid guidelines are not in place or exceptions are given. What draws young people is the beauty of the faith. So we expect homilies to reflect this while being grounded in liturgy and theology. The effectiveness of a homily relies on how engaging it is. Pop culture references can be useful to accomplish this, but they often feel forced and irrelevant. Examples and stories are quite engaging, as they ground the message in something memorable. The sermon must be relatable if it is to be engaging. Approach your sermon as a friend and ally of the crowd.

However, there are also elements of preaching that teens do not expect. For example, we do not want to receive abbreviated or watered-down messages. As not every homily will be written with teens in mind, we do not expect to understand everything all at once. Our questions can lead to fruitful conversations and deeper understanding.

As a teenager, the Catholic faith can be confusing. Our natural response to almost anything is to ask the question *why*. Why do we pray this or believe that? Why is it important to say this or do that? In a homily, it is helpful to learn not only what to do, but why we do it. It strengthens our faith and deepens our understanding.

SAIR DEL TORO
(LOS ANGELES, CALIFORNIA)

Sair left a successful radio career to serve Christ in surprising ways: working for the conversion of governors in Mexico, helping gang members find Jesus, teaching the beauty of human love, caring for the Hispanic community, and most especially, promoting the dignity and value of women. Her professional and charitable experience and her deep faith in the power of the Sacred Heart help her understand the power of a good word said at the right time.

It is always exciting to hear a priest preaching a homily, because when we practice our faith, we know Christ speaks through them. Personally, I love seeing a courageous priest who speaks with truth of the reality of our time, without fear of offending; many do seem to be afraid that their flock will leave and stop coming to Mass. But the reality is that when there is depth, we all like and are impacted to know that the Church still takes care of us.

Those who are really looking for Christ need well-founded and well-explained topics such as chastity, abortion, human dignity, euthanasia, purity of intention from the heart, moral life, the responsibility of a good Catholic before the world, the importance of the sacrament of matrimony, contraception, disorders of the heart, concupiscence, what pornography causes in the soul, new age, the true freedom Christ has freed us for, and the dogmas that most people don't understand anymore.

Special attention is needed for women, who are the heart of families and are particularly attacked by society so they won't desire matrimony and having children but rather live in constant competition against men. God made us for a perfect equilibrium. Our times don't allow the true value of families to be seen and we ought to overcome that.

There are also topics that lead us to an encounter with Christ and make us desire to live in holiness, such as the examples of the lives of saints, with which it is easy to relate when we see their humanity. Eschatological themes are also very important, and the importance of Holy Mary in the Church.

BEN HINTZ
(HEBRON, NEBRASKA)

Ben grew up working hard on a farm in Nebraska and then attended university in Lincoln. Becoming involved with the Newman Center, after graduation he decided to spend some time serving the homeless. As a young adult who cares for his faith and the service of the poor, Ben knows that a good homily can bring hope and purpose to the listeners.

I expect preachers to know their audience. I've been blessed with a wonderful diocese my whole life (Lincoln, Nebraska) and am continually amazed by those priests who take note of their parishioners. The most important homilies are those that are relevant to the congregation. Great shepherds know their sheep, where they tend to get lost, what their limitations are, and, most importantly, what they need to grow. When preachers know their audience, they can deliver a homily about almost anything. It doesn't so much matter how popular the preacher is, which topics he addresses, or even how long he speaks.

After understanding his audience, a preacher will benefit most from focusing on truth and practicality. Think about it. If you go to friend with a problem, you naturally have a few expectations. First, you must feel known by the person, otherwise you wouldn't seek their counsel. After that, you desire their honest opinions and realistic advice. A homily needs to be delivered in the same way. Don't be fearful of touchy subjects or a blunt message. Even if it's uncomfortable, our human hearts are made for loving truth and practical guidance.

In addition to making their homily relevant, truthful, and practical, I believe the best priests share themselves with their parishioners. Be vulnerable. Be yourself. Be bold. Be prayerful. Be guided by the Holy Spirit and under the mantle of the Blessed Virgin Mary. Let Jesus do the heavy lifting but put in enough effort to give him enough space to be effective. Have fun with your priestly vocation and be the best shepherd you can be.

CARLOS DE QUESADA
(SARASOTA, FLORIDA)

As a first generation American born to Cuban parents, Carlos understands the worlds of the Hispanic and Anglo communities. He has more than 30 years of experience in finance, business, and managerial work. With his wife and children, Carlos looks forward to homilies that can bring the wisdom of the Gospel to our daily lives.

As a 54-year-old lifelong Catholic who works with many pastors across the US and from all over the world, I reflect on today's alarming trends, be it in my own family or in research from credible sources such as CARA, Pew, or Barna, that show—across generations—a consistent, continued decline of Mass attendance and participation in the sacraments.

One thing that comes to mind is our pastors' preaching. I think of homilies I heard five, ten or twenty years ago that serve me to this day. I also think of the average homily or the 80 per cent that I cannot recall. While I do not attend Mass for the homily, a well-prepared, prayerfully delivered homily can enhance the worship experience and deepen one's faith.

As advice to our pastors, I offer the following guidance broken down into two areas: content and delivery. It's about the affective *and* the objective. Think about what you will say to that person or family that comes to Mass for the first time in years. Your homily is what may tip the balance for them to come back to the Church or not. What do you say to the teenager having trouble with chastity? How do you relate hope to an octogenarian that has had many hurts in her life? Having subject matter mastery *and* faith in the grace of the Holy Spirit will form a powerful, irresistible combination when they hear you. I encourage you to prepare by linking deep theological or biblical insights you have with practical application to circumstances that the congregation can relate to or apply in everyday life.

On delivery, repetition is helpful. Good storytelling is effective and remembered! Scripture tells us that three is important. Repetition is not going on and on. It means having clear, concise points augmented by stories from the Bible, saints, or sharing your own experiences (without seeking to become the center of attention) that captivate the mind and soul. I still recall (and apply) the point of homilies that told stories of saints' struggles or examples of Church teaching that can be applied in my business decision-making. These were not abstract or esoteric concepts, the parsing of details, or rhetorically asking about what we would do if we saw the resurrected Christ! Imagine that!

"ACTIVE NUNS"

A community of active nuns that work with the poor and the suffering offer their advice from their experience of bringing God's love and mercy with simplicity to those abandoned by society. They requested to remain anonymous.

What makes a good homily?

A homily should flow from the Scripture readings of the day. It could contain a personal testimony of the person who is giving the homily, related to the theme.

It could include thoughts or teachings of the fathers of the Church or saints. St. Augustine says, "before allowing his tongue to speak, the apostle ought to raise his thirsting soul to God and then give forth what he has drunk in [that is, the wisdom of God]."

What doesn't make a good homily?

When the homilist speaks too fast or cannot be heard or understood.

When he doesn't speak on the Scripture material or theme but emphasizes too much politics or secular or negative themes.

When he emphasizes his opinion and does not speak what the Church or our Catholic faith holds true.

Advice

The homilist should prepare initially with prayer and penance for himself and for those who will listen to his homily.

He should know the Scripture and have the goal that he wants his audience to come to know and understand.

He should have recourse to Our Lady when the topic is difficult. For example, St. Dominic begging Our Lady to help him with the heresy of the Albigensians.

Have a deep devotion to the Holy Spirit.

Help the listeners to develop a sense of sin, and love for the sacraments, especially confession.

Questions for Reflection and Conversation

• *Are there any common topics mentioned in the different contributions?*

• *Is there any advice that you had not considered before?*

• *Why is it important to pay attention to what the people in the pews really need?*

6

The Preparation

We have been considering the foundations of preaching:
why it is such a crucial ministry, what we can learn from
rhetoric, what it means to preach, why the Incarnation is a
key basis for preaching, and why we should attend to audience and
circumstances. It is time now to get down to brass tacks and turn
to the practical question of how to prepare our homilies. But first
we should go deeper into the reasons why preparation is necessary.

THE CASE FOR PREPARATION

We saw in our first chapter that the Magisterium has emphasized the
importance of preparing to preach. However, there is still a frequent
objection to preparing a homily that may be expressed like this:
rather than relying on our own wisdom and effort, we must let the
Holy Spirit inspire in us the right words at the right time. Did not
St. Paul say this when he wrote:

> When I came to you, I did not come with eloquence or human
> wisdom as I proclaimed to you the testimony about God. For I
> resolved to know nothing while I was with you except Jesus Christ
> and him crucified. I came to you in weakness with great fear and
> trembling. My message and my preaching were not with wise and
> persuasive words, but with a demonstration of the Spirit's power,
> so that your faith might not rest on human wisdom, but on God's
> power. We do, however, speak a message of wisdom among the
> mature, but not the wisdom of this age or of the rulers of this
> age, who are coming to nothing. No, we declare God's wisdom, a

mystery that has been hidden and that God destined for our glory before
time began (1 Cor 2:1–7).

Indeed, the wisdom necessary to proclaim "the testimony about God" is
not simply that of human rhetoric, but that of the Spirit, the real eloquence
that elevates our words and fills them with power. In the end, any honest
preacher can testify to this:.whenever a truly powerful homily has been delivered, there was a mystery at play, something, or rather someone, intervening.
Bernanos's young country priest learned this lesson from his mentor, the
priest of Torcy: "When the Lord has drawn from me some word for the good
of souls, I know, because of the pain of it."[1] Preaching a good homily is never
a matter of mere human accomplishment, but an experience of the Spirit.

That being said, there is nothing in St. Paul's words to the Corinthians
that indicates that we should not prepare our homilies. Nor should Christ's
instruction in Matthew's Gospel be applied to the liturgical homily: "When
they arrest you, do not worry about what to say or how to say it. At that time
you will be given what to say" (Mt 10:19). Rarely would a liturgical homily be
preached while being arrested. Openness to the inspiration of the Holy Spirit
does not mean mere passivity; being guided by the Spirit is not synonymous
with pure spontaneity. In fact, the patient and daily effort to open our hearts
and minds to the Spirit in the preparation of our preaching can be a more
honest and profound way of letting God work through us.

Pope Francis could not be more emphatic about this: "Trust in the Holy
Spirit who is at work during the homily is not merely passive but active and
creative. It demands that we offer ourselves and all our abilities as instru-
ments (see Rom 12:1) which God can use. A preacher who does not prepare is not 'spiritual'; he is dishonest and irresponsible with the gifts he has
received."[2] These are strong words that we must take to heart: there are no
excuses for not preparing our homilies. The more time we spend in prayer
and meditation on God's words for a specific celebration, the more open we
can be to the inspiration of the Holy Spirit and, therefore, the better we can
lead our flock.

Pope Francis also addresses the objection that priests are just too busy
to dedicate significant time to preparing their homilies: "Some pastors argue
that such preparation is not possible given the vast number of tasks which

---

1 Georges Bernanos, *The Diary of a Country Priest* (New York: Caroll & Graf Publishers, 2002), 54.
2 Francis, *Evangelii Gaudium*, 145.

they must perform; nonetheless, I presume to ask that each week a sufficient portion of personal and community time be dedicated to this task, even if less time has to be given to other important activities."[3] To see the demands of preparing our homilies only as another of the many things we have to do during the week is a mistake. In fact, the preparation of our Sunday preaching could be one of the best ways of bringing unity to our lives, as our prayer and study would become our work and our work as pastors would truly become our prayer. This point is decisive: the daily routine of praying and studying the different elements of a liturgical celebration can enrich our lives while at the same time progressively giving us the foundations for an effective homily.

Certainly, the life of many priests is filled with an unexpected number of tasks and demands. It is true that there will be some weeks in which we will not have the ideal amount of time for preparing our homilies. But these should be the exception; the rule is always to prioritize the time for our preparation, seeing in this activity the hinge between prayer, study, and pastoral work. In this way, the preparation of the homily can become a key for a healthy priestly life, in which permanent formation is not an isolated and disconnected activity but rather part of our daily lives. If we see that our schedule is organized in such a way that time for preparing a homily will not normally be found, then, following the request of Pope Francis, we must make a change in our planning and dedicate less time to other good works in order to find the time for this sacred task.

Unquestionably, there are times when a preacher experiences dryness and emptiness; there are moments when it is hard to find what to say, when we would prefer to cling to a good word said to us rather than by us. Many preachers are isolated and discouraged. Can it be realistically expected of them to prepare their homilies and preach well if their problems are not previously solved?

There is no simple answer to this, and all efforts should be made to promote the integral health and spiritual well-being of preachers. But the Lord has given us preaching as a path forward, a route to hope rather than an oppressive task. It is through our pastoral charity—in which preaching has a central place—that we can find meaning and light in those dark times.

In our pastoral experience we probably have accompanied families going through serious crises. More than once, at times when everything seemed lost, the love of their children has rescued the love between spouses. In our case, it is the paternal love that marks our vocation that can save what might seem lost. In the act of dying to ourselves and giving even of our poverty, we allow God's grace to access mysterious paths to renew and refresh our lives.

This truth is expressed in literary form in what might be the most moving paragraph in Bernanos's *Diary of a Country Priest*. After a decisive encounter of pastoral love experienced in the midst of dark days of loneliness and confusion, the parish priest of Ambricourt finds the unexpected gift of hope renewed in his heart and exclaims: "Oh, miracle—thus to be able to give what we ourselves do not possess, sweet miracle of our empty hands!"[4] When we feel our hands empty and still give, it is then that we become simple earthen vessels that let God's glory shine (see 2 Cor 4:7). It is then that God's love can occupy its true place in our hearts so that we can take care of the sheep he has given us. Augustine beautifully summarized the experience of Peter's triple confession of love that healed his triple denial with words than can be a program of pastoral love for any preacher: *Sit amoris officium.* "Let it be the service of love to feed the Lord's flock if it was the mark of fear to deny the Shepherd."[5] Preaching is truly a service of love; it comes from and renews charity in our lives.

Additionally, we could ask ourselves if, practically speaking, it would make sense to spend time in a myriad of other pastoral works and not in preparing our homilies. Will we be able to find another activity in which we can directly reach more people? Is there any better opportunity than a Sunday homily to be with our flock, to teach, to educate them in the art of praying, and to lead to the truth? We could hardly justify not dedicating enough time to the preparation of our preaching. Even from the most practical perspective, there is not a better way to "invest" our time.

This is true for those who are just beginning to preach as well as for more seasoned homilists, for naturally talented preachers and for those who are less gifted speakers. On this point, St. John Chrysostom said: "For since preaching does not come by nature, but by study, suppose a man to reach a high standard of it, this will then forsake him if he does not cultivate his power by constant application and exercise."[6] Coming from such an accomplished preacher, these words are even more compelling. Trained by Liban-

3 Francis, *Evangelii Gaudium*, 145.

4 Bernanos, *Diary of a Country Priest*, 180.

5 Augustine, *Tractates on John*, 123.5. Translation modified.

6 John Chrysostom, *On the Priesthood*, trans. William R. W. Stephens (New York: Christian Literature, 1889), V.5.

ius—arguably the best orator of his time—and deserving the title *Chrysostom* (golden mouth), he did not succumb to complacency but rather continued to nurture his speaking by study, exercise, prayer, and charity. Persistence in the cultivation of the art of preaching is a fruit of pastoral love and a manifestation and channel of personal holiness. This is, ultimately, what makes us effective preachers. For:

> It is not necessary to be a great orator in order to be an effective homilist…. What is essential … is that the preacher makes the Word of God central to his own spiritual life, that he knows his people well, that he be reflective on the events of the times, that he continually seeks to develop the skills that help him preach effectively and above all, that in his spiritual poverty, he invites in faith the Holy Spirit as the principal agent that makes the hearts of the faithful amenable to the divine mysteries.[7]

HOW TO PREPARE A HOMILY?

Preparation of an effective homily can be divided into three parts: remote, proximate, and immediate preparation.

Remote Preparation

This first step consists in the "indirect" efforts that allow us to be good preachers. I say "indirect" only in the sense that this aspect of the preparation of a homily does not necessarily imply actually composing or writing a speech. And yet, while it is not explicitly work for a particular homily, without this foundation it is not possible to preach well. As we have seen, a serious life of prayer and study, of growing familiarity with the sacred liturgy and its cycles, of an ever-deeper knowledge of God's Word, of being involved with the lives of our people, and of reflecting on the events of our times is the kind of life required for preaching well. This is what we term *remote preparation*.

Winston Churchill, one of the best orators of recent history, was particularly famous for precise and passionate speeches that gave the impression of extemporaneous delivery. Churchill's friend F. E. Smith said: "Winston has spent the best years of his life composing his impromptu speeches."[8]

---

7 Congregation for Divine Worship, *Homiletic Directory*, 3.

8 Found in Nicholas Soames, "Sweat and Tears Made Winston Churchill's Name," *The Telegraph*, May 4, 2011.

The paradox is evident and meaningful. Good impromptu speeches do not come out of a void. Commitment and hard work, study, reflection, and, for a preacher, prayer underlie effective speeches, both composed and improvised.

Even in situations in which a preacher may have to say some words without having previously thought about the occasion, those words could be memorable because of this indispensable remote preparation. The reason is simple: extemporization does not mean lack of preparation, but quite the opposite.

Remote preparation is a very important habit that seals the quality of any good homily. Nowadays we can easily find information about virtually any topic. If we were asked to give a speech on the recent pandemic or on the variation of gas prices, it would not be hard to put together some articles and offer a presentation on those topics. Nonetheless, even if the information presented was accurate, it would probably be noticeable that we were not experts, that our familiarity was limited. Such a speech would hardly be memorable. Sometimes, a homily is experienced as a speech prepared with disconnected information (probably found by a simple Internet search) that does not communicate the intensity and authority that come from dedicated acquaintance with the realities of the faith.

The first step in the process of preparing our homilies is, therefore, to grow in familiarity with the mysteries of our faith. This is a never-ending journey in which we should have for our best companions the great preachers of our tradition, including St. Ambrose, St. Augustine, St. John Chrysostom, St. Charles Borromeo, St. John Henry Newman, Ven. Fulton Sheen, and Benedict XVI, among many others.[9] Acquaintance with the history of the Church, in particular with the living proclamation of her best sons and daughters, constantly leads our preaching in the right direction. In the end, our message does not simply seek to please the demands of the majorities. As Joseph Ratzinger wrote, "the fortuitous majorities that may form here or there in the Church do not decide their and our path: they, the saints, are the true, the normative majority by which we orient ourselves."[10] The saints are our examples and friends: with their words and with their lives they teach us how to preach.

---

9 Several homilies from great preachers will be offered in the second section of this volume. On the Christian wisdom of preachers (not only Catholic), see Richard Lischer, ed., *The Company of Preachers: Wisdom on Preaching, Augustine to the Present* (Grand Rapids, Mich.: Eerdmans Publishing, 2002).

10 Joseph Ratzinger, *Called to Communion: Understanding the Church Today*, trans. Adrian Walker (San Francisco: Ignatius Press, 1991), 154.

Reading, reflecting, praying, shepherding: these priestly actions come together harmoniously as the remote preparation and the foundation of our faithful preaching. In the words of Michael Pasquarello, "learning to speak wisely is integrally related to learning to pray, think, love, and live within a community that exists to praise, know, and enjoy the one who speaks himself and his goodness through the creation and redemption of all things."[11]

Proximate Preparation

The second step, *proximate preparation*, consists in the "prolonged time of study, prayer and creativity" spent in preparation for the homily of the upcoming Sunday (or any other important celebration), described by Pope Francis as a priority in our ministry.[12]

Preparation demands, as Joshua Whitfield has rightly said, *attention* to the sacred texts, to the liturgy, to the world and to people, and to ourselves.[13] Thus, the proximate preparation of a homily begins by gaining familiarity with the occasion for preaching. For this, the first step is to take a look at the different elements of the liturgical celebration: the scriptural readings, the texts from the Ordinary or the Proper of the Mass of that day, as well as other aspects of the rite itself. These are the means through which the mystery to be renewed in a liturgical celebration is unfolded here and now. This initial reading should be done at the beginning of the week.

The second phase of proximate preparation is to begin a weeklong process of reading, studying, praying, and reflecting that will eventually bear the fruit of a mature homily. But before explicitly thinking about the composition of the homily, it is necessary to spend time in recollected meditation: to read and reread, to pray, to adore, to let those words and realities repose in our minds and hearts so that they can develop and take the form of a homily.[14]

The process of developing a homily follows the very process of faith: we have to accept the gift and let it grow. In one of his last Anglican sermons, St. John Henry Newman described how Mary "does not think it enough to

11 Michael Pasquarello III,*We Speak Because We Have First Been Spoken: A Grammar of the Preaching Life* (Grand Rapids, Mich.: Eerdmans Publishing, 2009), 57.

12 Francis, *Evangelii Gaudium*, 145.

13 See Whitfield, *The Crisis of Bad Preaching*, 78–96.

14 On the idea of expository preaching, which aims to bring out the message of a homily from the truths contained in the revealed text, see Bryan Chapell, *Christ-Centered Preaching: Redeeming the Expository Sermon*, 3rd ed. (Grand Rapids, Mich.: Baker Academic, 2018).

accept [the faith], she dwells upon it; not enough to possess, she uses it; not enough to assent, she develops it; not enough to submit the Reason, she reasons upon it."[15] Similarly, a preacher has to accept the mystery to be celebrated and assent to it with faith (and for this he first has to read and pray about it), so that, dwelling in that mystery, some worthy ideas for preaching can be developed throughout the week (and for this there is more to do, as we will see now).

The key for this development is a profound meditation throughout the week on the liturgical readings and prayers. This cannot be done well by simply reading an email with some commentaries or doing an online search a day before preaching. This process demands time.[16]

Along with time, proximate preparation requires knowledge of the *liturgical sources* already mentioned (readings and other liturgical texts and rites), and of additional *resources* that can assist us in this process, among which we can mention the following:

- **Lectionary**
  The lectionary is a mature fruit of the Council's desire that the treasures of Scripture be opened up more lavishly to the faithful.[17] It offers a rich sequence of Old and New Testament readings, exposing us to a significant review of the Bible (we read more than 70 per cent of the New Testament and more than 15 per cent of the Old Testament in the three year cycle.)[18]

- **Roman Missal**
  The book containing the priestly prayers for the Mass is a rich source of ancient and recent prayers, in which we can find the truths of our faith and its different celebrations expressed in a spiritual way. When a preacher pays greater attention to the antiphons, collects, and prefaces, as well as the

---

15 John Henry Newman, "Sermon 15: The Theory of Developments in Religious Doctrine," in *Fifteen Sermons Preached Before the University of Oxford*, eds. James David Earnest and Gerard Tracey (Oxford: Oxford University Press, 2006), 312–13.

16 It is important for this process to keep in mind the three criteria for interpreting Scripture "in accordance with the Spirit," as enunciated in *Dei Verbum*: attention to the content and unity of the whole Scripture—Scripture illumines Scripture; reading Scripture within the Tradition of the Church—attention to the life of the Church as vital context; finally, attention to the analogy of faith—the unity and harmony of mysteries. See *Dei Verbum*, 12. It would be worthwhile to revisit *Dei Verbum* and Pope Benedict XVI's apostolic exhortation *Verbum Domini* from time to time to stay close to the Church's recommended manner of reading the Scriptures.

17 See *Sacrosanctum Concilium*, 51. About the lectionary see also Waznak, *An Introduction to the Homily*, 72–89.

18 These data are taken from: http://catholic-resources.org/Lectionary/Statistics.htm

Eucharistic Prayers and the rest of the Order and Ordinary of the Mass, his homily is greatly enriched.

- **Fathers of the Church**
  These pastors who cared for their flocks and preached with passion and knowledge are our best guides to discover the spiritual meaning of Scripture. We learn from them how to discern images and figures of the Paschal mystery, the depth of each word, and the connections between Old and New Testament. Excellent editions that organize patristic commentaries according to books of the Bible or to the liturgical year are available.[19]

- **Biblical commentaries**
  There are many brilliant commentaries on Scripture that are extremely helpful for deepening our reflection on the passages to be explained in our preaching.

- **Papal homilies**
  The homilies of the popes contain wonderful spiritual treasures and homiletic lessons, from Leo the Great to Francis. The Vatican website contains the homilies of recent popes organized chronologically.

- **Homilies and reflections by saints and theologians**
  We can find another rich source for prayer and preaching in the different sermons and commentaries on Scripture and the mysteries by the great theologians of our tradition, for example, the reflections on the sacraments by St. Ambrose, the treatises on the Gospel of John by St. Augustine, or the sermons of St. John Henry Newman. There are other books, such as meditations on Christ and his life, that are helpful as well. Finally, commentaries on the liturgical year and rites of the Church offer valuable insights for mystagogical homilies that generate great interest among the people.

- *Catechism of the Catholic Church*
  The *Catechism* is a trustworthy source to which we should frequently refer as we prepare our homilies. An excellent table with references to the

---

19 Particular attention should be given to the two western patristic classics on preaching which became essential manuals for centuries of preaching: Augustine's *De Doctrina Christiana* and Gregory the Great's *Pastoral Rule*. See C. Colt Anderson, *Christian Eloquence: Contemporary Doctrinal Preaching* (Chicago: Hillenbrand Books, 2005), 19–37 and 56–73. For studies on patristic preaching, see *Preaching in the Patristic Era: Sermons, Preachers, and Audiences in the Latin West*, eds. Anthony Dupont, et al. (Leiden: Brill, 2018); Wendy Mayer, "Homiletics," in *The Oxford Handbook of Early Christian Studies*, eds. Susan Ashbrook Harvey and David G. Hunter (Oxford: Oxford University Press, 2008), 565–83; *Preaching in the Patristic Age: Studies in Honor of Walter J. Burghardt, S.J.*, ed. David G. Hunter (New York: Paulist Press, 1989).

Catechism in relation to each Sunday of the three cycles is offered in the *Homiletic Directory*.[20]

- ***Homiletic Directory***
  The recent *Homiletic Directory* offers a remarkable aid for preparing homilies, including sketches, examples, and suggestions for preaching throughout the liturgical year.

- **Dictionaries**
  Consulting different lexicons or dictionaries can be helpful, as the study of some biblical words, their roots, and their meanings can enrich a homily. Often what is ancient—a word's original meaning and context—can seem new, offering fresh insights to passages that have become stale to us through long familiarity. One can say the same of consulting various English translations. Of course, this has to be done in a pastoral way, avoiding an excessively academic tone.

- **Biblical software**
  There are a number of outstanding electronic resources, containing a wealth of content—commentaries, analyses, parallels, explanations, et cetera. Some resources are freely available online. Others are not necessarily inexpensive, but the depth and convenience of so much well-organized information may be worth the investment for a parish, as a source for preparation of homilies and other classes.

A Typical Week

How does the proximate preparation take place? I will suggest here a "typical week" of prayer and work toward the composition of a homily. This is, of course, only a suggestion that can be adapted in different ways.[21]

What follows is expected to normally take place during the daily time of prayer. The goal is not to start thinking or composing the homily at the beginning of the week, but to let God speak to us, allowing his voice move our minds and hearts slowly, so that we can recognize, after days of prayer and reflection, what he wants us to communicate to his people. As such, it is

---

20 Congregation for Divine Worship, *Homiletic Directory*, 157–160.

21 For other methods of homily preparation see, for example, O. C. Edwards, Jr., *Elements of Homiletic: A Method for Preparing to Preach* (Collegeville, Minn.: Liturgical Press, 1990); Peter Cameron, OP, *Why Preach: Encountering Christ in God's Word* (San Francisco: Ignatius Press, 2009), 168–82; Daniel E. Harris, *We Speak the Word of the Lord: A Practical Plan for More Effective Preaching* (Chicago: ACTA Publications, 2001), 61–65.

essential to keep a prayer journal in which we can write notes throughout the week. Certainly, if this in some way impairs the prayer life of a preacher, then he can find some other moment in the day. Finally, if a homilist regularly seeks advice from other people, whether in person or in group settings, he might integrate it with the personal steps described below.

- **Monday**
  The proximate preparation begins by prayerfully reading the passages from Scripture and the liturgical texts and other elements of the liturgy of the upcoming Sunday (or whatever day the homily will take place). *If something stands out, write it down.*

- **Tuesday**
  We read the texts again, perhaps focusing our attention on one or two of them. We can use some commentaries or other resources as we reflect on the texts or aspects of the celebration to which the Spirit is drawing us. *Whatever you find interesting or moving, write it down.*

- **Wednesday**
  We continue our meditation, now spending time in *lectio divina*. By letting the Word dwell in our hearts and minds (*lectio, meditatio, oratio, contemplatio*), we are letting the Spirit guide us in his direction. Indeed, as Pope Francis said, "before preparing what we will actually say when preaching, we need to let ourselves be penetrated by that word."[22] *Whatever strikes you, write it down.*

- **Thursday**
  By now there are some aspects of the celebration (its texts and rites) that are more relevant than others. If we are humbly trying to be open to his action, we can expect that the Spirit has been guiding our prayer, and so we continue in that direction. Perhaps we can continue with *lectio divina* of another text, or even the same one. *Surely something is becoming clear in our prayer. Write it down.*

---

22 Francis, *Evangelii Gaudium*, 149.

- **Friday**
  After a few days of praying and reflecting on the mysteries to be celebrated, it is good to go back and review our notes from the previous days, trying to "map out" the action of the Holy Spirit, to see the emphases and patterns of our meditation. We will be able to recognize some key topics. Now is a good moment for the preacher to "contemplate his people" as Pope Francis has asked, and, against the background of days of prayer, ask: What do my people need to hear? What has been going on in their lives? How can these readings illuminate their lives? *In prayer, ask the Lord: What do you want me to say to your people?* This might be the right time to work on an outline for the homily. Friday or Saturday, after days of prayer and reflection, is the time to write down the homily.

- **Saturday**
  This is the time in which we move on to the *immediate preparation* of the homily.[23]

Immediate Preparation

Finally, perhaps on Friday or Saturday morning, we spend time in prayer (around one hour or more) and begin the direct work of preparing our homily. For this, we must have our journal with the notes taken throughout the week. We read our notes, choose our topic, and make an outline.

However, St. John Eudes reminds us, "before beginning even to outline a sermon, kneel down and beg God's help,"[24] asking in particular to the Holy Spirit for the gift of knowledge, through which the preacher recognizes what his people ought to hear. In God's presence we come to the moment to think about our main goal, what we want to communicate. We need to choose one goal that is a fruit of the twofold contemplation: (1) what is the Word saying (2) to my people here and now? As a general rule a good homily is about one topic, one idea, found after days of searching.[25] As we saw earlier, any speech is like a journey, and the speaker is the guide. Where are we

---

23 The idea of actually composing the homily toward the end of the week corresponds to the importance of letting the days of prayer, study, and reflection bear a mature fruit. In my experience and that of many others, this is an effective way of letting the Holy Spirit work in us. However, if a preacher needs more time to write the homily, then, of course, he must adapt this method according to his own experience.

24 John Eudes, *The Priest*, 78.

25 See Thomas V. Liske, *Effective Preaching* (New York: The Macmillan Company, 1951), 100–105.

taking our people with this particular homily? What is the goal, and where is the route? Remembering the classical advice, we can also ask: What are we going to *teach*? How are we going to *delight*? How will we *move* them to conversion?[26] Put differently, we need to ask the "so what?" question: "If this Scripture originally meant this, and today, for us, it means this, what are called to do as a result of it? Preaching should never leave us self-satisfied or bored. It should invite us to action."[27] Where are we taking our people? How are we inviting them to action?

We can hardly exaggerate the importance of a good outline. It is there that we secure the choice of a topic, the flow of the discourse, the details of its composition (e.g., examples, explanations, quotes, transitions, introduction, conclusion), and the cohesion of its development. A good outline translates hours of prayer and study into a few minutes of clarity—a single homily with an effective message. It is never an optional step.

The next question is whether the homily should be written. Aware that there are different opinions about this, I will say that it is generally better to write down every single word of the homily, which does not mean that it will be read during its proclamation.[28] Writing down the text of a homily, after having carefully developed an outline, is a responsible way of ensuring that the riches of prayer and meditation guided by the Spirit throughout the week will illuminate the homily. It strengthens the definition of the topic; it helps keep a logical and convincing flow, as it helps us to think well about the connectors between ideas and paragraphs; it guides us in the discernment of which examples, quotations, or stories should be included; it provides a way to choose the right introduction and conclusion. A well-written homily is the mature fruit of days of prayer and work and can make the difference for a truly memorable homily that will teach, delight, and move, that will take our people, step by step, on a journey to a new discovery.

As we write the homily, we must keep in mind a couple of things. First, writing for a homily means writing for speaking; we should think as if we were saying what we write. Second, a prudent average length for a Sunday homily is between eight and ten minutes, which allows for developing one

---

26 Some have described the characteristics of a homily as personal, liturgical, inculturated, clarifying, and actualizing (PLICA). See DeLeers, *Written Text Becomes Living Word,* 50.

27 Charles Bouchard, OP, "How to Listen to the Sunday Homily," *Scripture in Church*, vol. 46, no. 183 (2016): 119.

28 See, for example, Alfred McBride, *How to Make Homilies Better, Briefer, and Bolder: Tips from a Master Homilist* (Huntington, Ind.: Our Sunday Visitor, 2007), 94.

idea while securing the attention of our people.[29] Generally speaking, we can follow this rule: one topic, around eight minutes. Typically, for homilies, less is more. Pope Francis says: "If the homily goes on too long it will affect two characteristic elements of the liturgical celebration: its balance and its rhythm."[30] If we speak well on one well-prepared topic, rather than several often-disconnected topics, our hearers will be more likely to remember it and therefore put it into practice. Needless to say, this is a general recommendation, and there will be many occasions in which these features will vary.

There are some other elements to consider for the composition of the homily, whether it is written in its entirety or not.

- **Introduction**
  Be intentional about a good introduction, which might simply indicate the occasion, enunciate the topic, or share a story. The purpose is to gain your audience's attention and benevolence, and to tell them where you are taking them on this journey.

- **Enunciate the topic**
  Whether it was mentioned in the introduction or not, it can be helpful to state the main topic of the homily clearly.

- **Kinds of homilies**
  Choose what kind of homily you will preach (and write). It can be about one verse, or about the connection between all the readings. The homily can meditate on a liturgical mystery, illuminated by the liturgical texts or rites, or on one of the Propers, such as the entrance antiphon. It can be a mystagogical or catechetical homily. It can explain, verse by verse, one of the readings. It can be a part of a series of homilies about a topic.

- **Develop the main idea**
  Some time must be dedicated to developing the main point in a clear way.

- **Illustrate**
  Choose some illustration for the idea—a story, a quotation, an example.

- **Suggest an application**
  It is beneficial to indicate some possible practical application of the truth

---

29 See about this Cameron, *Why Preach*, 176. Pope Francis has said a homily should normally "not last more than ten minutes." http://www.vatican.va/content/francesco/en/audiences/2018/documents/papa-francesco_20180207_udienza-generale.html

30 Francis, *Evangelii Gaudium*, 138.

explored in the homily, so that the experience can in fact move and win over the audience, inspiring them to want to put their learning into practice.

- **Resources for helping the audience**
  - **Ask questions**
    Before explaining something, you can begin by asking "What does that mean?"
  - **Personal experience**
    A homily has to be personal but need not always include stories or experiences of the preacher. However, on some occasions, for the good of souls, it is right to sing the great things done by God in us (see Lk 1:49). Mary can help us in our discernment.
- **Conclusion**
  Craft a simple and effective conclusion.
- We should always be able to summarize our homily in one sentence, or in what Chris Anderson calls the "throughline."[31] This is a simple and fruitful exercise that will prove that we have prepared and know what to say.

After the homily has been written, wait for some time, read it again, edit it, and read it aloud. Then rehearse it: there is nothing like practicing aloud in the place where you will preach. The preacher who limited rehearsal of the homily to mental reading would be like a violinist who limited his practice to reading the score in his room, rather than actually playing the instrument in the concert hall. Only by practicing aloud are we able to confirm that what we have prepared is the right thing to say, to notice where to add the emphases, how to say the words, and when to make the pauses. Practice makes all the difference. The effectiveness of a memorable homily, spoken with power and freshness, does not ordinarily come from the unprepared inspiration of the moment but rather from the hours of prayer, study, and practice that imprint the fruit of days of preparation into our hearts and memories so that, when we preach, the words can be pronounced with command and familiarity and thus penetrate the hearts and minds of our hearers. This has been the case for the most memorable speeches that have made a difference throughout history.[32] If we want to make a difference with our homilies, the path is clear.

Finally, right before preaching, we have to pray. St. Augustine says it clearly: "By praying then both for himself and for those he is about to address, let him be a pray-er before being a speaker. At the very moment he steps up to speak, before he even opens his mouth and says a word, let him lift up his thirsty soul to God, begging that it may belch forth what it has quaffed, or pour out what he has filled it with."[33]

We share of what we receive. For, indeed, how can we be certain that all our work throughout the week, translated into a prepared (and perhaps printed) homily, is what God wants us to say? We can unquestionably trust that a prolonged effort of being open to the Spirit will be blessed with his gifts, but we ultimately entrust ourselves to God and always beg him to give us his light and put into our mouth the right word, for "who knows what is the right thing for us to say, or for someone to hear from us, at precisely this time, but the one who can see into the hearts of us all?"[34]

Questions for Reflection and Conversation

• *How would you explain in a simple way the importance of preparing our homilies?*

• *What are the consequences of not spending time preparing our preaching? Have you experienced these?*

• *How would you envision a typical week of homily preparation?*

• *Why does practicing our homilies make such a difference?*

---

31 See Cameron, *Why Preach*, 173; Edwards, Jr., *Elements of Homiletic*, 72; see Chapter 2 above.

32 Abundant examples of this are found in Glover, *The Art of Great Speeches and Why We Remember Them*.

33 Augustine, *Teaching Christianity*, IV.15.32.

34 Augustine, *Teaching Christianity*, IV.15.32.

7

The Delivery

The homily is that sacred action in which a man, aided by God's grace, is called to help God's people enter into the mystery of the good news just announced to them. It is the epic work of a herald who comes to announce freedom to his friends; the exciting task of one guiding others to discover unknown treasures; the necessary mission of the one entrusted with a vital message. Augustine prefaced this action by saying: "We have heard what happened; let us search out the hidden meaning."[1] After the Gospel is proclaimed, the preacher leads his people on a journey through this "hidden meaning." How willingly they follow him depends in part on his delivery of the homily.

HOW TO DELIVER A HOMILY

As we have seen, it would be irresponsible for the preacher to arrive at the homily without having previously searched out the hidden meaning of the story renewed in that liturgical celebration so he can fruitfully lead his audience in that journey. It is clear that the trustworthy way of fulfilling our mission as preachers is to spend enough time in prayer, study, and practice in the days prior to our preaching. After doing that, we come to the moment of delivering the homily. It is a moment of grace.

As such, it has to be immediately preceded and accompanied by prayer. We need to pray during Mass: the homily is, as we have seen,

---

1 Augustine, *Tractates on John*, 50.6.

a liturgical event. The more we immerse ourselves in the celebration of the mysteries by actually praying as we perform the sacred rites, the more docile we will be to the action of the Holy Spirit in us. This demands attention and reverence. It is true that during Sunday Mass the church can be filled with potential distractions: noises, movements, the coordination of the ceremonies and music, et cetera. But a priest has to choose to pray, as St. Justin said in the first description of the rites of the Mass, "to the best of his ability."[2]

Praying, then, we listen to the liturgical prayers and readings and let the Spirit, "the gift of God" (Jn 4:10), refresh with his gifts what he has sown in us through days of prayer and study, and we remain open to any new light that might come to us in that moment. This openness, however, has to be prudent. St. John Eudes reminds us that not every idea that suddenly comes to the homilist while he is preaching necessarily originates in God.[3] As in any experience of spiritual discernment, the patient and prayerful discernment of what God wants for us should give us more confidence than sudden inspirations, which, needless to say, do sometimes come from God and achieve what we are unable to do.

After the proclamation of the Gospel, we pray as we make our way to the ambo. Those few seconds are precious occasions to lift our heart in humble petition for the gift of God, so that our poor words can bring some good to his people. If such a prayer is said with a contrite heart, how will the Good Shepherd not give us exactly what we need to feed his sheep? That short prayer right before preaching can be a precious encounter in which we ask for wisdom and humility, for docility and clarity, for boldness and gentleness.[4]

---

2 Justin Martyr, *First Apology*, 67.

3 See John Eudes, *The Priest*, 92.

4 See here a beautiful example of a prayer before preaching. Because of its length it is given here more as inspiration than as a model for an actual prayer for that moment: "O Lord Jesus Christ thou great Prophet arisen amongst us (Lk 7:6), yea, and more than a Prophet (cf. Mt 11:9), the very Word preached once and for all from eternity by the Father himself: Open, I pray thee, my lips, that my mouth shall show forth thy praises (Ps 50:17), and the wonderful works that thou hast done (Ps 77:4), to the generation of thy children which thou hast given me (Is 8:18; Heb 2:13). May divine utterance be given unto me, to speak of thee with great boldness, and to make known once again, to this little flock of mine, the mystery of the Gospel, for which I have been bound (Eph 6:19) in the sweet chains of thy service (cf. Mt 11:30). As when I know not what to ask thee in prayer (Rom 8:26), so also when I know not what to preach, send thou thy Holy Spirit from on high to help my weakness (Wis 9:17), and bring to mind whatsoever thou hast spoken to thy Saints in all times and in all places (Jn 14:26; cf. Ps 88:20). Through the prayers of thy immaculate Mother, of thy holy Apostles Peter and Paul, of the holy Patriarch Benedict, of thy holy Levite

Likewise, it is good to pray for our people, that their own hearts may be well disposed to receive to what God will communicate through our service.

As we walk to the ambo, we should do it with humility and confidence, as a simple liturgical gesture. The preacher communicates something by his every movement, especially because, as for Jesus when he preached for the first time in the synagogue of Nazareth, "the eyes of all are fixed on him" (Lk 4:20). Precisely because the eyes of all are fixed on us, it is essential to recognize one of the most common temptations for preachers: vanity. St. Francis Xavier wrote grave words about this in one of his letters: "How many great preachers have been lost eternally because they were consumed with vanity and self-esteem."[5] Aware of this temptation, we remember with gratitude that the faithful and humble response to our call to preach can lead us closer to the heart of Christ and his eternal joy, and with this confidence we begin our homily.

Where is the best place from which to preach the homily? The *General Instruction of the Roman Missal* indicates this: "The priest, standing at the chair or at the ambo itself or, when appropriate, in another suitable place, gives the homily."[6] The two "ordinary" places from which the homily is to be delivered are the chair or the ambo. The exception, justified by an appropriate reason and not mere personal preference, is "another suitable place," such as the center of the sanctuary.

There is something to be said for the ambo as the ideal place for preaching.[7] The ambo is the liturgical place for the proclamation of God's Word. It offers a solid, unspoken message about the centrality and stability of what happens there, no matter who comes and goes: "Heaven and earth will pass away but my words will never pass away" (Lk 21:33). The ambo also offers the possibility of visual helps for the preacher, such as notes, a passage to be quoted, or the printed homily. Finally, the ambo reminds us that the core of the event taking place at it is the breaking of the bread of the Word, as later the altar will be the place where the real presence of the Bread of Life will come to us. At the ambo, a posture of standing while delivering the homily

---

Martyrs Stephen and Benjamin, of thy blessed Doctor John Chrysostom, of Saint Dominic, and of all thy Saints, I beg of thee this grace, for the praise of thy glory, for the salvation of my hearers, and the edification of thy Mystical Body the Church. Amen." Found in https://vultuschristi.org/index.php/2018/11/a-priests-prayer-before-preaching/

5 Francis Xavier, *Letters*, IV.16. Quoted in John Eudes, *The Priest*, 77.

6 International Committee on English in the Liturgy, *General Instruction of the Roman Missal*, 136.

7 See about this DeLeers, *Written Text Becomes Living Word,* 175.

allows the preacher to communicate attentiveness and commitment, and more easily to enter into contact with his people.[8]

Now we come to the question of whether a homily should be read. In general, it is better not simply to read the text of the homily. Certainly, there are some occasions on which this could be done, especially on solemn and important celebrations, such as ceremonies where a bishop presides. The personal character of the communication may be more difficult to achieve when the homily is read, but depending on the occasion, the assembly, and the quality of the words, a homily can be memorable even though—and on occasion because—it is read. The *Oxford Sermons* of St. John Henry Newman and the fine homilies of Benedict XVI are examples of this.

However, the general paradigm is a homily in which remote, proximate, and immediate preparation have produced such familiarity with its contents that, after practicing what we have prepared, we will be able to preach freely in a personal and effective way, creating the communion of hearts that memorable speeches generate by teaching, delighting, and swaying the hearers.

We need hours of humble and generous practice in order to discern what works best for each one of us. One method is to print our text, highlighting key words so we can easily maintain the flow of the homily while not losing eye contact with the audience. For others, some bullet points will be a more effective strategy. Others will need to have with them only a passage they want to quote; some will speak without any notes at all. But what no one can afford to omit is the previous effort of preparing well. The right "translation" from the prepared homily to its delivery has to be discerned after practice and self-evaluation. The key question is not about how we can say more exactly what we have prepared, word by word, but about how we can be more effective in our preaching. The answer might vary in each case.

Then, trusting in God's power, we lend him our poor voice so that his Word can resound today, in the context of so many challenges. It will do any preacher good to remember what St. Paul said to Timothy:

> In the presence of God and of Christ Jesus, who is to judge the living and the dead, and in view of his appearing and his kingdom, I solemnly urge

---

8 On the appropriateness of standing, see *General Instruction of the Roman Missal*, 136. The option of preaching while seated on the chair is, significantly, only mentioned in the *Ceremonial for Bishops*, 142, perhaps as a sign of the teaching mission of a Bishop from his *cathedra*, a symbol particularly eloquent when the Bishop preaches in his cathedral. The now-outdated fashion of a few decades ago of walking around the sanctuary or the nave seems to have lost its popularity.

you: proclaim the message; be persistent whether the time is favorable or unfavorable; convince, rebuke, and encourage, with the utmost patience in teaching. For the time is coming when people will not put up with sound doctrine, but having itching ears, they will accumulate for themselves teachers to suit their own desires, and will turn away from listening to the truth and wander away to myths. As for you, always be sober, endure suffering, do the work of an evangelist, carry out your ministry fully. (1 Tm 4:1–5)

Indeed, we were born for this! "For if I preach the Gospel, that gives me no ground for boasting. For necessity is laid upon me. Woe to me if I do not preach the Gospel!" (1 Cor 9:16). Every homily is the fulfillment of our vocation, a liturgical act of praise, a work of charity, a happy encounter between God's grace and our best effort. Preaching should fill us with joy and a deep sense of mission. It ought to be done with a passion which is not sentimentality; with sobriety but also with the vulnerability of letting the Word pierce our hearts; with trembling for our tremendous responsibility (see Phlm 2:12), while trusting completely that the one "who began a good work in [us] will bring it to completion" (Phlm 1:6). God began the good work of our vocation and he will fulfill it with his grace; he begins every week the good work of our homilies; after our days of loving preparation, he will take it to completion as we preach for his people.

OTHER PRACTICAL POINTS

There are a number of practical elements that we should keep in mind for a good delivery, some of which were mentioned briefly in Chapter 2:

- **Eye contact**
  A homily is interpersonal communication, an experience of communion and conversation. Because of this personal character, the homilist must normally look at his people when he preaches. Eye contact is one of the most natural and evident expressions of this personal aspect of preaching: naturally, we look at those we are addressing. We must avoid certain defects as we preach, such as simply reading from a text, looking at a wall, or closing our eyes.

- **Voice**
  A preacher's voice has to be clear, natural, and understandable. It ought to be projected at the right volume: always loud enough to be heard by everyone, but also with some variations in tone and speed and added emphases according to *what* is said. A monotone delivery can undermine the power

of a well-prepared speech. Practicing our homilies aloud is the only way of finding the right way of saying the right words

- **Gestures**
Good homilists are aware of their gestures while preaching. Every movement expresses something: it either adds or subtracts. A preacher has to exercise self-mastery and confine himself to gestures that will help him effectively communicate his message. Oftentimes, simple and genuine gestures will be more than enough for the kind of sacred oratory demanded by a homily. The setting, as Pope Francis has reminded us, is mother Church: "This setting, both maternal and ecclesial, in which the dialogue between the Lord and his people takes place, should be encouraged by the closeness of the preacher, the warmth of his tone of voice, the unpretentiousness of his manner of speaking, the joy of his gestures."[9]

- **Questions**
A great device, used frequently by preachers like St. Augustine or St. John Chrysostom, is to ask questions throughout the homily. It is a natural way to highlight the most interesting or difficult aspects of the readings, in order to help our audience to find the meaning that is hidden in those opaque verses in which, according to Augustine's insight, charity is concealed.[10] The preacher is the guide on the journey towards that charity. Questions are excellent tools that help to gather and hold the attention of our audience and invite them to be part of the conversation.

- **Pauses**
Often, though not exclusively, related to asking questions, a pause can be an eloquent tool for a speech. It can offer variation to the simple exposition of ideas and attract the minds of the people.

- **Attention to the audience**
Because of the personal character of a homily, and related to the previous points, a preacher has to speak while actually looking at his audience, observing their reactions, noticing what works and what does not. This is perhaps a practice that is more difficult for beginners, but one that should be kept in mind: as in any conversation, we need to notice the reactions of our hearers and be able, if need be, to adapt what we are saying to what we see in them.

9 Francis, *Evangelii Gaudium*, 140.
10 See Augustine, *Expositions of the Psalms*, 140.2.

- **Technological tools**

  Is there room for using videos or presentations on screens during the homily? As the Church has reminded us more than once in recent times, the homily is a liturgical action, a unique kind of public speaking that is essentially sacred and, as such, different from other kinds of teaching. The celebration of the sacred liturgy should be kept sacred, and the "stewards of God's mysteries" (1 Cor 4:1) should try to preserve the distinct character of all the liturgical rites. Simply put, Mass should be one of the few oases in which the soul can rest from screens, so that communication can occur as directly as possible. There is a time for teaching with visual and audio aids, but it is not during Mass. If a church has screens, there might be room for such teaching before or after the liturgical celebrations, but just as Paul did not come with human wisdom when he proclaimed the testimony about God to the Corinthians (1 Cor 2:1), so we must leave plenty of space for the Spirit to fill our human words rather than relying on the quick effect of technology.

THE FRUITS OF A PRAYERFUL HOMILY

After preaching the homily, the priest will lead his congregation into the creed. The wise patristics scholar, Cardinal Tomáš Špidlík (1919–2010), said once with great wit that the reason the Church places the creed after the homily is to invite the faithful to believe, in spite of what they probably just heard.[11] Sadly, as we know, there is some truth to that. But we can also hope that a renewal in homiletics will actually lead to a renewal in the faith of the faithful who, being filled with fervor and love after hearing good homilies, will gladly profess their faith in God and then join in the sacrifice of thanksgiving offered on the altar.

A good homily comes from prayer and leads more fully into it. This is true for both preacher and assembly. In this sense, a homily is always a school of prayer, not only because it will include teachings about how to pray, but perhaps even more because a well-prepared and well-delivered homily shows the fruit of prayer, becomes an invitation to meditate on God's Word, and reveals the importance of letting God's grace work in us. In this sense, an essential teaching of the homily comes not from what is said but from what can be perceived by the assembly in the life of a preacher. Indeed, "when the

11 Taken from Claudio Dalla Costa, *Avete Finito di Farci la Predica? Riflessioni Laicali Sulle Omelie* (Cantalupa: Effatà Editrice, 2011), 9.

act of preaching is a prayer, the act of listening is more likely to be a prayer as well."[12] A preacher's personal holiness will move a congregation to greater openness to follow Christ even more than any exhortation about it. The faith, hope, and love of a homilist become a sincere enthusiasm that convinces the congregation more than what he says.

Homilies that come from what God works in the heart of a preacher always bear fruit at the right time. The man who has made the effort humbly to lead his people into this journey will have the joy of seeing the awe in the eyes of his audience as they rejoice in gazing at new things on this expedition of faith. Can anything more constantly refresh our faith and vocation than this? The preparation and delivery of our homilies can be a constant source of renewal in our faith. St. Augustine knew how good it was for us to share the mysteries of the faith and expressed it with these beautiful words that prepare us for our next chapter, in which we will learn from his brilliant example:

> Isn't this what generally happens when we are showing people who had never before seen them those impressive and beautiful sights, in the city or in the country, that we had grown used to passing by without the slightest pleasure because we had already seen them so often? In showing them to others do we not find that our own enjoyment is revived by sharing in the enjoyment that others derive from seeing them for the first time? And this we experience the more intensely, the closer our friendship with one another is, for the more the bond of love allows to be present in others, the more what has grown old becomes new again in our own eyes as well.[13]

Questions for Reflection and Conversation

• *Why is prayer the source and goal of preaching?*

• *What are the three practical points for delivering the homily that are most important for you?*

---

12 Burghardt, *Preaching: The Art & the Craft*, 117.

13 Augustine, *Instructing Beginners in Faith*, I.12.17.

8

A Brilliant Example:
St. Augustine and Some
Lessons for Today's Preaching

I n preaching, as in any art, anyone who aims at excellence must know the "classics," the timeless works in that field. Throughout history, people have flocked to hear the words of great preachers. We will review some classic homilies in the second section of this book; now, we will consider some lessons we can learn from one of the best preachers ever to proclaim the good news, Augustine of Hippo.[1]

The testimony and wisdom of St. Augustine, who has already appeared more than once in these pages, offer a great wealth of teaching for our preaching today. Of course, the North Africa of the late fourth and early fifth centuries was very different from our reality here and now, and yet there is an important, albeit counterintuitive, parallel. In that time, only around 10 percent of the population was literate. The bishop of Hippo once famously said to his congregation: "We here are your books" (*Codices vestres nos sumus*).[2] Though undoubtedly ambiguous, this statement is pow-

---

1 About Augustine's preaching see, among many: Michele Pellegrino, "General Introduction," in *Augustine: Sermons I (1–19)*, trans. Edmund Hill, OP (Brooklyn, N.Y.: New City Press, 1990), 13–136; F. Van der Meer, *Augustine the Bishop: Church and Society at the Dawn of the Middle Ages*, trans. Brian Battershaw and G.R. Lamb (New York: Harper & Row, 1961), 405–52; Peter T. Sanlon, *Augustine's Theology of Preaching* (Minneapolis: Fortress Press, 2014); William Harmless, *Augustine in His Own Words* (Washington, D.C.: The Catholic University of America Press, 2010), 122–55; George Lawless, OSA, "Preaching," in *Augustine through the Ages: An Encyclopedia*, ed. Allan D. Fitzgerald (Grand Rapids, Mich.: Eerdmans, 1999), 675–77.

2 Augustine, *Sermons*, 227.

erful: to a people who do not know how to read or how to interpret God's Word, the preacher becomes a book. Today's preachers face a kind of "illiteracy": whereas most people know how to read, and the average American household has 4.4 Bibles, nearly 60 percent of Americans read the Bible four times a year or less. Nor could many Catholics, even regular Sunday Mass attendees, easily recall the history of Israel or of the early Church, so the first two readings and psalm may sound to them like disconnected stories or oracles rather than revisited chapters of a story they already know.

And when we come to the problem of interpreting Scripture or understanding God's revelation—theology!—the "illiteracy" is even greater. In this context of decreasing familiarity with God's Word, preachers are the only "books" that most people will "read." Augustine can teach us how to fulfill that mission. We will learn three lessons from him: preaching as shared prayer; his common-sense style; and his appeal to the heart. Each lesson will shed light on a common false dilemma about preaching.

HOMILIES AS SHARED PRAYER

Augustine is famous for the "restless heart" that urged him on to his initial conversion and thereafter to a continuing search for God and a great labor of transmitting God's love effectively as a good preacher. His great achievements did not lead him to complacency, as he confessed: "I am nearly always dissatisfied with the address that I give ... and when I find that my actual address fails to express what I have before my mind, I am depressed by the fact that my tongue has been unable to keep up with my intellect."[3] The sudden insight into the truth does not last for long, whereas our speech needs to be articulated in syllables, taken from what has been impressed on the memory. Christ, however, is one syllable, one eternal Word said by the Father from all eternity. "Yet we should not find it surprising that to meet our weakness he descended to the discrete sounds that we use."[4] His Incarnation makes it truly possible to explain, albeit imperfectly, the Word through our words.

Our life is a pilgrimage towards eternal happiness and, while we walk on this path, our true and daily food, Augustine said, is the "absolutely necessary" bread of the Word of God: "Your daily food on this earth is the Word

---

3 Augustine, *Instructing Beginners in Faith*, Prologue.2.3.

4 Augustine, *Expositions of the Psalms*, 103.1.

of God, which is always being served up in the Churches."[5] Encountering this Word, he said, "it's our food, not our wages."[6] A disposition to prayer, as the encounter with Christ and his Word, is necessary for any believer, and this is keenly felt by anyone who has to share God's Word.

The bishop of Hippo was very fond of describing his mission as preacher in the following way: "I feed you on what I am fed on myself. I am just a waiter, I am not the master of the house; I set before you from the pantry which I too live on."[7] His own experience of prayer is what allowed him to share the good news with his people. His own search for Christ led him to search for the truth and find it in the revelation of charity. Everything in Scripture tends toward charity, as he taught his people: "You need look for nothing else in Scripture ... wherever there is an obscure passage of Scripture, charity is concealed in it, and wherever the sense is plain, charity is proclaimed. If it were nowhere plain to see, it would not nourish you; if it were nowhere concealed, it would not exercise you."[8] The life of a preacher is the constant search for that charity in prayer and the faithful effort to share that love with the people entrusted to his care.

Augustine understood that preparation for preaching was not primarily an intellectual or technical endeavor. He knew that all his years of teaching and training in the art of public speaking were insufficient to make him a good preacher upon ordination. He was deeply aware of the necessity of preparing his heart and mind through prayer for this important ministry. He wrote a moving letter to his bishop, Valerius, asking for some dedicated time "to examine carefully all the remedies of his scriptures and, by praying and reading, work that he may grant my soul health suited for such dangerous tasks."[9] This preparation was not only about a specific "time off," but about taking the time to be fed so as to be the good household servant who, like a waiter, offers the tray of God's Word to his people.[10]

We can look to Augustine's teaching and example for an answer to the question posed earlier of whether to prepare homilies or improvise them. Augustine certainly improvised *and* prepared his preaching, not alternately

---

5 Augustine, *Sermons,* 56.10.

6 Augustine, *Sermons,* 56.10.

7 Augustine, *Sermons,* 339.4.

8 Augustine, *Expositions of the Psalms,* 140.2.

9 Augustine, *Letters,* trans. Roland Teske, SJ (Hyde Park, N.Y.: New City Press, 2001), 21.3.

10 See Augustine, *Sermons,* 126.8.

but simultaneously. He was able to improvise and preach without notes *because* he prepared, even on those occasions in which he had planned a sermon for a reading different from the one the lector proclaimed:

> We had prepared a short psalm for our consideration today and indicated to the reader that this was the psalm to be recited. But at the last minute he apparently became flustered and read this one instead. We have deemed it preferable to see in the reader's mistake a sign of the will of God and to follow that rather than to do our own will by sticking to our original plan.[11]

Familiarity with the Word and dedicated years of prayer and training bear fruit in foreseen and unforeseen circumstances. If Augustine was able to rise to the occasion, it was because of his life of prayer and study, because of his years of dedicated training in the art of speaking, very much—according to the image used by William Harmless—like a jazz player who is able to play well because of the long hours of disciplined practice.[12]

In the end, the solution to this common pastoral dilemma—to prepare or not to prepare—is to be fed and to serve what we are fed on, as Augustine recommended. Although many priests might say that, because they are busy, they can preach without preparing their homilies, very few will say that, because they are busy, they can live without praying. In prayer we are fed by God; in preaching we feed our people. As we saw, the preparation of our Sunday preaching could be one of the best ways of bringing unity to our lives, as our prayer and study *become* our work and our work *becomes* our prayer. Preaching is, truly, our own prayer shared with our people.

COMMON-SENSE PREACHING

The contemplation of God's Word in prayer is the foundation but not the only prerequisite for effective preaching. Like a good waiter, the preacher needs to know what to serve and how to serve it, according to those who are being fed. Augustine is a great example of the art of accommodation not only, as we saw, in his capacity to preach about unexpected readings but

11 Augustine, *Expositions of the Psalms*, 138.1. It is fair to say that the cohesion of this remarkable (and long) sermon is not as strong as in other *Expositions*. *Dolbeau Sermon* 5 was preached in a similar circumstance. See George Lawless, "Preaching," in *Augustine through the Ages: An Encyclopedia*, ed. Allan D. Fitzgerald (Grand Rapids, Mich.: Eerdmans, 1999), 676.

12 See William Harmless, "A Love Supreme: Augustine's 'Jazz' of Theology," *Augustinian Studies* 43 (2012): 149–77.

especially in the art of adapting his speech to the needs and characteristics of his audience; his is a testimony to common-sense preaching.

This answers another common false dilemma often posed as a question: are homilies supposed to teach or share, to be doctrinal or pastoral, conceptual or personal? Augustine's common sense in preaching came from his knowledge of his people and the permanent aim of his prayer and preaching: conversion. Being one with his people, he was able to say, as he celebrated the anniversary of his episcopal ordination, "brothers and sisters, lighten my burden for me, lighten it, please, and carry it with me; lead good lives," and elsewhere, "do my job in your own homes."[13] According to Augustine biographer Peter Brown:

> This is the secret of Augustine's enormous power as a preacher. He will make it his first concern to place himself in the midst of his congregation, to appeal to their feelings for him, to react with immense sensitivity to their emotions, and so, as the sermon progressed, to sweep them into his own way of feeling. He could identify himself sufficiently with his congregation to provoke them to identify themselves completely with himself.[14]

The eloquence of Augustine's preaching was motivated not by the vain pursuit of excellent rhetoric but by a bond of love, an experience of communion that moved the preacher to dwell in his listeners and the listeners to dwell in the preacher.[15] Out of this love and compassion, he asks:

> What, after all, do I want? What do I desire? What am I longing for? Why am I speaking? Why am I sitting here? What do I live for, if not with this intention that we should all live together with Christ? That is my desire, that's my honor, that's my most treasured possession, that's my joy, that's my pride and glory. But if you don't listen to me and yet I have not kept quiet, then I will deliver my soul. But I don't want to be saved without you.[16]

This loving passion moves Augustine to teach doctrine as he preaches, explaining the mysteries of Scripture—as he did, for example, in his series of sermons on the Psalms, those preached commentaries which themselves are

---

13 Augustine, *Sermons*, 339.4; 94.

14 Peter Brown, *Augustine of Hippo: A Biography. A New Edition with an Epilogue* (Berkeley and Los Angeles: University of California Press, 2000), 248.

15 Augustine, *Instructing Beginners in Faith*, I.12.17.

16 Augustine, *Sermons*, 17.2.

a larger corpus than all other patristic commentaries on the Psalms together. Elsewhere, he explains the mysteries of the sacraments to the *infantes* (newly baptized) in a manner both personal and magisterial: "I haven't forgotten my promise. I had promised those of you who have just been baptized a sermon to explain the sacrament of the Lord's table, which you can see right now, and which you shared in last night.... If you receive them well, you are yourselves what you receive."[17]

The Bishop of Hippo's pastoral common sense shines forth in the images and simple phrases, very moving and easy to understand, that permeate his homilies. A few examples will suffice:

- "It's by the mercy of God that a man doesn't know when he is going to die. The last day is hidden from us, in order that every day may be taken seriously."[18]

- Preaching about Jesus being asleep in the boat, he said: "You have heard an insult—it's a high wind; you've got angry—it's a wave.... What does it mean that Christ is asleep in you? That you have forgotten Christ. So wake Christ up, remember Christ; let Christ stay awake in you."[19]

- Speaking about love of the things of this world, which "smiles on us with many things,"[20] he used the image of a ring. "Brothers, if a bridegroom made a ring for his bride, and she loved the ring ... more than her bridegroom ... if she said, 'the ring is enough. I do not want to see his face again', what sort of person would she be? Who wouldn't detest this crazy woman ... [the ring] is given her by the betrothed just that [in it] he himself may be loved. God, then, has given you all these things. Love Him who made them."[21]

- Finally, teaching about prayer, he was fond of the image of a doctor who knows better than we what we need: "God provides for our salvation even if he doesn't comply with our wish."[22] "You know what you desire, but he knows what's good for you.... So think yourself as being ill under a doctor.

---

17 Augustine, *Sermons*, 227.

18 Augustine, *Sermons*, 39.1.

19 Augustine, *Sermons*, 63.2.

20 Augustine, *Sermons*, 158.7.

21 Augustine, *Homilies on the First Epistle of St. John*, trans. Boniface Ramsey (Hyde Park, N.Y.: New City Press, 2008), 2.11.

22 Augustine, *Homilies on First John*, 6.8.

You have suddenly the lovely idea of asking the doctor to let you have a glass of wine…. Don't hesitate to ask … but if you don't get it, don't feel bad about it."[23]

Effective preaching is always personal *and* profound, it always teaches *and* touches the heart, and it always moves to conversion: "Do what he has told you, and hope for what he has promised."[24]

THE HEART AS A PATH

With this we come to our last point, in which we find a solution for another common false dilemma for preachers today: are our homilies supposed to address the mind or the heart? This question arises because we live in a culture of subjectivism and relativism that favors appeals to personal experience and emotion over appeals to reason and truth.

How can the Church teach the truth to our society? How can homilies be relevant for the youth? Augustine's example gives us an important key. The emotional mindset so common in our culture, while being a challenge, also presents an opportunity if we know how to rightly appeal to the heart.[25]

Augustine's own experience of search and conversion had a central and decisive role in the healing of his heart. His different emotions and affections found redemption, especially, in the words of the Psalms: "How copiously I wept at your hymns and canticles, how intensely was I moved by the lovely harmonies of your singing Church!"[26] He understood that love is at the root of who we become and so he prayed with the Song of Songs: "Set charity in order in me," *ordinate in me caritatem*.[27] This was, in the end, the dividing line for the history of humanity: "The citizens of the city of God, who live according to God during the pilgrimage of his life, feel fear and desire, pain and gladness, in accord with Holy Scripture and sound doctrine; and,

---

23 Augustine, *Sermons*, 80.2.

24 Augustine, *Sermons*, 80.8.

25 In order to more clearly apply Augustine's teachings in our context, I use the term "heart" in a broad contemporary sense as the center of emotions and love, rather than in the ancient sense of the locus of thoughts.

26 Augustine, *Confessions*, trans. Maria Boulding, OSB (Hyde Park, N.Y.: New City Press, 2016), IX.6.14.

27 Augustine, *The City of God*, trans. William Babcock (Hyde Park, N.Y.: New City Press, 1993), XV.22.

because their love is right, they have all these emotions in the right way."[28] True love is that force that orders our hearts and propels us upwards, towards the city of God: "If our foundation is in heaven, the weight of our building bears upward, toward heaven."[29]

Augustine teaches the preachers of our times to address their people just as he did in the early fifth century: "Question your heart: see what you have done and what you have been yearning for."[30] Everyone understands these perennial questions of the human heart, and this can be a fruitful emphasis in preaching today. Go to the heart, but to the real human heart; bypass the accretions of relativism and a politically correct sentimentalism. Go to the heart, with all its passion, with its questions, with its deep longing. Start with the heart.

St. Augustine knew how to do that. He would preach about the psalms of ascent, but not so much about the physical ascent to the city of Jerusalem. He would say: "Our ascent must be made in the hearts, by a good intention, in faith and hope and charity, in a desire for eternity," because "love is a powerful thing … we travel not on foot but by our affections."[31]

We can teach our people how to ascend in the heart through what we could call a pedagogy of desire. Desire is an experience of any human heart. All persons, of any age or background, will relate to the simple and profound insight of Augustine's commentary on the Gospel of John: *desiderium sinus cordis*, "desire is the bosom of the heart," or as Brown put it, "it is yearning that makes the heart deep."[32]

This profound human reality is no less central for a Christian because of his faith. A preacher can wake up a congregation consumed by routine: "Because now you are unable to see, let your task consist in desiring. The entire life of a good Christian is a holy desire."[33] A homilist can strengthen those who might be tired of praying: "He wanted to make them knock at his door in order to exercise them in desire."[34] He can give comfort to those who

---

28 Augustine, *City of God*, XIV.9.

29 Augustine, *Expositions of the Psalms*, 121.4.

30 Augustine, *Homilies on First John*, 6.3.

31 Augustine, *Expositions of the Psalms*, 120.3; 121.11–12.

32 Augustine, *Tractates on John*, 40.10; Brown, *Augustine of Hippo*, 150.

33 Augustine, *Homilies on First John*, 4.6.

34 Augustine, *Sermons*, 80.1.

do not know how to pray: "Desire is praying always."[35] He can offer hope to those who worry that their prayers are not heard: "God stretches our desire through delay, stretches our soul through desire, and makes it large enough by stretching it. Let us desire then, brothers, for we have to be filled."[36]

The goals of a good homilist today and always are to help his people, whether they are well-formed or not, to stretch that desire and go from there to God, and to help them recognize in their hearts the longing for eternity. Calling their attention to their restlessness and dissatisfactions, acknowledging their doubts, expressing aloud their fears, recognizing their longings—these can be steps in the journey towards seeing Christ as the true answer to their deepest needs, their Savior in reality and not just in theory. It can make clear that the call to conversion is not a moralistic imposition, but the path to freedom. Beginning with the heart, a preacher can open the conversation towards eternity, as St. Augustine did so well when he described "being possessed by yearning for the wellsprings": "Remember how we were gladdened by an inner sweetness, remember how we found it possible to perceive … something that does not change."[37] This is something that can be done in a particularly effective way in our mystagogical preaching. We can surprise our congregations, accustomed to the same well-known ideas, as the bishop of Hippo did when he preached during the dramatic rites of baptism about our deep thirst for God, the fountain of true water, or when he praised the shining night of our hearts as he described the lights of the Easter Vigil.

Allow me here to introduce a free comparison that helps us to see how modern Augustine can feel and how much we can learn from him today. In the 1930s James Agee wrote a beautiful poem, made famous by Morten Lauridsen's setting, expressing his gratitude for the beauty of the earth but also his deep longing for something more. It goes like this:

> Sure on this shining night
> Of star made shadows round,
> Kindness must watch for me
> This side the ground
>
> . . . .
> Sure on this shining night
> I weep for wonder

---

35 Augustine, *Sermons*, 80.7.

36 Augustine, *Homilies on First John*, 4.6.

37 Augustine, *Expositions of the Psalms*, 41.10.

Wand'ring far alone
Of shadows on the stars.

Some 1,500 years before, Augustine also sang about this shining night, brightly seen in the liturgical rites of Easter, revealing the true meaning of this night where all our human longings are fulfilled: "The sun has gone but not the day, for a shining earth has taken the place of the shining sky. With delighted eyes we behold the gleam of these lamps, and thus, with an illuminated spirit, we can understand the meaning of this shining night."[38] Our human desires are fulfilled in the mysteries of the Church.

Few ancient authors can be felt in such a powerful way by us today as Augustine. But, as much as we are moved when we peruse the written words of these homilies, we know that we are missing their tone, volume, and musicality; we know that the expression of his face and the movement of his hands are lost for us. As Possidius said about his friend, "those who read what Augustine has written in his works on divine subjects profit greatly, but I believe that the ones who really profited were those who actually heard him and saw him speak in church."[39] Though we have not seen him, we find delight in knowing him through his words, in learning from him how to preach today. His heartfelt letter to his friend St. Paulinus of Nola expresses well what we experience when we get to know Augustine and learn from him how to renew our preaching for the new evangelization:

> What has happened to me is strange, but true. I am in pain because I do not see you, and my pain itself consoles me. For I do not like the courage by which one patiently bears the absence of good persons, like yourself.... Who, then, can refrain from joy when he sees you in order that he may be able not to feel pain when he does not see you? Hence, I can do neither one, and since, if I could, I could do so only inhumanly, I am delighted in my inability, and there is some consolation in the fact that I am delighted.[40]

In the end, what makes Augustine's preaching so compelling is the harmony between his words and his life, and this is why we feel we are in his presence when he preaches to us. In this way, he embodies his own decisive advice for preachers: "But for us to be listened to with obedient compliance,

---

38 Augustine, *Sermon Guelferbytanus*, 5.1–2, cited in Van der Meer, *Augustine the Bishop*, 323.
39 Possidius of Calama, *Vita Augustini*, 31, cited in Harmless, *Augustine in His Own Words*, 122.
40 Augustine, *Letters*, 27.1.

whatever the grandeur of the speaker's utterances, his manner of life carries more weight."[41]

Questions for Reflection and Conversation

• *How do we learn from St. Augustine to overcome the following false dilemmas about preaching?*
  • *To prepare or to improvise?*
  • *To be conceptual or personal?*
  • *To address the mind or the heart?*

• *Is there any line of Augustine's homilies quoted here that you particularly liked? Why?*

---

41 Augustine, *Teaching Christianity*, IV.27.59.

9

Preaching as *Locus Theologicus*: The Power of Practicing Theology in the Twenty-First Century

We have reflected on how the ministry of preaching is much more than one of the many "chores" in our busy schedules. Preaching is indeed a central work not only as an important mission to fulfill but also as a potential key to bringing unity to our lives. In this last chapter, I want to explore one of the amazing possibilities of preaching for the strengthening of our priestly identity and mission.

Some time ago, in a homiletics class, I asked my students—deacons, or soon to be ordained deacons—if they were looking forward to their lives as theologians. Sensing their confusion, I asked directly if they would see themselves as theologians once their studies were completed. Not one of them said yes. They all agreed, quite honestly, that theology often felt more like a requirement for ordination than a reality meant to be a central part of their priestly life.

At the root of this outlook, we find an imperfect understanding which mistakenly confines the study of theology to the formal academic endeavors of research, writing, and teaching. Theology, however, is not the province solely of academics. To imply that only those who are writing articles or teaching at universities are engaged in theological work would be a mistake akin to alleging that a lawyer who does not publish in academic journals is not really lawyering, even though we see him in the courtroom applying the law as he learned to do in years of study.

When theology is confined to libraries and classrooms—as it often is—some problems arise. First, theology itself can become the profession of an elite in academic echo chambers, more interested in political or academic standards than in the urgent and real answers needed in our times. Second, what was learned in long years of theological study becomes a distant memory for priests who are not always rooted in the effort of deepening their meditation on God's truth but are distracted by the exigencies of myriad practical realities. When this is the case, theology is not integrated as it should be into daily priestly life.

A problem and an opportunity arise from this situation. The problem: homilies are often a poor and scattered collection of thoughts that, in unnecessarily long speeches, shed little light on the wonders of God's revelation and their meaning for our lives. The opportunity: the homily can become the site where the preacher recovers the living and necessary place of theology in his life. While only a small portion of a presbyterate will publish books, every single priest will preach. Rather than seeing the preparation for the homily as another of the many tasks to be fulfilled during the week, a priest can make this ministry become the regular space for theological study and reflection. In this way, theology will not be the restricted to a career for a few, and preaching can be renewed by the honest and constant quest for the truth and beauty of God.

PREACHING AS *LOCUS THEOLOGICUS*

This means that—freely borrowing a category from classic theology—preaching can be understood as *locus theologicus*.[1] Melchior Cano famously defined this concept as *domicilia omnium argumentorum theologicorum*.[2] The *loci* are the places where authority is found, and thus where we can encounter the "grammar" for articulating the faith (e.g., Scripture, Tradition, councils, fathers).

---

1 About this, see "Lieux Théologiques," in *Dictionnaire de Théologie Catholique* [DTC] 9, (Paris: Librairie Letouzey et Ané, 1929), 712–42; Louis Bouyer, *Dictionary of Theology* (New York: Desclee, 1965), 439–40. About Cano's contribution and shortcomings, see M. J. Congar, *Théologie*, in DTC 15, 422.

2 Melchior Cano, *De Locis Theologicis* (Salamanca: Mathias Gastius, 1563), 1.3.

It is important to see these places as the active and living spaces where argumentation occurs. It is in this way that we can say that preaching can be fruitfully understood as *locus theologicus*: a place, a domicile, a home for the real exercise of theology today. It is in a deeper understanding of the value and importance of preaching that theology can be renewed as a living and essential part of the daily life of priests. If we take preaching as a "home" for theology, let us explore three of its "areas" or "rooms."

A Place for Encountering the Word

A first room in this domicile is where we listen to the Word. The many urgencies of priestly life and the incessant distractions of our postmodern society can become obstacles for the first duty of any preacher: to actively listen the Word of God in prayer.

The positive disposition to preach should move a priest, first and foremost, to listen. Certainly, there are different ways of listening. St. Augustine would tell his people: "You, then, listen with care and attention, while we bishops should listen with fear and apprehension."[3] A preacher does not only listen attentively, but also with the reverent fear of knowing that he is accountable for speaking the truth. Mindful of his responsibility as a preacher, a priest must avoid distractions and be silent in order to listen in prayer to what God says to him, and through him, to his people. Cardinal Sarah expresses this with clarity and depth: "The priestly dignity requires us to realize the importance of our own words. Everything in the priest, body and soul, must proclaim the Glory of God.... Above all, in order to nourish this speech, it is terribly important to remain silent."[4] Indeed, without silence we cannot really preach; we might say words that come from noise and busyness and may add disorder and confusion. The old adage remains true today, *silentium pater praedicatorum* (silence is the father of preachers).[5]

A Place for the Celebration of God's Word

Moving on to another room in the *locus*, we come to the place to experience the liturgy of the word in all its depth. It certainly makes a difference when a

3 Augustine, *Sermons*, 46.1.

4 Robert Cardinal Sarah, *The Power of Silence: Against the Dictatorship of Noise* (San Francisco: Ignatius Press, 2017), 194.

5 See A. D. Sertillanges, OP, *L'Orateur Chrétien: Traité de Prédication* (Juvisy: Les Éditions du Cerf, 1930), 82.

preacher sees the proclamation of God's Word and his preaching as a mysterious and effective action and not just as a casual moment of human sharing.

There is a unique power when the words of Scripture resound in the liturgy. They are not only prayerfully remembered; they are pronounced *here* and *now* by God through the Church, especially in the Gospel, which is only read by ordained ministers. Reverently listening to God who speaks in the liturgical proclamation of his Word, the preacher has to constantly remind himself of the mystery at work when the Word is proclaimed, and therefore, of the mystery that unfolds when he breaks the bread of God's Word for the people in the homily.

A Place to Listen to Theology

The third area is where we listen to the Word *explained*. Reading is important, but there is something irreplaceable about hearing. We read God's Word, we read articles, books, and blogs. But "faith comes from what is heard" (Rom 10:17). A few years ago, at a conference on the Letter to the Galatians held at the University of St Andrews, the organizers had a simple and powerful idea: at the opening of the conference, all the participants gathered in a room and listened to one person read the entire Letter to the Galatians. It was an eloquent reminder that what we were actually reflecting on was not a theoretical work, not a text to be dissected in self-standing verses, but a letter to be heard by a community in which the author, illumined by the Holy Spirit, applied the Gospel to a concrete problem. Is this not real theology?

All the decisive developments in Pauline theology come from letters that were heard by communities. Around two-thirds of patristic literature was originally spoken, and much of what was written was dictated and frequently read aloud to groups of people. For the most part, the indispensable progress made in early Christian theology was made orally. As someone said, to read an early Christian text is to eavesdrop on a conversation.[6]

Here we come to a very important realization. The reason for the oral-auditory character of biblical and patristic literature is not only sociological—that is, the limited means for communication or the very restricted literacy of those times. Something more is at stake here.[7]

---

6 Harrison, *The Art of Listening in the Early Church*, 2.

7 On the oral character of Sacred Scripture, see Walter J. Ong, *Orality and Literacy: The Technologizing of the Word* (London: Methuen, 1982), esp. 74–75.

Theology is, essentially, a dialogical activity, an encounter between people and communities with questions and longings, a common exploration of God's mysteries, a true and necessary conversation. Thus, orality has an important place in theology. It not only reminds us of the foundational efforts of early Christians to understand and share their faith, but also takes us to what they heard, and what we must hear again today: the Word that was in the beginning and became flesh (see Jn 1:1,14). Christ, the eternal Logos, became one of us and assumed our human voice in order to tell us everything he had heard from his Father (see Jn 15:15). The Lord Jesus, in his infinite wisdom, chose to speak and not to write. The Word wanted us to keep his words and dwell in them, fulfilling in this way the prophecy of Isaiah:

> For as the rain and the snow come down from heaven, and do not return there until they have watered the earth, making it bring forth and sprout, giving seed to the sower and bread to the eater, so shall my word be that goes out from my mouth; it shall not return to me empty, but it shall accomplish that which I purpose, and succeed in the thing for which I sent it (Is 55:10–11).

The Word comes from on high to transform our hearts and thus, in the case of preachers, we are able to speak good things to God's people. If faith, as Joseph Ratzinger said, is "to re-think what has been heard," then theology is the experience of reflecting on the Word and letting it (him!) become words for others.[8] If it is not a dialogue, then it becomes vain human wisdom.[9]

Preaching, therefore, is the privileged home for the practice of theology: in it the Word still resounds and informs words that are pronounced and heard, thus leading the hearers to know and love God. It is true *homilein*: speaking and being in company with the other, communing and being in harmony with the listeners. In doing this, the Church is more than the human setting for this conversation: in this living communion preaching, as an ecclesial activity, becomes a true place, an indispensable domicile, for living theology.

A clarification is in order: preaching is the place to practice theology, understood as the reflection on the deposit of the faith here and now, but it

---

8 Joseph Ratzinger, *Storia e Dogma* (Milan: Jaca Book, 1993), 43.

9 An excellent example of a theological work born as a dialogue is Ratzinger's *Introduction to Christianity*. About this see Daniel Cardó, *What Does It Mean to Believe? Faith in the Thought of Joseph Ratzinger* (Steubenville, Ohio: Emmaus Academic, 2020), 9–12.

is not the place to experiment with new and uncertain theological theories. Preaching and theology come from the faith and lead to a deeper understanding and practice of it: "It follows that the chief points of our faith— God, Christ, the Holy Spirit, grace and sin, sacraments and Church, death and eternal life—are never outmoded. They are always the issues that affect us most profoundly. They must be the permanent center of preaching and therefore of theological reflection."[10]

THE PREACHER AS THEOLOGIAN

Two accomplished preachers—one ancient, one contemporary—who have been present in these pages before can help us to find some important keys for the task of being theologians *and* preachers, or rather, theologians who preach.

We can spend a lifetime learning from St. Augustine; in the present case we turn to his Christmas homilies, which are excellent models for concise, powerful, deeply theological, and eminently pastoral preaching. These sermons are very short, not more than two pages each. And perhaps precisely because of that they can express so powerfully the mystery of the Nativity, particularly the great paradox of the Incarnation. Jesus is the "speechless infant and Word."[11] Indeed, "he lies in a manger but he holds the whole world in his hands; he sucks his mother's breast, but feeds the angels; he is swaddled in rags, but clothes us in immortality; he is suckled, but also worshipped."[12] He became man "that He, the Bread, might be hungry; that He, the Fountain, might thirst."[13] Because of this, the Child Jesus, God and man, is "amiable and terrible, severe and serene." Therefore, Augustine exhorts, "since we are not yet ready for the banquet of our Father, let us grow familiar with the manger of our Lord Jesus Christ."[14] He continues in the vein of paradox in teaching about Mary: "She fed our bread" and was "ruling our Ruler" because of the power of Christ himself, who "created his own mother."[15] These profound insights of spoken theology are not only deep but also effective: the

10 Joseph Ratzinger, *Gospel, Catechesis, Catechism: Sidelights on the Catechism of the Catholic Church* (San Francisco: Ignatius Press, 1995), 24.

11 Augustine, *Sermons*, 184.3; 185.1; 187.1; 190.3.

12 Augustine, *Sermons*, 190.4.

13 Augustine, *Sermons*, 191.1.

14 Augustine, *Sermons*, 195.4; 194.3.

15 Augustine, *Sermons*, 184.3; 186.1; 195.2.

stark contrast of the paradoxes becomes a powerful way of inviting an audience to reflect on the mystery.

Augustine also knows how to bring these theological reflections into a very personal conversation with his people. He has a gift for reaching people in different states of life by speaking about different aspects of the mystery, and relates the two nativities of Christ—eternal from the Father and in time from Mary—to the dignity of both sexes.[16] He speaks to each person in front of him: "Consider, O man, what God became for your sake; understand this lesson of surpassing humility presented by a teacher who, as yet, says no word," and famously, "wake up, O man, it was for you that God was made man!"[17]

Finally, Augustine constantly invites his congregation to rejoice, to "let astonishment give way to thanksgiving and praise" by a "joyous gathering and appropriate festivity."[18] Is there any other possible response in those who have been led by good preaching to the true celebration of so great a grace as the birthday of Christ? Indeed, "look for merit, look for a cause, look for justice; and see whether you can find anything but grace."[19]

Pope Emeritus Benedict XVI gives us our second example of profound and appealing preaching as spoken theology. The seven Easter homilies of his pontificate are jewels of prayer and Christian reflection on the Paschal Mystery. Benedict himself indicates that, unlike the mystery of Christ's Nativity, the Easter story is something very foreign to our experience.[20] Because of this difficulty, he frequently follows a mystagogical approach, unfolding the meaning of the rites perceived by the senses. With depth and beauty, he explains the symbols of baptism (water and light), those of the Easter Vigil liturgy (light, water, and the alleluia), and again the mystery of light in the context of the new creation.[21]

16 Augustine, *Sermons*, 184.2; 188.3; 192.2; 196.2.

17 Augustine, *Sermons*, 188.3; 185.1.

18 Augustine, *Sermons*, 189.4; 184.2.

19 Augustine, *Sermons*, 185.3.

20 Benedict XVI, *Homily at the Easter Vigil of 2006*, in https://w2.vatican.va/content/benedict-xvi/en/homilies/2006/documents/hf_ben-xvi_hom_20060415_veglia-pasquale.html

21 Benedict XVI, *Homily at the Easter Vigil of 2008*, in https://w2.vatican.va/content/benedict-xvi/en/homilies/2008/documents/hf_ben-xvi_hom_20080322_veglia-pasquale.html; *Homily at the Easter Vigil of 2009*, in https://w2.vatican.va/content/benedict-xvi/en/homilies/2009/documents/hf_ben-xvi_hom_20090411_veglia-pasquale.html; *Homily at the Easter Vigil of 2012*, in https://w2.vatican.va/content/benedict-xvi/en/homilies/2012/documents/hf_ben-xvi_hom_20120407_veglia-pasquale.html

The homilies of the pope emeritus provide excellent examples of the pastoral application of theological knowledge. Hear how he shares the information transmitted by Gregory of Tours about the ancient practice of lighting the fire for the Easter Vigil directly from the sun, using a crystal: "Light and fire, so to speak, were received anew from heaven, so that all the lights and fires of the year could be kindled from them."[22] Or how he utilizes the apocryphal *Life of Adam and Eve* (probably 1 AD) to reflect on the search for a medicine for death and the need for a different cure: "The true cure for death must be different. It cannot lead simply to an indefinite prolongation of this current life. It would have to transform our lives from within."[23]

Certainly, Benedict does not leave things there; he shows also that Easter has concrete meaning for our lives. Bringing the mystery to a very personal dimension, he comments on the *Introit* of the Easter Sunday Mass: "'I arose and now I am still with you,' he says to each of us. My hand upholds you. Wherever you may fall, you will always fall into my hands. I am present even at the door of death. Where no one can accompany you further, and where you can bring nothing, even there I am waiting for you, and for you I will change darkness into light."[24] Easter, indeed, means a real change. But how can a typical person in our postmodern world understand this mystery? Benedict dares to "borrow the language of the theory of evolution." The Resurrection of Christ:

> Is the greatest "mutation", absolutely the most crucial leap into a totally new dimension that there has ever been in the long history of life and its development.... It is a qualitative leap in the history of "evolution" and of life in general towards a new future life, towards a new world which, starting from Christ, already continuously permeates this world of ours, transforms it and draws it to itself.[25]

This mystery becomes a reality for us in baptism, a theme very frequently present in these homilies.

---

22 Benedict XVI, *Homily at the Easter Vigil of 2008.*Gregory of Tours is a great witness to many customs and traditions. See Peter Brown, *The Cult of the Saints: Its Rise and Function in Latin Christianity* (Chicago: University of Chicago Press, 2015), 81.

23 See "Life of Adam and Eve" [Latin] in *The Old Testament Pseudepigrapha*, ed. and trans. James Charlesworth (New York: Doubleday, 1985), II:274; Benedict XVI, *Homily at the Easter Vigil of 2008.*

24 Benedict XVI, *Homily at the Easter Vigil of 2007.*

25 Benedict XVI, *Homily at the Easter Vigil of 2006.*

In the homilies of these great thinkers, we do not find the dry and theoretical diversions of academics but true theology, based on a real life of prayer
and of deep knowledge, expressed with concern for the good of the people.
We do not find a trace of some of the common defects of today's homilies:
self-centeredness, a simplistic or paternalistic tone, or even a condescending
didacticism that ultimately excludes the presence of the mystery being celebrated. Rather, we find in them the words of shepherds who raise the minds
and hearts of their people to what God offers in the liturgical celebrations.
In their preaching we encounter true and courageous explorations of the
mysteries, significant developments in theological reflection, and concrete
applications. We see how preaching is truly the place for practicing theology.

The search for eloquence in preaching should not be primarily about
tools, arrangement of words, or stories, but about the truth. A preacher
searches for the truth and thus speaks, according to the words of Christ: "Out
of the abundance of the heart the mouth speaks" (Mt 12:34). Our homilies
must come from our prayer and study, and because of that, they should
express the truth with beauty. Newman said: "Thought and speech are inseparable from each other.... Style is a thinking out into language."[26] Similarly,
Pascal wrote about eloquence: "There must be both the pleasing and the real,
but what is pleasing must itself be drawn from what is true."[27] Because of this,
with Ratzinger we believe that "proclamation is the measure of theology."[28]

A simple and important goal for priestly formation should be to foster
the awareness that priests *are* theologians, and that the ministry of preaching
which will be exercised in some way throughout our lives will be the constant
place to practice theology. Everything learned will prove useful as new situations require us to think theologically and let God's revelation illumine the
challenges and questions of today's Church.

Seeing the homily not as a burden but as an occasion to teach from
theological reflection will inspire ongoing formation and will motivate the
preparation of good homilies. These in turn will edify the people of God

---

26 Newman, *Idea of a University*, 208.

27 Blaise Pascal, *Pensées*, trans. Honor Levi (Oxford: Oxford University Press, 1995), 547.

28 Joseph Ratzinger, *The Nature and Mission of Theology: Approaches to Understanding its Role
in the Light of Present Controversy* (San Francisco: Ignatius Press, 1995), 63. Significantly, in the
times of St. Thomas Aquinas, a requirement for a bachelor's degree in theology was to preach
two sermons. Preaching was seen as a test of theology. See *Thomas Aquinas: The Academic
Sermons*, trans. Mark-Robin Hoogland, CP (Washington, D.C.: The Catholic University of America
Press, 2010), 4.

and enrich the Church with new insights on God and the world. This is how theology became a reality; this is how it should fulfill its mission today.

Finally, the encounter with the God we lovingly search for in our prayer and study will be the source of the authentic enthusiasm and the cheerfulness necessary in preaching.[29] *Quaerere Deum* (seek God) continues to be the lifelong journey of a preacher and the constant wellspring of what he says.

Questions for Reflection and Conversation

• *Do you see yourself as a theologian? Why?*

• *How can preaching help priests to put their theological learning into practice? Give some concrete examples.*

---

29 This is what Augustine called *hilaritas*, See Augustine, *Instructing Beginners in Faith*, I.2.4 and I.10.14.

Part II

A Homiletics Reader

Introduction

In the previous chapters we have explored the richness and complexity of the art of preaching, reviewing its human and theological foundations and studying the practical elements of its preparation and delivery. In the last chapter we remembered that the homily is at the core of the life of anyone who, by virtue of the sacrament of orders, *is* a preacher. Indeed, the homily is one of the most privileged places where a priest exercises what he has learned in his years of formation, and where his busy life finds constant renewal and harmony.

The humble cultivation of good lives bears—albeit in varied forms—good preaching. This is the first lesson we learn from the best preachers of our tradition: if we try to know and love Jesus Christ, and live according to the Gospel, we will have something valuable to say. The second lesson is that preaching can be effective *and* beautiful. As such, it can be memorable. Not in vain will we read now some homilies that are hundreds of years old and yet have lost nothing of their poignant freshness.

In this section I will provide a sample of exemplary homilies for personal reflection and group discussion, because we need to learn from the best. This is, in fact, the advice of one among them: "So then, infants only become speakers by learning the speech and pronunciation of speaker; why cannot people become eloquent without any formal training in the art of public speaking, but simply by reading and hearing the speeches of the eloquent and, as far as they have the chance to follow this up, by imitating them?"[1] Most of us

1 Augustine, *Teaching Christianity*, IV.5.

have not been sufficiently trained in the art of public speaking, but we have in front of us a vast treasure of immortal homilies from which we can learn to preach well by studying with the best among us.

One clarification is in order at this point: to learn does not mean to copy. We would gain little by simply copying what Chrysostom or Newman said, trying to replicate their words and style in so different a context as ours. Rather, the invitation is to learn *from them*, to imitate their wisdom, to tune our ear to the beautiful melodies of homilies that are so different in style, approach, and length, as similar in essence.

There is another benefit of reading good homilies: if we lack inspiration to compose great speeches, then we can use what has already been brilliantly composed by celebrated preachers.[2] Simply put, there are many ideas and lines that we can use and quote for our homilies. Neither Leo nor Bossuet would mind.

A third benefit of reading classic homilies is access to the great minds of these theologians, who, because they were shepherds, were "forced" by their pastoral charity to condense into short, oral compositions the depth of their reflection on the Christian faith. How can we get acquainted with Augustine or Newman? Rather than aiming first for *De Trinitate* or *A Grammar of Assent* it would be easier, and probably more fruitful, to start with their homilies.

In the end, the most important reason for reading great homilies is the least pragmatic one: familiarity with the best makes us better. The dedicated reading of these wonderful texts shapes our minds and hearts with the depth, wisdom, and beauty of their words. An architect who has only learned the theoretical principles of building houses, and who has grown in a time and place in which the norm was to see white (or beige) boxes of drywall as homes, offices, and churches, will find it difficult to design something truly beautiful and lasting. But if he gets acquainted with beautiful buildings by studying (and travelling, if possible), he will add a quality to his work that mere technique, good intentions, or resignation to the current standards will never achieve. If we want to preach in an effective and moving way, we need the experience of our best preachers.[3]

---

2 Augustine, *Teaching Christianity*, IV.62.

3 Reading the sermons of the best preachers of our tradition also invites us to take the risk—in the words of Bishop Robert Barron—to "preach the strange Word," as we learn how they "took their listeners/readers on a careful tour of the densely-textured world of the Bible." See his insightful reflections on: https://www.wordonfire.org/resources/article/preaching-the-strange-word/4965/

For this, we will read here fourteen homilies, chronologically organized, and thus offering the opportunity to appreciate the different emphases of preaching throughout history. Of course, the selected homilies are only a very small sample of the abundant treasure of sacred preaching. These texts vary in length, occasion, and style. Some are very biblical, others more liturgical. Some are quite passionate, others deeply theological. I will offer very brief introductions and commentaries in order to highlight some noteworthy aspects of the homilies, not so much—as I said—to simply copy them, but to "distill" their essence and "extract" their scent, applying them to our contexts, in which we have to proclaim the same Word with our voices, as the Spirit teaches us to do it today.

St. Gregory Nazianzen
(329–390)

Oration 38—On the Theophany, or Birthday of Christ

Along with John the Evangelist and Symeon, Gregory is one of three saints called "the theologian" by the Byzantine tradition. His theology was expressed in orations, poems, and letters, and his oratorical style became the accepted model for forthcoming generations. Oration 38 (AD 379–380) is his first Christmas homily and is a good example of his elegant and theological preaching. As this oration is particularly long, we will read only the first and last paragraphs. Pay attention to his careful use of words to describe the mystery of the Incarnation.

1.

Christ is born, glorify him. Christ from heaven, go out to meet him. Christ on earth; be exalted. Sing unto the Lord all the whole earth; and that I may join both in one word, let the heavens rejoice, and let the earth be glad, for him who is of heaven and then of earth. Christ in the flesh, rejoice with trembling and with joy; with trembling because of your sins, with joy because of your hope. Christ of a virgin; O you matrons live as virgins, that you may be mothers of Christ. Who does not worship him that is from the beginning? Who does not glorify him that is the last?

2.

Again the darkness is past; again light is made; again Egypt is punished with darkness; again Israel is enlightened by a pillar. The people that sat in the darkness of ignorance, let it see the great light of full knowledge. Old things are passed away, behold all things are become new. The letter gives way, the Spirit comes to the front. The shadows flee away, the Truth comes in upon them. Melchizedek is concluded. He that was without mother becomes without father (without mother of his former state, without father of his second). The laws of nature are upset; the world above must be filled. Christ commands it, let us not set ourselves against him. O clap your hands together all you people, because unto us a Child is born, and a son given unto us, whose government is upon his shoulder (for with the Cross it is raised up), and his name is called The Angel of the Great Counsel of the Father. Let John cry, "Prepare the way of the Lord:" I too will cry the power of this day. He who is not carnal is incarnate; the Son of God becomes the Son of man, Jesus Christ the same yesterday, and today, and forever. Let the Jews be offended, let the Greeks deride; let heretics talk till their tongues ache. Then shall they believe, when they see him ascending up into heaven; and if not then, when they see him coming out of heaven and sitting as Judge.

3.

Of these on a future occasion; for the present festival is the Theophany or Birthday, for it is called both, two titles being given to the one thing. For God was manifested to man by birth. On the one hand being, and eternally being, of the Eternal Being, above cause and word, for there was no word before the Word; and on the other hand for our sakes also becoming, that he who gives us our being might also give us our well-being, or rather might restore us by his Incarnation, when we had by wickedness fallen from well-being. The name *Theophany* is given to it in reference to the manifestation, and that of *Birthday* in respect of his birth.

16.

A little later on you will see Jesus submitting to be purified in the river Jordan for purification, or rather, sanctifying the waters by his purification (for indeed he had no need of purification, he who takes away the sin of the world) and the heavens cleft asunder, and witness born to him by the Spirit that is of one nature with him; you shall see him tempted and conquering and served by angels, and healing every sickness and every disease, and giving life to the dead, and driving out demons, sometimes himself, sometimes by his disciples; and feeding vast multitudes with a few loaves; and walking dry-shod upon seas; and being betrayed and crucified, and crucifying with

himself my sin; offered as a lamb, and offering as a priest; as a man buried in
the grave, and as God rising again; and then ascending, and to come again
in his own glory. Why, what a multitude of high festivals there are in each of
the mysteries of the Christ; all of which have one completion, namely, my
perfection and return to the first condition of Adam.

17.

Now then I pray you accept his conception, and leap before him; if not
like John from the womb, then like David, because of the resting of the Ark.
Revere the enrolment on account of which you were written in heaven, and
adore the birth by which you were loosed from the chains of your birth,
and honor little Bethlehem, which has led you back to paradise; and worship the manger through which you, being without sense, were fed by the
word. Know, as Isaiah bids you, your owner, like the ox, and like the ass your
master's crib; if you be one of those who are pure and lawful food, and who
chew the cud of the word and are fit for sacrifice. Or if you are one of those
who are as though unclean and uneatable and unfit for sacrifice, and of the
gentile portion, run with the star, and bear your gifts with the magi, gold
and frankincense and myrrh, as to a king, and to God, and to one who is
dead for you. With shepherds glorify him; with angels join in chorus; with
archangels sing hymns. Let this festival be common to the powers in heaven
and to the powers upon earth. For I am persuaded that the heavenly hosts
join in our exultation and keep high festival with us today … because they
love men, and they love God … just like those whom David introduces after
the Passion ascending with Christ and coming to meet him, and bidding one
another to lift up the gates.

18.

Travel without fault through every stage and faculty of the life of Christ.
Be purified; be circumcised; strip off the veil which has covered you from
your birth. After this teach in the Temple, and drive out the sacrilegious trad-
ers. Submit to be stoned if need be, for you shall be hidden from those who
cast the stones; you shall escape even through the midst of them, like God. If
you be brought before Herod, answer not for the most part. He will respect
your silence more than most people's long speeches. If you be scourged, ask
for what they leave out. Taste gall for the taste's sake; drink vinegar; seek for
spittings; accept blows, be crowned with thorns, that is, with the hardness
of the godly life; put on the purple robe, take the reed in hand, and receive

mock worship from those who mock at the truth; lastly, be crucified with him, and share his death and burial gladly, that you may rise with him, and be glorified with him and reign with him. Look at and be looked at by the great God, who in the Trinity is worshipped and glorified, and whom we declare to be now set forth as clearly before you as the chains of our flesh allow, in Jesus Christ our Lord, to whom be the glory forever.

Amen.[1]

Questions for Reflection

• *This homily uses several antitheses as a device that invites the audience to reflection: earth-heaven, light-darkness, new-old, letter-spirit, et cetera. How can we use paradoxes in our homilies today?*

• *There are a number of important theological truths expressed in elegant oratorical style. Which are the key theological ideas of this sermon?*

• *A wonderful aspect of this homily is that the preacher invites his audience to be part of the mysteries: honor Bethlehem, worship the manger, "travel without fault through every stage and faculty of the life of Christ." You are there; the mysteries are real; our history is a path to God. Why is this an important and effective way of preaching?*

1 Gregory Nazianzen, "Oration 38" in *S. Cyril of Jerusalem, S. Gregory Nazianzen*, ed. Philip Schaff and Henry Wace, trans. Charles Gordon Browne and James Edward Swallow, vol. 7 of *A Select Library of the Nicene and Post-Nicene Fathers of the Christian Church, Second Series* (New York: Christian Literature Company, 1894), 350–51. [Translation modified]

11

St. Ambrose of Milan
(339–397)

On the Death of his Brother Satyrus

When the catechumen and former governor Ambrose became bishop of Milan, his older brother Satyrus left his post as prefect to help Ambrose in the administration of his imperial diocese. Satyrus accomplished this job with great diligence for only four years, as he died unexpectedly in 378. His death was a painful experience for the holy bishop, who eulogized his brother in two lengthy, graceful, and heartfelt sermons that he later edited, of which here we can read a few paragraphs.

1.

We have brought here, dearest brothers, my sacrifice, a sacrifice undefiled, a sacrifice well pleasing to God, my lord and brother Satyrus. I did not forget that he was mortal, nor did my feelings deceive me, but grace abounded more exceedingly. And so I have nothing to complain of, but have cause for thankfulness to God, for I always desired that if any troubles should await either the Church or myself, they should rather fall on me and on my house. Thanks, therefore, be to God, that in this time of common fear, when everything is dreaded from the barbarian movements, I ended the trouble of all by my personal grief, and that I dreaded for all which was turned upon me. And may this be fully accomplished, so that my grief may be a ransom for the grief of all.

3.

To this must be added that I cannot be ungrateful to God; for I must rather rejoice that I had such a brother than grieve that I had lost a brother, for the former is a gift, the latter a debt to be paid. And so, as long as I might, I enjoyed the loan entrusted to me, now he who deposited the pledge has taken it back. There is no difference between denying that a pledge has been deposited and grieving at its being returned. In each there is untrustworthiness, and in each [eternal] life is risked. It is a fault if you refuse repayment; is it piety if you refuse a sacrifice? Since, too, the lender of money can be made a fool of, but the author of nature, the lender of all that we need, cannot be cheated. And so the larger the amount of the loan, so much the more gratitude is due for the use of the capital.

6.

For why should I weep for you, my most loving brother, who was thus torn from me that you might be the brother of all? For I have not lost but changed my intercourse with you; before we were inseparable in the body, now we are undivided in affection; for you remained with me, and ever will remain. And, indeed, while you were living with me, our country never tore you from me, nor did you yourself ever prefer our country to me; and now you have become surety for that other country, for I begin to be no stranger there where the better portion of myself already is. I was never wholly engrossed in myself, but the greater part of each of us was in the other, yet we were each of us in Christ, in whom is the whole sum of all, and the portion of each severally. This grave is more pleasing to me than your natal soil, in which is the fruit not of nature but of grace, for in that body which now lies lifeless lies the better work of my life, since in this body, too, which I bear is the richer portion of yourself.

8.

But now, brother, where shall I advance, or where shall I turn? The ox seeks his fellow, and conceives itself incomplete, and by frequent lowing shows its tender longing, if perchance that one is wanting with whom it has been wont to draw the plough. And shall I, my brother, not long after you? Or can I ever forget you, with whom I always drew the plough of this life? In work I was inferior, but in love more closely bound; not so much fit through my strength, as endurable through your patience, who with the care of anxious affection did ever protect my side with yours, as a brother in your love, as a father in your care, as older in watchfulness, as younger in respect. So in the one degree of relationship you did expend on me the duties of many, so that I long after not one only but many lost in you, in whom alone flattery was unknown, dutifulness was portrayed. For you had nothing to which to add by pretense, inasmuch as all was comprised in your dutifulness, so as neither to receive addition nor await a change.

10.

But we have not incurred any grievous sin by our tears. Not all weeping proceeds from unbelief or weakness. Natural grief is one thing, distrustful sadness is another, and there is a very great difference between longing for what you have lost and lamenting that you have lost it. Not only grief has tears, joy also has tears of its own. Both piety excites weeping, and prayer waters the couch, and supplication, according to the prophet's saying, washes the bed. Their friends made a great mourning when the patriarchs were buried. Tears, then, are marks of devotion, not producers of grief. I confess, then, that I too wept, but the Lord also wept. He wept for one not related to him, I for my brother. He wept for all in weeping for one, I will weep for you in all, my brother.[1]

Questions for Reflection

• *These words are an expression of the polished and spiritual oratory of Ambrose, which so moved Augustine. In this sermon we find precise language (Ambrose was trained as a lawyer) and spiritual theology (his theological training was based on Eastern exegesis). At the same time, it is a very human and heartfelt speech. How can we bring together these different elements in our preaching?*

• *Note that Ambrose uses some relatable figures to illustrate his ideas, such as his time with his brother as a "loan," and his absence as the ox missing his fellow to plough with the yoke.*

• *The great bishop is not afraid to show his sentiments. Where do we find this in this sermon?*

---

1 Ambrose of Milan, "The Two Books on the Decease of His Brother Satyrus," in *St. Ambrose: Select Works and Letters*, ed. Philip Schaff and Henry Wace, trans. Henry de Romestin, Eugene de Romestin, and Henry T. F. Duckworth, vol. 10 of *A Select Library of the Nicene and Post-Nicene Fathers of the Christian Church, Second Series*, (New York: Christian Literature Company, 1896), 159–62. [Translation modified]

12

St. John Chrysostom
(347–407)

On Eutropius, the Eunuch, Patrician and Consul

Soon after his death, John was known as Chrysostom *(Golden Mouth). Formed in the best of classical oratory, he is one of the most eloquent preachers in history, and the most prolific Greek father: we have 800 authentic sermons and thousands of dubious ones. More than creative explorations in theology, John's homilies are an outstanding and eloquent witness to tradition. His preaching teaches us to explore revelation and connect spiritual reflection with the moral demands of the Gospel. The following sermon is an excellent example of this: Eutropius was a corrupt official who fell into disgrace and ran to the cathedral for asylum. The bishop of Constantinople preached to an angry crowd seeking for violent revenge, as they both contemplated the disgrace of this man, lying next to the altar.*

1.

"Vanity of vanities, all is vanity"—it is always seasonable to utter this but more especially at the present time. Where are now the brilliant surroundings of your consulship? Where are the gleaming torches? Where is the dancing, and the noise of dancers' feet, and the banquets and the festivals? Where are the garlands and the curtains of the theater? Where is the applause which greeted you in the city, where the acclamation in the hippodrome and the flatteries of spectators? They are gone—all gone: a wind has blown upon the tree shattering down all its leaves, and showing it to us quite bare, and shaken from its very root; for so great has been the violence of the blast, that it has given a shock to all these fibers of the tree and threatens to tear it up from the roots. Where now are your feigned friends? Where are your drinking parties, and your suppers? Where is the swarm of parasites, and the wine which used to be poured forth all day long, and the manifold dainties invented by your cooks? Where are they who courted your power and did and said everything to win your favor? They were all mere visions of the night, and dreams which have vanished with the dawn of day: they were spring flowers, and when the spring was over they all withered: they were a shadow which has passed away—they were a smoke which has dispersed, bubbles which have burst, cobwebs which have been rent in pieces. Therefore we chant continually this spiritual song—"Vanity of vanities, all is vanity." For this saying ought to be continually written on our walls, and garments, in the marketplace, and in the house, on the streets, and on the doors and entrances, and above all on the conscience of each one, and to be a perpetual theme for meditation. And inasmuch as deceitful things, and maskings and pretense seem to many to be realities it behooves each one every day both at supper and at breakfast, and in social assemblies to say to his neighbor and to hear his neighbor say in return "Vanity of vanities, all is vanity." Was I not continually telling you that wealth was a runaway? But you would not heed me. Did I not tell you that it was an unthankful servant? But you would not be persuaded. Behold actual experience has now proved that it is not only a runaway, and ungrateful servant, but also a murderous one, for it is this which has caused you now to fear and tremble. Did I not say to you when you continually rebuked me for speaking the truth, "I love you better than they do who flatter you?" "I who reprove you care more for you than they who pay you court?" Did I not add to these words by saying that the wounds of friends were more to be relied upon than the voluntary kisses of enemies? If you had submitted to my wounds their kisses would not have wrought you this destruction: for my wounds work health, but their kisses have produced an incurable disease. Where are now your cupbearers, where are they who cleared the way for you in the marketplace, and sounded your praises end-lessly in the ears of all? They have fled, they have disowned your friendship, they are providing for their own safety by means of your distress. But I do not act thus, no, in your misfortune I do not abandon you, and now when you are fallen I protect and tend you. And the Church which you treated as an enemy has opened her bosom and received you into it; whereas the theaters which you courted, and about which you were oftentimes indignant with me have betrayed and ruined you. And yet I never ceased saying to you "Why do you do these things?" "You are exasperating the Church, and casting yourself down headlong," yet you hurried away from all my warnings. And now the hippodromes, having exhausted your wealth, have whetted the sword against you, but the Church which experienced your untimely wrath is hurrying in every direction, in her desire to pluck you out of the net.

2.

And I say these things now not as trampling upon one who is prostrate, but from a desire to make those who are still standing more secure; not by way of irritating the sores of one who has been wounded, but rather to preserve those who have not yet been wounded in sound health; not by way of sinking one who is tossed by the waves, but as instructing those who are sailing with a favorable breeze, so that they may not become overwhelmed. And how may this be effected? By observing the vicissitudes of human affairs. For even this man, had he stood in fear of vicissitude, would not have experienced it; but whereas neither his own conscience, nor the counsels of others wrought any improvement in him, do you at least who plume yourselves on your riches profit by his calamity: for nothing is weaker than human affairs. Whatever term therefore one may employ to express their insignificance it will fall short of the reality; whether he calls them smoke, or grass, or a dream or spring flowers, or by any other name; so perishable are they, and nothing more than nonentities; but that together with their nothingness they have also a very perilous element we have a proof before us. For who was more exalted than this man? Did he not surpass the whole world in wealth? Had he not climbed to the very pinnacle of distinction? Did not all tremble and fear before him? Yet behold, he has become more wretched than the prisoner, more pitiable than the menial slave, more indigent than the beggar wasting away with hunger, having every day a vision of sharpened swords and of the criminal's grave, and the public executioner leading him out to his death; and he does not even know if he once enjoyed past pleasure, nor is he sensible even of the sun's ray, but at midday his sight is dimmed as if he were encompassed by the densest gloom. But even let me try my best I shall not be able to present to you in language the suffering which he must naturally undergo, in the hourly expectation of death. But indeed what need is there of any words from me, when he himself has clearly depicted this for us as in a visible image? For yesterday when they came to him from the royal court intending to drag him away by force, and he ran for refuge to the holy furniture [i.e. the altar], his face was then, as it is now, no better than the countenance of one dead: and the chattering of his teeth, and the quaking and quivering of his whole body, and his faltering voice, and stammering tongue, and in fact his whole general appearance were suggestive of one whose soul was petrified.

3.

Now I say these things not by way of reproaching him, or insulting his misfortune, but from a desire to soften your minds towards him, and to induce you to compassion, and to persuade you to be contented with the punishment which has already been inflicted. For since there are many inhuman persons among us who are inclined, perhaps, to find fault with me for having admitted him to the sanctuary, I parade his sufferings from a desire to soften their hardheartedness by my narrative.

For tell me, beloved brother, why are you indignant with me? You say it is because he who continually made war upon the Church has taken refuge within it. Yet surely we ought in the highest degree to glorify God, for permitting him to be placed in such a great strait as to experience both the power and the loving-kindness of the Church:—her power in that he has suffered this great vicissitude in consequence of the attacks which he made upon her: her loving-kindness in that she whom he attacked now casts her shield in front of him and has received him under her wings, and placed him in all security not resenting any of her former injuries, but most lovingly opening her bosom to him. For this is more glorious than any kind of trophy, this is a brilliant victory, this puts both Gentiles and Jews to shame, this displays the bright aspect of the Church: in that having received her enemy as a captive, she spares him, and when all have despised him in his desolation, she alone like an affectionate mother has concealed him under her cloak, opposing both the wrath of the king, and the rage of the people, and their overwhelming hatred. This is an ornament for the altar. A strange kind of ornament, you say, when the accused sinner, the extortioner, the robber is permitted to lay hold of the altar. No, do not say so: for even the harlot took hold of the feet of Jesus, she who was stained with the most accursed and unclean sin: yet her deed was no reproach to Jesus, but rather redounded to his admiration and praise: for the impure woman did no injury to him who was pure, but rather was the vile harlot rendered pure by the touch of him who was the pure and spotless one. Grudge not then, O man. We are the servants of the crucified one who said, "Forgive them for they know not what they do."

But, you say, he cut off the right of refuge here by his ordinances and diverse kinds of laws. Yes, yet now he has learned by experience what it was he did, and he himself by his own deeds has been the first to break the law, and has become a spectacle to the whole world, and silent though he is, he utters from there a warning voice to all, saying "do not such things as I have done, that you suffer not such things as I suffer." He appears as a teacher by means of his calamity, and the altar emits great luster, inspiring now the greatest awe from the fact that it holds the lion in bondage; for any figure of royalty might be very much set off if the king were not only to be seen seated on his throne arrayed in purple and wearing his crown, but if also prostrate at the feet of the king barbarians with their hands bound behind their backs were bending low their heads. And that no persuasive arguments have been used, you yourselves are witnesses of the enthusiasm, and the concourse of the people. For brilliant indeed is the scene before us today, and magnificent the assembly, and I see as large a gathering here today as at the Holy Paschal Feast. Thus the man has summoned you here without speaking and yet uttering a voice through his actions clearer than the sound of a trumpet: and you have all thronged here today, maidens deserting their boudoirs, and matrons the women's chambers, and men the marketplace that you may see human nature convicted, and the instability of worldly affairs exposed, and the harlot-face which a few days ago was radiant (such is the prosperity derived from extortion) looking uglier than any wrinkled old woman, this face I say you may see denuded of its enamel and pigments by the action of adversity as by a sponge.

4.

Such is the force of this calamity: it has made one who was illustrious and conspicuous appear the most insignificant of men. And if a rich man should enter the assembly he derives much profit from the sight: for when he beholds the man who was shaking the whole world, now dragged down from so high a pinnacle of power, cowering with fright, more terrified than a hare or a frog, nailed fast to yonder pillar, without bonds, his fear serving instead of a chain, panic-stricken and trembling, he abates his haughtiness, he puts down his pride, and having acquired the kind of wisdom concerning human affairs which it concerns him to have he departs instructed by example in the lesson which Holy Scripture teaches by precept:—"All flesh is grass and all the glory of man as the flower of grass: the grass withers and the flower fails" or "They shall wither away quickly as the grass, and as the green herb shall they quickly fail" or "like smoke are his days," and all passages of that kind. Again the poor man when he has entered and gazed at this spectacle does not think meanly of himself, nor bewail himself on account of his poverty, but feels grateful to his poverty, because it is a place of refuge to him, and a calm haven, and secure bulwark; and when he sees these things he would many times rather remain where he is, than enjoy the possession of all men for a little time and afterwards be in jeopardy of his own life. Do you see how the rich and poor, high and low, bound and free have derived no small profit from this man's taking refuge here? Do you see how each man will depart here with a remedy, being cured merely by this sight? Well, have I softened your passion, and expelled your wrath? Have I extinguished your cruelty? Have I induced you to be pitiful? Indeed I think I have; and your countenances and the streams of tears you shed are proof of it. Since then your hard rock has turned into deep and fertile soil let us hasten to produce some fruit of mercy, and to display a luxuriant crop of pity by falling down before the emperor or rather by imploring the merciful God so to soften the rage of the emperor, and make his heart tender that he may grant the whole of the favor which we ask. For indeed already since that day when this man fled here for refuge no slight change has taken place; for as soon as the emperor knew that he had hurried to this asylum, although the army was present, and incensed on account of his misdeeds, and demanded him to be given up for execution, the emperor made a long speech endeavoring to allay the rage of the soldiers, maintaining that not only his offences, but any good deed which he might have done ought to be taken into account, declaring that he felt gratitude for the latter, and was prepared to forgive him as a fellow creature for deeds which were otherwise. And when they again urged him to avenge the insult done to the imperial majesty, shouting, leaping, and brandishing their spears, he shed streams of tears from his gentle eyes, and having reminded them of the Holy Table to which the man had fled for refuge, he succeeded at last in appeasing their wrath.

5.

Moreover let me add some arguments which concern ourselves. For what pardon could you deserve, if the emperor bears no resentment when he has been insulted, but you who have experienced nothing of this kind display so much wrath? And how after this assembly has been dissolved will you handle the holy mysteries, and repeat that prayer by which we are commanded to say "forgive us as we also forgive our debtors" when you are demanding vengeance upon your debtor? Has he inflicted great wrongs and insults on you? I will not deny it. Yet this is the season not for judgment but for mercy; not for requiring an account, but for showing loving-kindness: not for investigating claims but for conceding them; not for verdicts and vengeance, but for mercy and favor. Let no one then be irritated or vexed, but let us rather beseech the merciful God to grant him a respite from death, and to rescue him from this impending destruction, so that he may put off his transgression, and let us unite to approach the merciful emperor beseeching him for the sake of the Church, for the sake of the altar, to concede the life of one man as an offering to the Holy Table. If we do this the emperor himself will accept us, and even before his praise we shall have the approval of God, who will bestow a large recompense upon us for our mercy. For as he rejects and hates the cruel and inhuman, so does he welcome and love the merciful and humane man; and if such a man be righteous, all the more glorious is the crown which is wreathed for him: and if he be a sinner, he passes over his sins granting this as the reward of compassion shown to his fellow servant. "For," he says, "I will have mercy and not sacrifice,"[2] and throughout the Scriptures you find him always enquiring after this and declaring it to be the means of release from sin. Thus then we shall dispose him to be propitious to us, thus we shall release ourselves from our sins, thus we shall adorn the Church, thus also our merciful emperor, as I have already said, will commend us, and all the people will applaud us, and the ends of the earth will admire the humanity and gentleness of our city, and all who hear of these deeds throughout the world will extol us. That we then may enjoy these good things, let us fall down in prayer and supplication, let us rescue the captive, the fugitive, the suppliant from danger that we ourselves may obtain the future blessings by the favor and mercy of our Lord Jesus Christ, to whom be glory and power, now and forever, world without end. Amen.[1]

---

1 John Chrysostom, "First Homily on Eutropius, the Eunuch, Patrician and Consul," in *Saint Chrysostom: On the Priesthood, Ascetic Treatises, Select Homilies and Letters, Homilies on the Statues*, ed. Philip Schaff, trans. William R. W. Stephens, vol. 9 of *A Select Library of the Nicene and Post-Nicene Fathers of the Christian Church, First Series* (New York: Christian Literature Company, 1889), 249–52. [Translation modified]

Questions for Reflection

• *While certainly the style of this homily is characteristic of its time and place, here we find a masterpiece of persuasion. Chrysostom was able to convince his audience to change their conduct: he saw tears in their eyes, and they forgave their enemy (at least for now).*

• *In terms of the composition of the sermon: how did Chrysostom use Scripture? How did he develop his arguments, mostly through images or concepts?*

• *Note the effectiveness of switching his subject: at times he spoke to Eutropius (and through him to the audience) and at times to the audience (and through them to Eutropius). How can this be done today?*

• *Chrysostom improvised this sermon because of the urgency of the situation. Was he prepared to improvise? How?*

13

St. Leo the Great
(400–461)
Sermon 74—On the Lord's Ascension

Pope Leo was a courageous leader who defended the faith of the Church in a time of theological and social crises. He is the first pope whose homilies have been transmitted in written form, in two collections probably edited by Leo himself, including the sermon pronounced at his ordination. Leo is a great example of classical conciseness, expressing his ideas in carefully formulated phrases, offering key theological truths imprinted for generations to come, such as the idea of Christ's presence in the sacraments that we will find in this homily.

The mystery of our salvation, dearly beloved, which the creator of the universe thought worth the price of his blood, has, from the day of his bodily birth to the end of his suffering, been carried to completion through the condition of his humility. Although many signs of the divinity in the "form of a servant" have been evident, strictly speaking, the action of that time pertained to demonstrating the truth of the humanity he assumed. After his Passion, when the chains were broken of that death which had destroyed its own strength by proceeding against one who "had no acquaintance with sin," then weakness was turned to strength, mortality to eternity, disgrace to glory. The Lord Jesus made this obvious in the sight of all "by many" and clear "signs," until he carried the triumph of victory that he had brought back from death up into heaven.

As the Resurrection of the Lord was a cause of rejoicing for us in the Paschal liturgy, so his Ascension into heaven is a matter of present delight for us. We recall and rightly venerate that day when our lowly nature was carried in Christ above all the hosts of heaven, over all the angelic orders and beyond the height of all powers, to the seat of God the Father. We have been established, we have been built in this order of divine works, that the grace of God becomes the more wonderful when those things which are felt to invite proper reverence are removed from the sight of human beings and still faith does not weaken, hope does not waver, love does not grow cold.

This is the strength of great souls, and it is the light of intensely faithful spirits to believe unhesitatingly what is not seen by bodily perception, and to fix their desire where they cannot fix their sight. From where would this devotion be born in our hearts; or how would anyone be "justified through faith," if our salvation consisted only in those things that lie under our eyes? For this reason the Lord even said to that one who seemed to doubt the Resurrection of Christ unless, by sight and touch, he tested the marks of the Passion in his very flesh: "Because you have seen me, you have believed; blessed are those who have not seen and yet believe."

2.

So then, that we can be fit for this blessedness, dearly beloved, after all had been fulfilled that belonged to the preaching of the Gospel and the mysteries of the New Testament, our Lord Jesus Christ was raised to heaven. He made an end to his bodily presence in the sight of his disciples on the fortieth day after the Resurrection. He was to remain at the Father's right hand until the time predetermined by God for filling the number of the children of the Church should come, and he would return to judge the living and the dead in the same flesh with which he ascended. What was to be seen of our Redeemer has passed over into the sacraments. In order that faith might be more perfect and more firm, teaching has taken the place of sight, and to this authority the hearts of believers, illumined by heavenly rays, have conformed.

3.

This faith, reinforced by the Ascension of the Lord and strengthened by the gift of the Holy Spirit, has not been terrified by chains, by prison, by exile, by hunger, by fire, by the mangling of wild beasts, nor by sharp suffering from the cruelty of persecutors. Throughout the world, not only men but also women, not just immature boys but also tender virgins, have struggled on behalf of this faith even to the shedding of their blood. This faith has cast out demons, driven away sicknesses, and raised the dead.

Those blessed apostles, strengthened as they were by so many miracles, taught by so many sermons, although they had been terrified at the Lord's Passion and had not accepted the truth of his Resurrection without hesitation, advanced so much at the Lord's Ascension that whatever had brought fear to them before was turned into joy. They had raised the whole gaze of their souls to the divinity of the one sitting at the right hand of the Father. No longer are they held back by any use of bodily sight which would prevent them from looking with sharpness of soul on that one who had neither been absent from the Father by his coming down, nor had departed from the disciples by his Ascension.

4.

Then, dearly beloved, the son of a human being became more eminently and more sacredly as the Son of God when he entered into the glory of his Father's majesty. In an ineffable way, he began to be more present in the divinity as he became more remote from our humanity. Then, by a spiritual step, a more instructed faith began to give assent to the Son equal to the Father, and it did not need the touch of the bodily substance in Christ, by which he is less than the Father, because, with the nature of the glorified body remaining, the faith of believers was drawn there where the Only Begotten Son equal to the Father might be touched not by fleshly hand but by the spiritual intellect.

Hence, it is that after his Resurrection, where Mary Magdalene, manifesting the person of the Church, was hastening to approach to touch him, he said to her: "Do not touch me because I have not yet ascended to my Father." He was in fact saying, I do not want you to come to me bodily, nor to acknowledge me with the perception of your flesh. I am taking you to higher things. I am preparing greater things for you. When I have ascended to my Father, then you will feel me more perfectly and more truly. You will embrace what you do not touch and believe what you do not see. When the searching eyes of the disciples were following the Lord with keen wonder as he ascended into heaven, two angels stood before them shining in marvelously radiant clothing and said: "Men of Galilee, why do you stand looking up into the sky? This Jesus, who was taken up from you, will so come as you have seen him going into heaven."

By these words all the children of the Church are taught that we believe Jesus Christ is going to come, visible, in the same flesh in which he ascended. No one can doubt that "All things have been made subject to him," whom, from the very beginning of his natural birth, the angelic household had served. Just as the angel announced to the Blessed Virgin that Christ would be conceived through the Holy Spirit, so the voice of the heavenly choir sang to the shepherds that he was born from the Virgin. As the first witness of the heavenly messengers told that he had risen from the dead, so the service of the angels was to announce that he would come to judge the world in the very same flesh. In this way we might understand how many powers there will be with him when he comes to judge, to whom such a great number "ministered" even when he was about to be judged.

5.

Let us exult, therefore, with a spiritual gladness, dearly beloved, and joy-fully, with fitting gratitude to God, let us freely raise the eyes of our hearts to that height where Christ is. Let not earthly desires hold down the souls called upwards. Let perishable things not hold those ordained for eternity. Let false pleasures not delay those who have entered the "way of truth." Let the faithful so travel over these temporal things that they may realize they are pilgrims in this valley of the world, where, even though certain pleasures attract, these are not to be vainly embraced, but must be passed over bravely. The blessed apostle Peter urges us to this devotion, and according to that desire for "feeding the sheep of Christ" which he conceived at the threefold avowal of his love to the Lord, he begged them saying: "I urge you, my dear people, just as visitors and pilgrims, to keep yourselves free from the selfish passions that attack the soul."

For whom, if not for the devil, do the worldly pleasures make war? Who is it that delights in hindering, by the pleasures of corruptible goods, the souls reaching for heaven, and in leading them away from that home from which he himself fell? Against his snares all faithful souls ought wisely to keep watch, so that, from that which is made a temptation against them, they might be able to crush this enemy.

Nothing is stronger, dearly beloved, against the wiles of the devil than the kindness of mercy and the generosity of love, through which "every sin" is either avoided or conquered. But the sublimity of this virtue is not gained until what is contrary to it has been broken down. What is so inimical to the works of mercy and charity as greed, from which "root" the seed of "all evil" comes? Unless this be cut down in its first growth, it is certain that in the field of that heart in which the plants of this evil become strong, spines and thorns of sins will rise, rather than any seed of true virtue. Let us resist then, dearly beloved, this rankling evil, and "strive after" charity, without which no virtue can shine. Through this way of love, by which Christ descended to us, we also can ascend to him, to whom are honor and glory with God the Father and with the Holy Spirit forever and ever. Amen.[1]

Questions for Reflection

• *Leo the Great's style is theological and precise. What can we learn from this approach?*

• *Faith grows with the Ascension. Can you explain why?*

• *"What was visible in our Redeemer has come to us in the sacraments." This sentence has become a sort of axiom for sacramental theology. Do you see how a homily can contain deep insights while keeping an oral style?*

1 Leo I, *Sermons*, trans. Jane Patricia Freeland, CSJB, and Agnes Josephine Conway, SSJ (Washington, D.C.: The Catholic University of America Press, 1996), 325–29.

14

St. Bernard of Clairvaux
(1090–1153)

Sermon on the Song of Songs 61, 3-5

St. Bernard, the Doctor Mellifluous, spoke indeed with poignant beauty of his love for his Lord and helped his monks, and all generations after them, to receive the mystery of God with deep affection. Immersed in Scripture, Bernard makes the mystery feel real for us. The following is a section of one of his sermons on the Song of Songs in which he reflects on these words: 'Arise my love, my bride, and come. My dove in the clefts of the rock, in the crannies of the wall, show me your face, let your voice sound in my ears.'

Someone else has expounded this passage interpreting the "clefts of the rock" to mean the wounds of Christ, which I entirely approve of, since "Christ is the Rock." O blessed clefts, which fortify our faith in the resurrection and in the divinity of the Savior! "My Lord and my God," exclaimed Thomas the Apostle. But from where did he derive this confession save from the clefts of the Rock? There, "the sparrow has found herself a house, and the turtledove a nest for herself, where she may lay her young ones." Therefore, the Bridegroom here calls his spouse, "my dove in the clefts of the Rock." And it is the voice of the dove we hear in the psalm saying, "He has exalted my upon a Rock," and, "He has set my feet upon a Rock." The wise man builds his house upon the Rock, because on such a foundation he shall have nothing to fear from the violence of floods or tempests. What can be found in the Rock except what is most excellent? It lifts me up from the ground, it renders me secure, if affords me firm footing. On the Rock I am safe from my enemies, I am prevented from falling, and that because, standing on the Rock, I am exalted above the earth. For everything on the earth is unstable and insecure. But if "our conversation is in heaven," then we need have no fear either of falling or of being thrown down. In heaven is the Rock, where alone can be found strength and security. And in truth where shall the weak find a safe rest or a secure refuge except in the wounds of our Savior? There shall I dwell with a confidence proportionate to the greatness of his power to save me. Let the world rage, let the body bear me down, let the devil plot against me: I shall not fall, for I am founded on the Rock. I have sinned most grievously; my conscience is indeed much disquieted, yet is not confounded, because I will call to mind the wounds of my Savior. For "he was wounded for our iniquities." What sin can be so much "unto death" as that it cannot be "loosed" by the death of Christ? Therefore, no disease, however desperate, shall have power to drive me to despair, if only I keep in mind so potent and efficacious a remedy.

Cain consequently was in error when he said, "My iniquity is greater than I may deserve pardon"; unless it be that he was not one of Christ's members, and had no share in Christ's merits, entitling him to regard them as his own and to call them his own, just as the members can claim as its own what belongs to the heard. But as for me, of whatever I perceive to be lacking, I appropriate for myself with all confidence from the heart of my Lord Jesus. For that heart overflows with mercy, and there is no lack of clefts for the outpouring of its treasures. They dug his hands and feet and opened his side with a lance. And through these clefts I am permitted to "suck honey out of the Rock, and oil out of the hardest stone." That is to say, I am enabled to "taste and see that the Lord is sweet." He was thinking "thoughts of peace" and I knew it not. For "who has known the mind of the Lord? Or who has been his counselor?" But the nail that pierced him has been for us a key to unlock the mind of the Lord and to expose to our view his secret counsels. Why should I not look through these fissures into the heart of the Rock? The nails announce to me, the wounds proclaim to me that "God indeed is in Christ, reconciling the world to himself." "The iron pierced his soul" and "his heart has drawn near" to us in order that he may no longer be as one "who cannot have compassion on our infirmities." The secret of his heart is revealed to us through the clefts of his body; the "great mystery of godliness" is revealed to us; and revealed also are "the tender mercies of our God, in which the dawn from on high has visited us." Surely the heart of Christ can be seen through the openings of his wounds. For what can prove to me so clearly as your wounds that you, O Lord Jesus, "are good and forgiving and abounding in mercy"? "Greater mercy that this no man has, that a man lay down his life," not for his friends, but for his enemies, criminals devoted and doomed to death.

My merit, therefore, is nothing but the mercy of the Lord. Hence, I cannot be poor in merits so long as he is rich in compassion. And if "the mercies of the Lord are many," many too must my merits be. I may be "conscious to myself" of a multitude of sins, but what of that? For "where sin abounded, grace abounded all the more." And if "the mercies of the Lord are from eternity and unto eternity," "the mercies of the Lord I sing forever" also. But shall I sing my own justice? "O Lord, I will be mindful of your justice alone." For your justice is also my justice, because you are made unto me "justice of God," as the Apostle declares.

As for me, my brethren, I will go to these storerooms thus replenished with good things. Following the Prophet's advice, I will "leave the cities and dwell in the Rock."[1]

Questions for Reflection

• *St. Bernard was a master in the use of Scripture, both in direct quotes, but also in the way in which many of his sentences are rooted in Scriptural verses. As you read this homily, try to pay attention and find his several references to Scripture.*

• *In this homily we can also find a wonderful example of spiritual exegesis that unifies the Old and New Testaments with Christ as the hermeneutical key.*

• *What do you think of Bernard's spiritual applications of Christ's love and mercy? Can you tell the power of his beautiful eloquence?*

---

1 Bernard of Clairvaux, *Sermons on the Canticle of Canticles*. Translated from the Original Latin by a priest of Mount Melleray. Vol. II (Dublin, Belfast, Cork, Waterford: Browne and Nolan, 1920), 196–200. Translation modified. Omits the second half of paragraph 5 and includes the first two lines of paragraph 6.

15

St. Thomas Aquinas
(1225–1274)

Celum et Terra Transibunt—
Sermon on the First Sunday of Advent

The Angelic Doctor is mostly known as the author of works such as his Summa Theologiae *or other academic writings. However, as a member of the Order of Preachers (Dominicans), and as a* Magister in Sacra Pagina *[Master on the Sacred Page] in Paris, preaching was an essential part of his vocation and service. We will read a homily preached on the first Sunday of Advent before the University of Paris. It is an example of a homily given in an academic setting, in which the preacher explores the meaning of each word of a small verse.*

Luke 21:33: *Heaven and earth will pass*
"Heaven and earth will pass" [Lk 21:33]. Dearest brethren, how great the delight, how great the pleasure, how great the sweetness that is in the heavenly words of wisdom! This is even obvious in the words of the natural philosopher, who writes in Book 10 of *Ethics* about created knowledge: "All delights are at some point cut off. The greatest, however, is the delight that is in accordance with the operation of wisdom." Also the theological philosopher writes in Wisdom 7:8 that he "loved (*diligo*) it more than gold and outward appearance"; "it" is the heavenly wisdom about which we speak.

Because of this we will ask, at the beginning of this homily, our Lord Jesus Christ, the fountain of all wisdom [see Sir 1:5], who is, according to St. Dionysius in Book 6, part c of *The Hierarchy of the*

Angels, the principal instructor of all heavenly spirits and devout souls, to illumine our understanding, to kindle our hearts, and to make my mouth eloquent for the honor of his name in accordance with the Gospel teaching and the edification of our souls.

Part I

"Heaven and earth will pass" [Lk 21:33], et cetera. In these words the situation of the just and the unjust is described according to a spiritual knowledge. Our most providential and meek Savior commended these words—out of care for his sheep's salvation in faith [see Jn 10:13]—to his disciples and in them to all believers for serious attention to the Last Judgment, without mentioning the term, because it is clear. (1) By the noun "heaven" the marvelous loftiness of the heavenly man is mentioned, and (2) by the noun "earth" the deserved lowliness of the worldly person is mentioned, and (3) by the verb "will pass" he carefully refers to a distinctive quality of each.

(1) So, as he describes the marvelous loftiness and the worthy eminence of the heavenly man, he calls him "heaven." Yet we must consider that the heavenly man is signified by the noun "heaven" for four reasons:

(1.1) Heaven is of a great brightness, as the Philosopher demonstrates in Book 2 of *On Heaven and Earth*. Thus it is shown that the just man ought to be full of light by heavenly wisdom, as we read in Sirach 24:4: "I have made (my home) in heaven, so that perfect light may rise."

(1.2) It has a splendid appearance, as the Philosopher demonstrates in Book 2 of *On Heaven and Earth*. Thus it is shown that the just man ought to be like a circle by a wide mercy, or like an orbit by a broad devotion and perfect love (*caritas perfecta*). "I alone have gone round the canopy of heaven," says eternal Wisdom in Sirach 24:5.

(1.3) It sets in motion, as the Philosopher shows in Book 8 of *Physics*. Thus it is shown that the just man ought to be moved always by a spiritual carefulness. Job 38:37 reads: "Who will narrate the heavens' thoughts, and who will put to sleep what they contain?"

(1.4) It is high in location, as the sight and the effect of it prove. By this it is pointed out that the just man ought to excel in holiness by eminence. Because, as we read in Sirach 43:1: "The firmament of highness"—that is, the highness of the firmament—"is his beauty, the sight of heaven in a vision of glory."

Part II

(2) The worldly man is absolutely not comparable to him; he is compared to the earth, [as follows:]

(2.1) On the ground of his capacity of understanding, as we read in Genesis 1:2: "Darkness was over the face of the abyss. The earth was void and empty."

(2.2) On the ground of the weakness of avarice, as we read in Colossians 3:2: "Taste the things that are above, not those under the earth" and Psalm 44:25 says: "Our stomach is stuck to the ground."

(2.3) On the ground of the aridity of wickedness [Jn 4:10–15], as we read in Genesis 1.:0: "And God called the arid land 'earth.'"

(2.4) On the ground of the immutability of the soul, or of the life, or opinion, as we find it in Ecclesiastes 1:4: "The earth truly stands forever." And this is preceded by: "The generation" of the good ones "passes, and the generation" of the just ones "arrives" [Eccl. 1:4]. Why? Because an evil person is not led in the right direction, nor is he changed.

(3) Well, now that the most deserved disdain toward the worldly man and the marvelous loftiness of the just have been described, the quality of the way of life of each of them must be distinguished, in view of the verb "to pass," (*transire*). Indeed, we must note that passing is said (3.1) of the just in a different way than (3.2) of the unjust.

(3.1) For the just passes on,

(3.1.1) firstly, from sin to justice, as it says in Isaiah 45:14: "Lofty man" and proud sinners "will pass over to you, and they will be yours."

(3.1.2.) He passes, secondly, by advancing from virtue to virtue, as it says in Sirach 29:26: "Pass, stranger; prepare the table," meaning, "prepare your conscience for the heavenly spouse" [cf. Prv 9:1–6].

(3.1.3) He passes, thirdly, from labor in the present to the eternal refreshment, as it says in Psalm 66:12: "we have come through fire and water, and you have led us out into refreshment."

(3.2) Yet the unjust passes,

(3.2.1) first of all, from innocence to guilt, as Sirach 28 reads: "He passes from justice to sin" [Sir 26:19 or 26:28].

(3.2.2) He passes, secondly, from guilt into guild, as Proverbs 14:16 has it: "A wise man fears and turns away from evil; (a foolish man passes on and is self-confident)."

(3.2.3) He passes, thirdly, from guilt into eternal punishment, as Job 36:12 reads: "If they will not listen, they will pass through the sword," namely, through eternal punishment.

So in view of the short description of the marvelous loftiness of the heavenly man in the noun "heaven," also in view of the very well deserved disdain toward the worldly man in the noun "earth," and in view of the difference of the life of these two in respect of the verb "to pass," let us apply ourselves to renouncing earthly things and to loving (*amo*) heavenly things [cf. Col 3.1], in such a way that we disdain the worldly life and embrace the heavenly life, that we may pass over from labor to rest [cf. Heb 4.10], from the world to glory, which he may grant us, et cetera.[1]

Questions for Reflection

- *This is probably not how we envision a Sunday homily at a typical parish. However, this sermon shows that preaching can vary in style and approach depending on the context. A theological conference and a youth gathering will call for different kinds of preaching.*

- *Note also that this sermon is deeply rooted in Scripture and philosophical wisdom. Why is this always important for preaching?*

- *What else can we learn from this sermon? How can we apply its wisdom for our different circumstances?*

---

1 Thomas Aquinas, "Sermon 06: Celum et Terra Transibunt," in *Thomas Aquinas: The Academic Sermons*, trans. Mark-Robin Hoogland (Washington, D.C.: The Catholic University of America Press, 2010), 79–84.

16

St. Charles Borromeo
(1538–1584)
Sermon to Priests on his Last Synod

Borromeo was an outstanding bishop in Milan during the Catholic Reformation. His fame has recently grown, as he is a model of spiritual leadership during a pandemic. He worked hard to implement the renewal of the Council of Trent, and as a good shepherd, understood that the true reform of the Church begins with the reform of the hearts, particularly the hearts of her priests. This sermon retains all its validity for us today.

I admit that we are all weak, but if we want help, the Lord God has given us the means to find it easily. One priest may wish to lead a good, holy life, as he knows he should. He may wish to be chaste and to reflect heavenly virtues in the way he lives. Yet he does not resolve to use suitable means, such as penance, prayer, the avoidance of evil discussions and harmful and dangerous friendships. Another priest complains that as soon as he comes into church to pray the office or to celebrate Mass, a thousand thoughts fill his mind and distract him from God. But what was he doing in the sacristy before he came out for the office or for Mass? How did he prepare? What means did he use to collect his thoughts and to remain recollected?

Would you like me to teach you how to grow from virtue to virtue and how, if you are already recollected at prayer, you can be even more attentive next time, and so give God more pleasing worship? Listen, and I will tell you. If a tiny spark of God's love already burns within you, do not expose it to the wind, for it may get blown out. Keep the stove tightly shut so that it will not lose its heat and grow cold. In other words, avoid distractions as well as you can. Stay quiet with God. Do not spend your time in useless chatter.

If teaching and preaching is your job, then study diligently and apply yourself to whatever is necessary for doing the job well. Be sure that you first preach by the way you live. If you do not, people will notice that you say one thing, but live otherwise, and your words will bring only cynical laughter and a derisive shake of the head.

Are you in charge of a parish? If so, do not neglect the parish of your own soul, do not give yourself to others so completely that you have nothing left for yourself. You have to be mindful of your people without becoming forgetful of yourself.

My brothers, you must realize that for us churchmen nothing is more necessary than meditation. We must meditate before, during and after everything we do. The prophet says: "*I will pray, and then I will understand.*" When you administer the sacraments, meditate on what you are doing. When you celebrate Mass, reflect on the sacrifice you are offering. When you pray the office, think about the words you are saying and the Lord to whom you are speaking. When you take care of your people, meditate on the Lord's blood that has washed them clean so that "*all that you do becomes a work of love.*"

This is the way we can easily overcome the countless difficulties we have to face day after day, which, after all, are part of our work: in meditation we find the strength to bring Christ to birth in ourselves and in other men.[1]

Questions for Reflection

• *This excerpt is an example of a spiritual sermon that is also down-to-earth. It is both loving and challenging. In other words, these are the words of a pastor whose experience allows him to help his audience. Can you see how pastoral love is necessary for fruitful preaching?*

• *What other important and timely lessons can we draw from this sermon for today's preachers?*

---

1 *Saint Charles Borromeo (Acta Ecclesiae Mediolanensis, Mediolani 1599, 1177–1178). Taken from the Office of Readings for the memorial of St. Charles Borromeo on November 4th.*

17

Jean-Bénigne Bossuet
(1627–1704)

Sermon on Death

Bossuet was a French theologian and bishop who is regarded as one of the most brilliant preachers of all time. He simplified the grandiose style of Baroque preaching in orations and homilies that exude eloquence and highlight the moral consequences of the faith. The Sermon on Death, preached in the presence of King Louis XIV, is a masterpiece, where the beauty of the words comes from the truth of the mystery celebrated, and leads the hearers to conversion. Needless to say, this is a much longer sermon than one we would normally preach today, but its expressiveness and the manner in which Bossuet develops his argument are exemplary in several ways.

Domine, veni et vide—"Lord, come and see" (Jn 11:34)

Will the Court permit me to open a tomb today? Or will your delicate eyes be offended by such a deathly sight? I do not think that Christians should refuse to join Jesus Christ before such a spectacle, Jesus to whom the words of our Gospel were spoken: "Lord, come and see" where the body of Lazarus has been laid. It was he who commanded that the stone be rolled away. And it is he who says to us in turn: come and see for yourselves. Jesus did not decline to see that dead body, which was for him both an object of pity and a subject for a miracle. Yet we, wretched mortals, prove our errors by refusing to look on. Come with Jesus and see. And let us forever forsake the things that death can strip away.

It is an odd weakness of mankind that death is never present to our minds, though it surrounds us in its myriad forms. At funerals one hears only words of astonishment at the death of a fellow mortal. Each calls to mind the last time he spoke with the deceased and about what. Then, suddenly, he was dead. And we say: how fleeting are a man's days! But who makes these observations? One who is himself a man; one who does not apply the lesson to himself; one who is not mindful of his own destiny. If a transitory wish to prepare himself for death does pass through his mind, he soon casts it off. It may even be said that mortals take no less care to bury the thoughts of death than they do the dead themselves. Yet perhaps these thoughts will have more of an effect in our hearts if we meditate upon them with Jesus Christ at the tomb of Lazarus. Let us ask him to imprint them upon our minds by the grace of his Holy Spirit, and let us strive to merit that grace through the intercession of the blessed Virgin. *Ave Maria...*

Of all the passions of the human mind, one of the fiercest is the desire to know. Our curiosity drives us to find either some undiscovered secret in the order of nature, or some unknown skill in the works of art, or some unusual refinement in the conduct of our affairs. Yet in our keen desire to enrich our minds with new discoveries, we are like those who by looking far ahead fail to see the objects nearby. By this I mean that our mind, devoting itself to great efforts upon things far afield and, as it were, wandering about the world, passes so quickly over things near at hand that we spend our entire lives not knowing the very things that touch upon us, and not only the things that touch upon us, but also not knowing what we are ourselves.

We must immediately marshal these straying thoughts. It is to this end, Christians, that I invite you today to accompany the Savior to the tomb of Lazarus: "*Veni et vide*; Come and see." Come and contemplate the spectacle of mortal things. Come to learn what you are.

You may be surprised that I would speak to you of death in order to teach you what you are, and you may think that man is misrepresented if he is depicted when he no longer exists. Yet if you carefully attend to what the tomb presents to us, you will surely agree that there is neither a more truthful interpreter, nor a more faithful mirror of humanity.

The nature of a composite being is never more distinctly to be perceived than in the dissolution of its parts. When joined, they mutually alter one another, and so they must be separated in order to be understood well. In fact, the fellowship of the body and the soul is such that the body seems to us to be more than it really is while the soul seems to be something less. But when, having been separated from one another, the body returns to the earth while the soul is made fit to return to heaven whence it came, then we see each of them in its purity. We have, therefore, only to consider what death takes from us and what it leaves to us, which part of our being falls under its blows and which sustains itself amidst the ruin. Then we shall understand what is man, and so I shall not fear to affirm that it is in the bosom of death and in its dark shadow that an immortal light shines to illumine our minds about the condition of our nature. Let us run then, and see what humanity is by gazing into the tomb of Lazarus. Come and see in one view the end of all your designs and the beginning of all your hopes. Come and see both the dissolution of your being and its renewal. Come and see the triumph of life amidst the victory of death: *Veni et vide*.

O Death, we give you thanks for the light that you shine upon our ignorance. You alone can convince us of our lowliness; you alone can teach us of our dignity. If man thinks too well of himself, you know how to beat down his pride. If man disdains himself overmuch, you know how to rekindle his courage. And to bring all of these thoughts together in their proper balance, you teach him these two truths that open his eyes to accurate self-knowledge: that he is contemptible when he passes away, but infinitely worthy when he attains eternity. These two important considerations will form the subject of our discourse.

First Point

It is a bold enterprise to tell man of his littleness. Each of us is jealous of what he is and would rather be blind than know his own weaknesses. Those who enjoy great wealth especially want to be treated delicately. They take no pleasure in the notice of their failings; they would prefer that, if we were to see them, at least we should pretend not to see. Nevertheless, thanks to death, we are at liberty to speak. From the vantage of death, none is so great in this world that he cannot recognize his littleness. Long live the Eternal One! O human greatness, from whatever side I look upon you—unless, of course, I consider you as having come from God and as owing everything to God, for in that case I discover in you a ray of divinity that rightly attracts my regard; when, however, I look upon you as something purely human—I say it again, from whatever side I look upon you—I see nothing in you to esteem. Wherever I turn I always find myself facing death, which casts its shadow upon everything that worldly brilliance would light, and then I no longer know what I should call great, nor do I see anything worthy of being so called.

Let us be convinced of this important truth by an irrefutable course of reasoning. The accident cannot be nobler than the substance, nor the subaltern more important than the commander, nor the building more secure than its foundation, nor, finally, can what is added to our being be greater or more important than our very being itself. Now, just what is our being? Tell us, O Death, for proud man no longer believes me. And yet you are mute; you speak only to our eyes. A great king will lend you his voice, so that our ears might hear you and our hearts might receive the most incisive of truths.

Here is what David pronounced from the throne and amidst his court. It merits your attention, Sire: *Ecce mensurabiles posuisti dies meos, et substantia mea tanquam nihilum ante te* (Ps 38:6). O Eternal King of the ages! You are always with yourself and in yourself. Your being, forever enduring, neither passes away, nor changes, nor has limits; "and behold, my days you have measured, and my substance is nothing before you." No, my substance is nothing before you, and every finite being is nothing, because what has limits has an end, and when it has arrived at that end, a final moment suffices to destroy everything as if it had never existed. What are a hundred years, what are a thousand, when they can be erased by a single moment? Multiply your days like the deer that fable or natural history would make to live for so many centuries. Live as long as the great oaks under which our ancestors lie and which will continue to shade our descendants. And fill that immense space with honors, riches, and pleasures. What shall any of it profit you, when death's final breath, weak and languid though it be, will cast down this vain display as if it were a house of cards, a mere child's plaything. What will it serve you to have written so much in this book, to have filled all its pages with beautiful script, when in the end a single stroke will erase it all? And does this one last stroke leave any trace even of itself? Or will not the last stroke of that final moment be itself lost in the great gulf of nothingness? There will not remain on earth even a single vestige of what we are: the flesh will change its nature, the body will take on another name, "even that of cadaver will not long remain, for it will become," as Tertullian says, "something that has no name in any language," so true it is that everything dies in it, including even those funeral terms with which we describe its wretched remains: *Post totum ignobilitatis elogium, caducae in originem terram, et cadaveris nomen; et de isto quoque nominae periturae in nullum inde jam nomen, in omnis jam vocabuli mortem.*

What, then, is my substance, O great God? I come into life only to leave it soon after. I show myself like the others but must disappear. Everything calls us unto death. Nature, almost envious of the gift she gives us, often tells us and shows us that she cannot allow us to keep for very long the little bit of matter she has loaned us, that it must not remain in the same hands, that it must forever be exchanged. She has need of it for other forms; she requires it for other works.

The constant stream of recruits to mankind—that is, the children who are born—as they grow and advance, seem to push us from behind, saying, "Get out of our way; now it is our turn." And just as we have seen others go before us, so others will see us pass, and they will present the same spectacle to their successors. I ask again, what are we? If I look to the years that preceded me, what an infinite space do I see in which I was not! And if I glance to the years ahead, what a horrible succession of years in which I will no longer be! What a small place do I occupy in the immense abyss of time! I am nothing. So small an interval cannot distinguish me from nothingness. I was sent here to be a mere number. There would have been no part waiting for me, and the play would have been no less well-played had I remained behind the curtain.

Let us consider the matter again in more subtle terms. We see that it is not the length of our lives that distinguishes us from nothingness. And you know, Christians, that we are never separated from death by more than a single moment. Now we lay hold of one such moment, and now it dies. And with it, we should all die, if we did not immediately lay hold of another just like it. Until at last, there comes one which we cannot grasp, no matter what efforts we make to reach out for it. And then we shall immediately fall for lack of support. O fragile purchase of our being! O ruinous foundation of our substance! *In imagine pertransit homo.* (Ps 38:7) Does not man himself pass for a shade, or even an image? And as he himself is nothing solid, so also does he pursue vain things, the image of the good, and not the good itself.

How little is the place that we occupy in this world! So little indeed and of such scant importance that it seems that my whole life is but a dream. Sometimes, with Arnobius, I wonder whether I sleep or wake: *Vigilemus aliquando, an ipsum vigilare, quod dicitur, somni sit perpetui portio*? I do not know whether what I call waking is not perhaps a somewhat more excited part of a deep sleep, and whether I am seeing things that are real, or whether I am only troubled by fantasies and illusions. *Praeterit figura huius mundi.*

(1 Cor 7:31) The shape of this world is passing away, and, compared to God, my substance is nothing.

Second Point

We must not doubt, Christians, that although we be relegated to this lowest part of the cosmos, to the theater of change and the empire of death, and although we carry it in our very bosom, nevertheless, through the shadowy knowledge that we gain from our prejudiced senses, if we know how to return to ourselves, we will find therein a principle whose vigor testifies to a heavenly origin, a principle that does not fear corruption.

I am not one of those who place great stock in human knowledge; and yet I confess that I cannot contemplate without admiration those marvelous discoveries by which science has sounded the depths of nature, nor the many fine inventions that art has found to make it suitable for our use. Man has almost changed the face of the earth. By his mind he has tamed animals that surpass him in strength. He has known how to discipline their brutish temper and channel their heedless liberty. He has even placed his mark upon the inanimate creatures. Has not his industry forced the earth to give him more suitable food, plants to adjust their wild bitterness in his favor, and even poisons to change into medicines for the love of him? It is needless to tell you how he has controlled the elements, after all of the miracles he daily performs with the most intractable of them, that is, with his two great enemies fire and water, who nevertheless agree to serve him in so many useful and necessary works. What else? He has climbed to the very heavens. In order to travel more safely, he has taught the stars to guide his voyages; to measure his life more accurately, he has obliged the sun to keep an account of all of his steps. Yet we must leave the long and scrupulous enumeration to rhetoric and be content as theologians to remark that God, intending man to be the head of the universe—as the oracle of Scripture says—formed him upon so noble a foundation that, although deformed by his crime, he has retained a certain instinct to seek what he lacks throughout the whole course of nature. That is why, if I may say so, he boldly delves everywhere, as if upon his own domain; and there is no part of the universe in which he has not set the sign of his industry.

How could such ascendancy have been gained by a creature with a body so weak and so liable to be assailed by other creatures? It would not have happened unless his mind had a force superior to the whole of visible nature, an immortal breath of the Spirit of God, a ray of light from his face, an aspect of his countenance.

No, it could not be otherwise. If a skilled artisan makes a machine, no one is able to use it except with his instructions. God made the world as an immense machine that his wisdom alone could have invented and that his power alone could have built. He established you to make use of it. He placed in your hands the whole of nature, that you might apply it to your ends. He even allowed you to decorate and embellish it by your art: for what is art but the embellishment of nature? You can add a little color to decorate this marvelous canvas; but how could you move even slightly a machine at once so strong and so delicate? Or in what way could you add even a single correct brush stroke to so rich a painting if you did not have in yourself and in some part of your being some art derived from that first art, some secondary ideas derived from the original ones, in a word, some resemblance, some spilling over, some portion of that artisan Spirit that made the world? If this be true, who cannot see that all of nature drawn together is unable to extinguish so beautiful a ray of the power that sustains it, and that our soul, superior to the world and to all the powers that compose it, has nothing to fear except from its author?

Let us prolong this beneficial meditation upon the image of God in us, and let us see by what maxims that beloved creature man, destined to make use of all the others, prescribed for himself what he ought to do. I admit that, in our state of corruption we discover our weakness. Nevertheless, I do marvel at those unchanging moral rules that reason has laid down. What! This soul, immersed in the body, so closely married to all of the passions, who languishes, who is no longer herself when the body suffers: by what light has she been able to perceive that her felicity lies apart from it? By which she might boldly say—while all her senses, all her passions, and almost all of nature cry out against her—"Death, to me, is gain" (Phlm 1:21), and "I rejoice in my afflictions" (Col 1:24). It must be that she has discovered within herself a most exquisite beauty in what is called duty, in order to dare to affirm that for friends, country, throne, and altar one ought fearlessly to face immense labors, incredible sorrows, and the certitude of death. It is a kind of miracle that these maxims of courage, probity, and justice have not ever been abolished—I do not say by the passage of time, but by contrary practice—and that to the benefit of the human race there have always been many fewer persons who deny them than there have been those who have practiced them perfectly.

It may not be doubted that there is a divine light within us: "A ray of light from your face, O Lord, has been lodged in our souls: *Signatum est super nos lumen vultus tui, Domine*" (Ps 4:7). Here we discover, as in a globe of light, an immortal goodness in rectitude and virtue. It is the first Reason that reveals itself to us by its image. It is Truth himself who speaks to us and who causes us to understand that there is something in us that does not die, for God has made us capable of finding happiness even in death.

All of this is but nothing, Christians, for here is the most marvelous brush stroke of the divine likeness. God knows himself and contemplates himself. His life is to know himself, and because man is his image, he also wants man to know that he is eternal, immense, infinite, wholly immaterial, free from every limit, alien to every imperfection. Christians, what is this miracle? We who sense only what has limits, who see nothing but what changes, whence have we been able to understand this eternity? Whence have we dreamt this infinity? "O eternity, O infinity," says St. Augustine, "that our senses do not even suspect: how is it that you have entered our souls?" But if all that we are is body and matter, how have we been able to conceive of pure spirit? And how have we been able even to invent the name?

I know what will be said at this point, and rightly: that, when we speak of these spirits we do not understand what we are saying. Our weak imagination, unable to sustain so pure an idea, always presents some little body with which to clothe it. Yet after reason has made its utmost effort to make those bodies subtle and fine, do you not sense that at the same time from the bottom of our soul there arises a heavenly light that clears away all those delicate phantoms by which we have imagined them? If you press onward and ask what it is, a voice rises from the center of the soul: I do not know what it is, yet it is certainly not that. What power, what energy, what secret strength does the soul find with which to correct itself, to undeceive itself, and to reject its own thoughts? Who does not see the hidden resource which has not yet used all of its strength, and which, though it be constrained, though it does not enjoy freedom of movement, nevertheless demonstrates by its vigor that it is not wholly bound to matter and that it is attached to some higher principle?

It is true, and I confess it: we cannot long maintain such noble ardor. The soul soon returns into her matter. The soul has her languor and frailty, and, as it were, her baseness, which—should she not be enlightened from elsewhere—almost force her to doubt what she is. This is why the worldly wise, in seeing man on the one hand so great and on the other so wretched, have not known what to think or to say: some making him out to be a god, others nothingness; some say that nature cherishes him like a mother and delights in him; others that, like an evil stepmother, she exposes him and counts him the runt. And a third group, not knowing what to conclude from this mixture, responds that nature has been at play in uniting two parts that have nothing to do with one another, and so, by a kind of caprice, has formed this prodigy called man.

You will judge rightly, Christians, that none of these has arrived at the terminus, and that only the faith can solve so great a riddle. You mislead yourselves, O wise men of this age: man cannot be nature's delight, for she offends him in so many ways. Nor can he be her runt, for there is something in him worth more than nature herself—I speak of the nature presented to us by the senses. Now, to speak of caprice in the works of God is to blaspheme against his wisdom. Yet whence so strange a disproportion? Must I tell you, Christians? Do not these ramshackle cabins with such magnificent foundations declare plainly enough that the work is not complete? Contemplate this grand edifice: you will see in it the marks of the divine hand. Yet the unevenness of the work will soon cause you to see that sin has mixed in its own. O God! What is this mixture? I am lost, and am almost ready to cry out with the prophet: "*Haeccine est urbs perfecti decoris, gaudium universae terrae*? Is this Jerusalem? Is this the city, is this the temple, the honor, the joy of the whole world?" (Lam 2:15). And for my part I say: is this the man made in the image of God, the miracle of his wisdom, and the masterpiece of his hands?

Truly, it is he. Whence this discord? Why do I see such ill-assorted parts? Because man wanted to build upon his Creator's work in his own way; he departed from the plan. And so, in opposition to the orderliness of the initial design, the immortal and the corruptible, the spiritual and the carnal, in a word, the angel and the beast found themselves joined together in one. Here is the clue to the riddle, here is the unraveling of the tangle: faith has restored us to ourselves, and our shameful failings can no longer hide our natural dignity.

But, alas, what does this dignity profit us? Even though we still breathe some air of greatness amidst our ruins, we are no less prostrate beneath them. Our former immortality serves only to make the tyranny of death all the more unbearable. And although our souls escape it, if they are made wretched by sin then they have nothing to boast about so burdensome an eternity. What shall we say then? How shall we reply to so pressing a complaint? Jesus Christ will respond to it in our Gospel. He has just seen the dead Lazarus. He has just visited human nature groaning under the empire of death. This visit was not without cause: it is the artisan himself who comes in person to see what is lacking in the building, for he has a plan to renovate it in accord with his initial design: *secundum imaginem ejus qui creavit illum* (Col 3:10).

O soul, weighted with crimes, rightly do you fear an immortality that would render your death eternal! Yet behold in the person of Jesus Christ the resurrection and the life. He who believes in him shall not die. He who believes in him is already living with a spiritual and interior life, living by the life of grace that draws after it the life of glory. But the body is nevertheless subject to death! O soul, console yourself. If this divine architect who has undertaken to repair you allows the old structure of your body to fall piece by piece, it is so that he may return it to you in a better state and may rebuild it in a better order. For a little while, the body will fall under the empire of death, but it will not leave anything in his hands save mortality itself.

Do not let yourselves be convinced by medical reasoning that corruption is a natural result of composition and mixture. We must lift our minds higher and believe according to the principles of Christianity that what involves the flesh in the necessity of corruption is that it is an attraction to evil, a source of evil desires, indeed, as the holy apostle says, a "flesh of sin" (Rom 8:3). Such a flesh ought to be destroyed, I say, even in the elect, because in its condition of a flesh of sin it deserves neither to be joined to the souls of the blessed nor to enter into the kingdom of God: *caro et sanguis regnum Dei possidere non possunt* (1 Cor 15:50). It must, therefore, change its initial form in order to be renewed, and to lose its first condition in order to receive a second from the hand of God. Like an old and haphazard building that is allowed to fall into disrepair in order that a new one may be built in a more lovely architectural style, so also this flesh, made unruly by sin and concupiscence, was allowed to fall into ruin in order that God may remake it in his way and according to the initial design of his creation. It must be reduced to rubble because it gave service to sin.

Do you not see the divine Jesus who has opened the tomb? It is the Prince who opens the prison doors for the suffering captives. The dead bodies shut up within will one day hear his word, and they will be raised up like Lazarus. They will be raised up better than Lazarus, because they will be raised up never to die again, and because death, as the Holy Spirit says, will be drowned in the abyss, never to appear again: *et mors ultra non erit* (Rv 21:4).

What then do you fear, Christian soul, from death's approach? Perhaps in seeing your house fall you fear that you will lack shelter? But listen to the holy apostle: "We know," we know, he says, we are not led to believe by uncertain guesses, but we know most assuredly and with complete certitude, "that if this house of dirt and mud in which we live is destroyed, we have another dwelling place prepared for us in heaven" (2 Cor 5:1). O merciful conduct of the one who anticipates our needs! He has a plan, as St. John Chrysostom fittingly said, to repair the house he has given us. When he destroys it and casts it down in order to make it anew, we must move out. Yet he himself offers us his palace, and within it, gives us rooms wherein we may await in peace the complete reconstruction of our former abode.[1]

Questions for Reflection

• *While the style and length of this sermon are different from those of a typical homily today, there are many things we can learn from it. Bossuet carefully crafted a speech in which Scripture illumines a situation and developed a flow of ideas expressed with beauty and poignancy, which moved the audience to conversion.*

• *This sermon shows great insight on the human condition. What ideas called your attention? What insights can be used in our preaching today?*

• *An exemplary aspect of this sermon is its structure. The preacher guides his audience step by step in his speech. Can you describe the structure of this homily?*

• *One final detail to note: towards the beginning of the sermon Bossuet asks for the intercession of Mary and prays an* Ave Maria.

1 Sermon for the Wednesday of the Fourth Week of Lent, preached in the royal chapel of the Louvre, in the presence of King Louis XIV, on March 22, 1662. The text is from Jean-Bénigne Bossuet, *Oeuvres Oratoires*, édition critique de l'abbé Joseph Lebarq, revue et augmentée par Charles Urbain et Eugène Levesque (Paris: Desclée, 1926), 4:262–81. Translation by Christopher O. Blum.

18

St. John Henry Newman
(1801–1890)

The Mental Sufferings of Our Lord in His Passion

John Henry Newman was a master of language. He has given us some of the most insightful and memorable homilies spoken in English, many of which were preached while he was an Anglican priest in Oxford. It is known that Newman's oratory was not particularly impressive, yet his words held the power of their depth and of the spiritual authority of the preacher.

This sermon is a spiritual jewel, consisting in a long meditation on the mental sufferings of Christ. Pay attention to the development of his argument and let the flow and beauty of his words take you to the mystery he presents to us.

Our Lord and Savior, though he was God, was also perfect man; and hence he had not only a body, but a soul likewise, such as ours, though pure from all stain of evil. How would he have sanctified our nature by taking a nature which was not ours? Man without a soul is on a level with the beasts of the field; but our Lord came to save a race capable of praising and obeying him, possessed of immortality, though that immortality had lost its promised blessedness. Man was created in the image of God, and that image is in his soul. When then his Maker, by an unspeakable condescension, came in his nature, he took on himself a soul in order to take on him a body. He himself created the soul which he took on himself, while he took his body from the flesh of the Blessed Virgin, his Mother. Thus he became perfect man with body and soul, and as he took on him a body of flesh and nerves, which admitted of wounds and death and was capable of suffering, so did he take a soul, too, which was susceptible of that suffering, and moreover was susceptible of the pain and sorrow which are proper to a human soul. And, as his atoning passion was undergone in the body, so it was undergone in the soul also.

His sufferings in the body—his seizure, forced journeyings, blows and wounds, scourging, the crown of thorns, the nails—are all summed up in the crucifix. They are represented all at once on his sacred flesh, as it hangs up before us, and meditation is made easy by the spectacle. It is otherwise with the sufferings of his soul. They cannot be painted for us, nor can they even be duly investigated. They are beyond both sense and thought, and yet they anticipated his bodily sufferings. The agony, a pain of the soul, not of the body, was the first act of his tremendous sacrifice. "My soul is very sorrowful, even to death" (Mt 26:38), he said.

It was the soul and not the body which was the seat of the suffering of the Eternal Word. There is no real pain, though there may be apparent suffering, when there is no kind of inward sensibility or spirit to be the seat of it. A tree, for instance, has life, organs, growth, and decay; it may be wounded and injured; it droops, and is killed; but it does not suffer, because it has no mind or sensible principle within it. But wherever this gift of an immaterial principle is found, there pain is possible, and greater pain according to the quality of the gift. Had we no soul, we should not feel pain more acutely than a brute feels it; but, being men, we feel pain in a way in which none but those who have souls can feel it.

This it is what makes pain so trying: we cannot help thinking of it, while we suffer it. It is before us; it possesses the mind; it keeps our thoughts fixed upon it. Whatever draws the mind off the thought of it lessens it. Hence friends try to amuse us when we are in pain, for amusement is a diversion. And hence it continually happens that in violent exercise or labor, men meet with blows or cuts so considerable and so durable in their effect as to bear witness to the suffering which must have attended their infliction, of which nevertheless they recollect nothing. And in quarrels and in battles wounds are received which, from the excitement of the moment, are brought home to the consciousness of the combatant not by the pain at the time of receiving them but by the loss of blood that follows.

Hardly any one stroke of pain is intolerable; it is intolerable when it continues. Patients feel as if they could stop the surgeon's hand, simply because he continues to pain them. Their feeling is that they have borne as much as they can bear, as if the continuance and not the intensity was what made it too much for them. What does this mean, but that the memory of the foregoing moments of pain acts upon the pain that succeeds? If the third or fourth or twentieth moment of pain could be taken by itself, if the succession of the moments that preceded it could be forgotten, it would be no more than the first moment, as bearable as the first; but what makes it unbearable is that it is the twentieth. Hence it is that brute animals would seem to feel so little pain. They do not know they exist; they do not contemplate themselves; they do not look backwards or forwards; every moment as it succeeds is their all. And hence, as their other feelings, so their feeling of pain is but faint and dull, in spite of their outward manifestations of it. It is the intellectual comprehension of pain, as a whole diffused through successive moments, which gives it its special power and keenness.

Now apply this to the sufferings of our Lord. They offered him wine mingled with myrrh when he was on the point of being crucified, but he would not drink of it. Why? Because such a portion would have stupefied his mind, and he was bent on bearing the pain in all its bitterness. You see from this the character of his sufferings. He would have willingly escaped them had that been His Father's will. "If it be possible," he said, "let this chalice pass from me" (Mt 26:39), but since it was not possible, he says calmly and decidedly to the apostle, who would have rescued him from suffering, "shall I not drink the chalice which the Father has given me?" (Jn 18:11). If he was to suffer, he gave himself to suffering. And as men are superior to brute animals and are affected by pain more than they by reason of the mind within them, so, in like manner, our Lord felt pain of the body, with a consciousness, and therefore with a keenness and intensity, and with a unity of perception, which none of us can possibly fathom or compass, because his soul was so absolutely in his power, so simply free from the influence of distractions, so fully directed upon the pain, so utterly surrendered, so simply subjected to the suffering. And thus he may truly be said to have suffered the whole of his passion in every moment of it.

Recollect that our Blessed Lord was in this respect different from us, that, though he was perfect man, yet there was a power in him greater than his soul, which ruled his soul, for he was God. The soul of other men is subjected to its own wishes, feelings, impulses, passions, perturbations. His soul was subjected simply to his Eternal and Divine Personality. Nothing happened to his soul by chance or on a sudden. He never was taken by surprise.

Nothing affected him without his willing beforehand that it should. When we suffer, it is because outward agents and the uncontrollable emotions of our minds bring suffering upon us. We are brought under the discipline of pain involuntarily. We suffer from it more or less acutely according to accidental circumstances. We find our patience more or less tried by it according to our state of mind, and we do our best to provide alleviations or remedies of it. We cannot anticipate beforehand how much of it will come upon us, or how far we shall be able to sustain it; nor can we say afterwards why we have felt just what we have felt, or why we did not bear the suffering better.

It was otherwise with our Lord. His Divine Person was not subject to the influence of his own human affections and feelings, except so far as he chose. He was not open to emotion, but he opened upon himself voluntarily the impulse by which he was moved. Consequently, when he determined to suffer the pain of his vicarious passion, whatever he did, he did not do it by halves. He did not turn away his mind from the suffering as we do. He said, "sacrifices and offerings you have not desired, but a body you have prepared for me" (Heb 10:5). He took a body in order that he might suffer. He became man, that he might suffer as man, and when his hour was come, that hour of Satan and of darkness, the hour when sin was to pour its full malignity upon him, it followed that he offered himself wholly; as the whole of his body, stretched out upon the cross, so the whole of his soul, his whole consciousness, a mind awake, a sense acute, a living cooperation, a present, absolute intention, not a virtual permission, not a heartless submission, this did he present to his tormentors. His passion was an action. He lived most energetically while he lay languishing, fainting, and dying. Nor did he die except by an act of the will, for he bowed his head, in command as well as in resignation, and said, "Father, into your hands I commend my Spirit" (Lk 23:46).

Had our Lord only suffered in the body, and in it not so much as other men, still as regards the pain, he would have really suffered indefinitely more, because pain is to be measured by the power of realizing it. God was the sufferer. God suffered in his human nature. The sufferings belonged to God, and were drunk up, were drained out to the bottom of the chalice, because God drank them; not tasted or sipped, not flavored, disguised by human medicaments, as man disposes of the cup of anguish.

Our Lord said, when his agony was commencing, "My soul is very sorrowful, even to death" (Mt 26:38); now we may ask whether he had not certain consolations peculiar to himself, impossible in any other, which diminished or impeded the distress of his soul, and caused him to feel, not more, but less than an ordinary man. For instance, he had a sense of innocence which no other sufferer could have; even his persecutors, even the false apostle who betrayed him, the judge who sentenced him, and the soldiers who conducted the execution, testified his innocence. And if even they, sinners, bore witness to his sinlessness, how much more did his own soul! And we know well that even in our own case, sinners as we are, on the consciousness of innocence or of guilt mainly turns our power of enduring opposition and calumny; how much more in the case of our Lord, did the sense of inward sanctity compensate for the suffering and annihilate the shame. Again, he knew that his sufferings would be short, and that their issue would be joyful, whereas uncertainty of the future is the keenest element of human distress; but he could not have anxiety, for he was not in suspense; nor despondency or despair, for he never was deserted. And in confirmation you may refer to St. Paul, who expressly tells us that, "for the joy that was set before him," our Lord "endured the cross, despising the shame" (Heb 12:2). And certainly there is a marvelous calm and self-possession in all he does.

He was always himself. His mind was its own center and was never in the slightest degree thrown off its heavenly and most perfect balance. What he suffered, he suffered because he put himself under suffering, and that deliberately and calmly. His composure is but the proof how entirely he governed his own mind. He drew back, at the proper moment, the bolts and fastenings, and opened the gates, and the floods fell right upon his soul in all their fullness. That is what St. Mark tells us of him; and he is said to have written his Gospels from the very mouth of St. Peter, who was one of three witnesses present at the time. "And they went to a place which was called Gethsemane; and he said to his disciples, 'Sit here, while I pray.' And he took with him Peter and James and John, and began to be greatly distressed and troubled" (Mk 14:32–33). Thus he walks forth into a mental agony with as definite an action as if it were some bodily torture, the fire or the wheel.

It is nothing to the purpose to say that he would be supported under his trial by the consciousness of innocence and the anticipation of triumph; for his trial consisted in the withdrawal, as of other causes of consolation, so of that very consciousness and anticipation. The same act of the will which admitted the influence upon his soul of any distress at all, admitted all distresses at once. It was not the contest between antagonist impulses and views, coming from without, but the operation of an inward resolution. As men of self-command can turn from one thought to another at their will, so much more did he deliberately deny himself the comfort and satiate himself with the woe.

What was it he had to bear when he thus opened upon his soul the torrent of this predestinated pain? Alas! He had to bear what is well known to us, what is familiar to us, but what to him was woe unutterable. He had to bear the weight of sin. He had to bear our sins. He had to bear the sins of the whole world. Sin is an easy thing to us; we think little of it. We do not understand how the Creator can think much of it. We cannot bring our imagination to believe that it deserves retribution. But consider what sin is in itself. It is rebellion against God. Sin is the mortal enemy of the All-holy. And here observe that when once Almighty Love, by taking flesh, entered this created system, and submitted himself to its laws, then forthwith this antagonist of good and truth, taking advantage of the opportunity, flew at that flesh which he had taken, and fixed on it, and was its death. The envy of the Pharisees, the treachery of Judas, and the madness of the people were but the instrument or the expression of the enmity which sin felt towards Eternal Purity as soon as, in infinite mercy towards men, he put himself within its reach. Sin could not touch his Divine Majesty, but it could assail him in that way in which he allowed himself to be assailed, that is, through the medium of his humanity.

In that most awful hour, there knelt the Savior of the world, putting off the defenses of his divinity, dismissing his reluctant angels, who in myriads were ready at his call, and opening his arms, baring his breast, sinless as he was, to the assault of his foe. There he knelt, motionless and still, while the vile and horrible fiend clad his spirit in a robe steeped in all that is hateful and heinous in human crime, which clung close round his heart, and filled his conscience, and found its way into every sense and pore of his mind and spread over him a moral leprosy. Oh, the horror, when he looked and did not know himself, and felt as a foul and loathsome sinner, from his vivid perception of that mass of corruption which poured over his head and ran down even to the skirts of his garments! Oh, the distraction, when he found his eyes, and hands, and feet, and lips, and heart, as if the members of the Evil One and not of God! Are these the hands of the Immaculate Lamb of God, once innocent, but now red with ten thousand barbarous deeds of blood? Are these his lips, not uttering prayer, and praise, and holy blessings, but as if defiled with oaths, and blasphemies, and doctrines of devils? Or his eyes, profaned by all the evil visions and idolatrous fascinations for which men have abandoned their adorable Creator? And his ears, they ring with sounds of revelry and of strife; and his heart is frozen with avarice, and cruelty, and unbelief. His very memory is laden with every sin which has been committed since the fall.

Who does not know the misery of a haunting thought which comes again and again, in spite of rejection, to annoy, if it cannot seduce? Or of some odious and sickening imagination, in no sense one's own, but forced upon the mind from without? Or of evil knowledge, gained with or without a man's fault, but which he would give a great price to be rid of at once and for ever? And adversaries such as these gather around you, Blessed Lord, in millions now. Of the living and of the dead and of the as yet unborn, of the lost and of the saved, of your people and of strangers, of sinners and of saints, all sins are there. Your dearest are there, your saints and your chosen are upon you, your three apostles, Peter, James, and John, but not as comforters, but as accusers, heaping curses on your head. All are there but one. One only is not there, one only, for she who had no part in sin, she only could console you, and therefore she is not nigh. She will be near you on the cross, she is separated from you in the garden. None was equal to the weight but God. It is the long history of a world, and God alone can bear the load of it. Hopes blighted, vows broken, lights quenched, warnings scorned, opportunities lost; the innocent betrayed, the young hardened, the penitent relapsing, the just overcome, the aged failing; the sophistry of misbelief, the willfulness of passion, the obduracy of pride, the tyranny of habit, the canker of remorse, the wasting fever of care, the anguish of shame, the pining of disappointment, the sickness of despair. Such cruel, such pitiable spectacles, such heartrending, revolting, detestable, maddening scenes: they are all before him now. They are upon him and in him. They are with him instead of that ineffable peace which has inhabited his soul since the moment of his conception. They are upon him. They are all but his own. He cries to his Father as if he were the criminal, not the victim. His agony takes the form of guilt and compunction. He is doing penance. He is making confession. He is exercising contrition, with a reality and a virtue infinitely greater than that of all saints and penitents together, for he is the One Victim for us all, the sole Satisfaction, the real Penitent, all but the real sinner. He rises languidly from the earth and turns around to meet the traitor and his band, now quickly nearing the deep shade. He turns, and lo there is blood upon his garment. No soldier's scourge has touched his shoulders, nor the hangman's nails his hands and feet. He has bled before his time. He has shed blood, and it is his agonizing soul which has broken up his framework of flesh and poured it forth. His passion has begun from within. That tormented heart, the seat of tenderness and love, began at length to labor and to beat with vehemence beyond its nature. The red streams rushed forth so copious and fierce as to overflow the veins, and bursting through the pores, they stood in a thick dew over his whole skin. Then, forming into drops, they rolled down full and heavy, and drenched the ground.[1]

Questions for Reflection

* *This sermon is about one topic: the mental sufferings of Christ in his passion. One topic, unfolded in a lengthy spiritual meditation. This is another example of how to approach a homily.*

* *It is evident that the preacher had put in a long period of thought and prayer before being able to say these things. What can we learn from this fact for the preparation of our own homilies?*

* *Certainly, it would be hard to try to do a homily like this today, and yet, there are many things that are indeed exemplary in it. Can you give some examples of this?*

1 John Henry Newman, "Discourse 16: Mental Sufferings of Our Lord in His Passion," in *Discourses Addressed to Mixed Congregations* (London and New York: Longmans, Greene, 1906), 323–341.

19

Ronald Knox
(1888–1957)

Homily on the Sacred Heart

Ronald Knox is another of the great English preachers of recent times. The son of the Anglican bishop of Manchester, and an Anglican priest himself, he converted to Catholicism and became a Catholic priest. He spent his ministry teaching and writing in a wide variety of subjects, and he made a new translation of the Bible. He has left many eloquent sermons, in which we find excellent models of preaching that is pastoral and spiritual.

Come to me, all you that labour and are burdened, and I will refresh you. Take up my yoke upon you and learn of me, because I am meek and humble of heart, and you shall find rest to your souls. —Matthew 11:28–29

Come—it is not enough to stand still; the movement will not be all on God's side. Christ stretches out his arms, as if the gesture of crucifixion had become habitual even to the glorified body; it is your part to respond to the invitation, to come to him, though your steps be weak and tottering, like the first steps of a child. The Sacred Heart of the Crucified would draw all men to him, yet draws them, not by any chain of necessity, but with cords of love; it must be a free choice of your will by which you step forward from the ranks that waver and hang back, to consecrate yourself to him. True, in this devotion we consecrate ourselves as a family, but it is the individual surrender he prizes, not the mere herd-instinct that bids us, to avoid singularity, associate ourselves in a public act of homage: the word is addressed to each soul individually—Come unto me.

Come unto me—other voices, maybe, in later years will endeavour to distract us, the false religious systems of yesterday, the world with its easy standards, ambition with its insistent call for action, or money, the hardest master of them all: their prizes will seem more ready to our hand, their voices closer in our ear, but none will woo so gently or so patiently as the Sacred Heart, the Heart that loves so much and is loved so little in return, no one else dares to ask or claims to offer as he does. Unto me—not as if your devotion to the Sacred Heart could rival or replace your devotion to Almighty God: for that Heart is the life-centre of the Sacred Humanity, wherein, not by some overshadowing influence, as in Mary and the saints, but by a real and personal union, the fullness of revealed Godhead dwells. Unto me—not to some abstract idea, some expressive image, some memory of a dead past, but a Human Heart, real, concrete, living as your own, living now amid the splendours of the glorified Humanity in heaven.

All you that labour—it is a fashion, a pose you affect among your friends, to despise anything that comes to you openly under the name of work: but labour is rightly measured not by the distastefulness of the occupation or by the value of the results achieved, but by what it costs you, the strain that tells on you, the disturbance and distraction it sets up in your thoughts. At this moment, ask yourself if there is not some day-dream or some project humming in your brain, distracting your attention or ready to do so the instant your vigilance is relaxed. That day-dream, that project, however trivial and however distant, though it be only some scheme for your enjoyment, innocent or misapplied, some affection, some grievance, some grudge, is the labour with which you labour under the sun, the prisoner of your own brooding thoughts. You know that at times when these worries and distractions interfere with your sleep, or when you feel dull and jaded after long hours of them. You that labour, leave here on one side for a moment the petty cares which tyrannize over you: be still, and see that I am God.

Come to me, all you that are burdened—labour distracts the mind; it is sin that weighs upon the shoulders and clogs the feet. That burden, too, we must lay down for a little, if we are to lift up our eyes to the tabernacle. Last time we kept the first Friday, there was some resolution, an occasion of sin to be avoided, a bad habit to be checked, an improvement to be made in our rule of prayer. Nothing very much has come of it, and conscience feels uneasy at this reminder. Put it aside just for the moment; we must turn our faces towards the future and consecrate ourselves anew.

And I will refresh you—this is to be a breathing-space from the dusty business of life, the daily, common round of earthly occupations in which we seldom catch a glimpse of the supernatural. We are to draw ourselves up, breathe deep in the fresh air of grace, stretch the cramped muscles of the soul and rejoice to find them still responsive to the will. We shall forget for a while the work that lies at our feet as our cheek catches the cooling influence of grace that comes from Him.

Take my yoke upon you—not the yoke of a conqueror, imposed on his unwilling vassal, but the yoke which eases your burden by distributing the weight so that all but all of it rests on him. It is not servitude he offers, but partnership. Oh, if we could believe what we see so often in lives which have greatly devoted themselves to him, that, in proportion as we resign ourselves to his love, care and sorrow and all the burden of mortality lies lightly on us, till we have to ask for suffering lest we should lose the sense of the privilege that partnership bestows! We will make an offering here of all the work and all the suffering God will have us undergo, in union with the merits of the Sacred Heart, Fountain of all Consolation.

And learn of me—not the lessons we learn in class, not Christian doctrine or apologetics, nothing that tires the brain and wrinkles the forehead, not the dreary formulas that seem only intended to catch us out by being so difficult to remember. In this lesson it is not mind that speaks to mind, but heart to heart, no elaborate considerations are necessary, no theological subtleties. You have only to stand still and contemplate the Sacred Heart, bruised for our sins and made obedient unto death; only to remember one simple formula—how easy to remember, how difficult to mean: "Heart of Jesus, full of love for us, make our hearts like thy Sacred Heart".

Because I am meek and humble of heart—meekness that will not be driven to resentment even by ill-usage, humility that will not be puffed up even where there is cause for self-congratulation. Meekness that in our case—not in his—sees its own sinfulness and acknowledges that the discomforts and reverses of life are only its lawful due; not assuming that the word which wounded you was aimed with intent, that you were right when

1 Ronald Arbuthnott Knox, "Homily on the Sacred Heart of Jesus," *University and Anglican Sermons of Ronald A. Knox Together with Sermons Preached on Various Occasions*, edited by Philip Caraman (New York: Sheed and Ward, 1963), 342–45.

you quarreled, unfairly hampered where you failed to come off; not for ever engaged in drawing up that long list of grievances against your fellow-men which leaves behind it no satisfaction, but only a character soured and blasé, a nature suspicious and difficult to please. Humility that in our case—not in his—realizes its own insignificance; humility that will not let you stand on your dignity, or lose your peace of mind when you are criticized and held up to ridicule; humility that, above all, approaches God with infinite reverence, and does not seek either to search out his hidden counsels or to presume on the graces he bestows.

And you shall find rest to your souls; rest in this life, when the wayward passions of your heart have been calmed and regulated by learning to beat in time with his; rest in the world to come, when you shall contemplate openly the Heart from which those graces used to flow, and, as you have been faithful yoke-fellows and docile scholars of your Lord below, be made partakers of his eternal glory in heaven.[1]

Questions for Reflection

- *This is a remarkable model for a specific kind of homily: to preach about one verse, word by word. When done well, as in this case, the effect can be memorable.*

- *How would you describe the style of this homily? How is Knox's use of images?*

- *Note, finally, how the words sometimes come from Christ, sometimes from the preacher, and sometimes from the audience.*

20

St. Paul VI
(1897–1978)

Homily at the Mass at the "Quezon Circle" in Manila

Pope Paul VI led the Church during and after the Second Vatican Council. More than any pope before him, he had the opportunity to travel to distant parts of the Earth to proclaim the Gospel. The homily we will read was delivered in front of close to a million people in Manila, Philippines. He did one thing: proclaim Jesus Christ.

I Paul, the successor of Saint Peter, charged with the pastoral mission for the whole Church, would never have come from Rome to this far-distant land, unless I had been most firmly convinced of two fundamental things: first, of Christ; and second, of your salvation.

Convinced of Christ: yes, I feel the need to proclaim him, I cannot keep silent. "Woe to me if I do not preach the gospel!" (1 Cor 9:16). I am sent by him, by Christ himself, to do this. I am an apostle, I am a witness. The more distant the goal, the more difficult my mission, the more pressing is the love that urges me to it (Cf. 2 Cor 5:13). I must bear witness to his name: Jesus is the Christ, the Son of the living God (Mt 16:16). He reveals the invisible God, he is the firstborn of all creation, the foundation of everything created. He is the teacher of mankind, and its Redeemer. He was born, he died and he rose again for us. He is the center of history and of the world; he is the one who knows us and who loves us; he is the companion and the friend of our life. He is the man of sorrows and of hope. It is he who will come and who one day will be our judge and—we hope—the everlasting fulness of our existence, our happiness. I could never finish speaking about him: he is the light and the truth; indeed, he is "the way, the truth and the life" (Jn 14:6). He is the bread and the spring of living water to satisfy our hunger and our thirst. He is our shepherd, our guide, our model, our comfort, our brother. Like us, and more than us, he has been little, poor, humiliated; he has been a worker; he has known misfortune and been patient. For our sake he spoke, worked miracles, and founded a new kingdom where the poor are happy, where peace is the principle for living together, where the pure of heart and those who mourn are raised up and comforted, where those who hunger and thirst after justice have their fill, where sinners can be forgiven, where all are brothers.

Jesus Christ: you have heard him spoken of; indeed the greater part of you are already his: you are Christians. So, to you Christians I repeat his name, to everyone I proclaim him: Jesus Christ is the beginning and the end, the Alpha and the Omega; he is the king of the new world; he is the secret of history; he is the key to our destiny. He is the mediator, the bridge, between heaven and earth. He is more perfectly than anyone else the Son of man, because he is the Son of God, eternal and infinite. He is the son of Mary, blessed among all women, his mother according to the flesh, and our mother through the sharing in the Spirit of his Mystical Body.

Jesus Christ is our constant preaching; it is his name that we proclaim to the ends of the earth (cf. Rom 10:18) and throughout all ages (Rom 9:5). Remember this and ponder on it: the pope has come here among you and has proclaimed Jesus Christ!

In doing this I express also the second dynamic idea that brings me to you: that Jesus Christ is to be praised not only for what he is in himself; he is to be exalted and loved for what he is for us, for each one of us, for every people and for every culture. Christ is our Savior. Christ is our greatest benefactor. Christ is our liberator. We need Christ, in order to be genuine and worthy men in the temporal order, and men saved and raised to the supernatural order.

At this point several questions present themselves. They are questions that torment our times, and I am sure that they are in your minds too. These questions are: Can Christ really be of any use to us for solving the practical and concrete problems of the present life? Did he not say that his kingdom is not of this world? What can he do for us? In other words, can Christianity give rise to a true humanism? Can the Christian view of life inspire a real renewal of society? Can that view harmonize with the demands of modern life, and favor progress and well-being of all? Can Christianity interpret peoples' yearnings and identify with the tendencies special to your culture?

These questions are many, and we cannot answer them with one single formula which would take account of the complexity of the problems and the different needs of man, spiritual, moral, economic, political, ethnic, historical and social. Yet, as far as the positive and happy development of your social conditions is concerned, we can give a positive answer: Christianity can be salvation also on the earthly and human level. Christ multiplied the loaves also to satisfy the physical hunger of the crowds following him. And Christ continues to work this miracle for those who truly believe in him, and who take from him the principles of a dynamic social order, that is, of an order that is continually progressing and being renewed.

For example, Christ, as you know, constantly proclaims his great and supreme commandment of love. There exists no social ferment stronger and better than this. In its positive aspect it unleashes incomparable and unquenchable moral forces; in its negative aspect it denounces all forms of selfishness, inertia, and forgetfulness that do harm to the needs of others. Christ proclaims the equality and brotherhood of all men: who but he has taught and can still effectively teach such principles which revolution, while benefitting from them, rejects? Who but he, we say, has revealed the fatherhood of God, the true and unassailable reason for the brotherhood of men? And whence comes the genuine and sacred freedom of man if not from human dignity, of which Christ made himself the teacher and champion? And who, if not he, has made available temporal goods, when he took from them the nature of ends in themselves and declared that they are means, means which must to some extent suffice for all, and means which are of less value than the supreme goods of the spirit? Who but Christ has planted in the hearts of his followers the talent for love and service on behalf of all man's sufferings and needs? Who has proclaimed the law of work as a right, a duty, and a means of providence? Who has proclaimed the dignity that raises it to the level of cooperation with and fulfillment of the divine plan? Who has freed it from every form of inhuman slavery, and given it its reward of justice and merit?

To you who are students and can well grasp these fundamental ideas and these higher values, I would say this: Today while you are challenging the structures of affluent society, the society that is dominated by technology and by the anxious pursuit of productivity and consumption, you are aware of the insufficiency and the deceptiveness of the economic and social materialism that marks our present progress. You are truly able to reaffirm the superiority, richness and relevance of authentic Christian sociology, based on true knowledge of man and of his destiny.

Workers, my message to you is this: While today you have become aware of your strength, take care that in the pursuit of your total rehabilitation you do not adopt formulas that are incomplete and inaccurate. These, while offering you partial victories of an economic and hedonistic nature, under the banner of a selfish and bitter struggle, may later increase the disappointment of having been deprived of the higher values of the spirit, of having been deprived of your religious personality and of your hope in the life that will not end. Let your aspirations be inspired by the vigor and wisdom that only the Gospel of the divine Worker can give you.

To you, the poor, I have this to say: Remember that you have a supreme friend—Christ who called you blessed, the privileged inheritors of his kingdom. He personified himself in you, so as to turn to you every good person, every generous heart, every man who wishes to save himself by seeking in you Christ the Savior. Yes, strive to raise yourselves: you have a right and duty to do so. Demand the help of a society that wishes to be called civilized, but do not curse either your lot or those who lack sensitivity, for you know that you are rich in the values of Christian patience and redemptive suffering.

A final word, to you who are rich: Remember how severe Christ was in your regard, when he saw you self-satisfied, inactive and selfish. And on the other hand, remember how responsive and grateful he was when he found you thoughtful and generous; he said that not even a cup of cold water given in a Christian spirit would go unrewarded. Perhaps it is your hour: the time for you to open your eyes and hearts to a great new vision not dedicated to the struggles of self-interest, hatred and violence, but dedicated to solicitous and generous love and to true progress.

All this, dear sons and daughters, dear brothers and sisters, is part of the message of the Catholic faith. I have the happy duty to proclaim it here, in the name of Jesus Christ, our Lord and Savior.[1]

1 Paul VI, "Homily at the Mass at the 'Quezon Circle' in Manila" (Manila, Philippines, November 29, 1970). Available at: http://www.vatican.va/content/paul-vi/en/homilies/1970/documents/hf_p-vi_hom_19701129.html

Questions for Reflection

• *This homily is kerygma, the proclamation of the good news here and now. Have you heard many homilies simply about Jesus Christ?*

• *Is there anything that called your attention in a special way?*

• *St. Paul VI was able to bring some concrete applications from the mystery of Christ for those who were present there. What can we learn in terms of "suitable adaptation" for our preaching?*

21

St. John Paul II
(1920–2005)
Inaugural Homily of his Pontificate

For us the name John Paul II—Karol Wojtyla—is a household name. But when, in 1978, he became the first non-Italian pope in more than four hundred years, this son of Poland was a rather unknown man. With what words would he begin a pontificate marked by the recent and short memory of John Paul I, and by the heritage of a century of wars and tensions? His inaugural homily captures the ethos of him who would be popularly acclaimed after his death as John Paul II, the Great.

1.

"You are the Christ, the Son of the living God" (Mt 16:16). These words were spoken by Simon, son of Jonah, in the district of Caesarea Philippi. Yes, he spoke them with his own tongue, with a deeply lived and experienced conviction—but it is not in him that they find their source, their origin: "Because it was not flesh and blood that revealed this to you but my Father in heaven" (Mt 16:17). They were the words of faith.

These words mark the beginning of Peter's mission in the history of salvation, in the history of the people of God. From that moment, from that confession of faith, the sacred history of salvation and of the people of God was bound to take on a new dimension: to express itself in the historical dimension of the Church.

This ecclesial dimension of the history of the people of God takes its origin, in fact is born, from these words of faith, and is linked to the man who uttered them: "You are Peter—the rock—and on you, as on a rock, I will build my Church."

2.

On this day and in this place these same words must again be uttered and listened to:

"You are the Christ, the Son of the living God."

Yes, brothers and sons and daughters, these words first of all.

Their content reveals to our eyes the mystery of the living God, the mystery to which the Son has brought us close. Nobody, in fact, has brought the living God as close to men and revealed him as he alone did. In our knowledge of God, in our journey towards God, we are totally linked to the power of these words: "He who sees me sees the Father." He who is infinite, inscrutable, ineffable, has come close to us in Jesus Christ, the only-begotten Son of God, born of the Virgin Mary in the stable at Bethlehem.

All of you who are still seeking God, all of you who already have the inestimable good fortune to believe, and also you who are tormented by doubt: please listen once again, today in this sacred place, to the words uttered by Simon Peter. In those words is the faith of the Church. In those same words is the new truth, indeed, the ultimate and definitive truth about man: the son of the living God—"You are the Christ, the Son of the living God."

3.

Today the new bishop of Rome solemnly begins his ministry and the mission of Peter. In this city, in fact, Peter completed and fulfilled the mission entrusted to him by the Lord.

The Lord addressed him with these words: "When you were young you put on your own belt and walked where you liked; but when you grow old you will stretch out your hands and somebody else will put a belt round you and take you where you would rather not go" (Jn 21:18).

Peter came to Rome!

What else but obedience to the inspiration received from the Lord guided him and brought him to this city, the heart of the empire? Perhaps the fisherman of Galilee did not want to come here. Perhaps he would have preferred to stay there, on the shores of the lake of Genesareth, with his boat and his nets. But guided by the Lord, obedient to his inspiration, he came here!

According to an ancient tradition (given magnificent literary expression in a novel by Henryk Sienkiewicz), Peter wanted to leave Rome during Nero's persecution. But the Lord intervened: he went to meet him. Peter spoke to him and asked, "*Quo vadis, Domine?*"—"Where are you going, Lord?" And the Lord answered him at once: "I am going to Rome to be crucified again." Peter went back to Rome and stayed here until his crucifixion.

Yes, brothers and sons and daughters, Rome is the See of Peter. Down the centuries new bishops continually succeeded him in this See. Today a new bishop comes to the chair of Peter in Rome, a bishop full of trepidation, conscious of his unworthiness. And how could one not tremble before the greatness of this call and before the universal mission of this See of Rome!

To the See of Peter in Rome there succeeds today a bishop who is not a Roman. A bishop who is a son of Poland. But from this moment he too becomes a Roman. Yes—a Roman. He is a Roman also because he is the son of a nation whose history, from its first dawning, and whose thousand-year-old traditions are marked by a living, strong, unbroken and deeply felt link with the See of Peter, a nation which has ever remained faithful to this See of Rome. Inscrutable is the design of Divine Providence!

4.

In past centuries, when the successor of Peter took possession of his see, the triregnum or tiara was placed on his head. The last pope to be crowned was Paul VI in 1963, but after the solemn coronation ceremony he never used the tiara again and left his successors free to decide in this regard.

Pope John Paul I, whose memory is so vivid in our hearts, did not wish to have the tiara; nor does his successor wish it today. This is not the time to return to a ceremony and an object considered, wrongly, to be a symbol of the temporal power of the popes.

Our time calls us, urges us, obliges us to gaze on the Lord and immerse ourselves in humble and devout meditation on the mystery of the supreme power of Christ himself.

He who was born of the Virgin Mary, the carpenter's son (as he was thought to be), the Son of the living God (confessed by Peter), came to make us all "a kingdom of priests".

The Second Vatican Council has reminded us of the mystery of this power and of the fact that Christ's mission as Priest, Prophet-Teacher and

King continues in the Church. Everyone, the whole people of God, shares in this threefold mission. Perhaps in the past, the tiara, this triple crown, was placed on the pope's head in order to express by that symbol the Lord's plan for his Church, namely that all the hierarchical order of Christ's Church, all "sacred power" exercised in the Church, is nothing other than service, service with a single purpose: to ensure that the whole people of God shares in this threefold mission of Christ and always remains under the power of the Lord; a power that has its source not in the powers of this world but in the mystery of the Cross and Resurrection.

The absolute and yet sweet and gentle power of the Lord responds to the whole depths of the human person, to his loftiest aspirations of intellect, will, and heart. It does not speak the language of force but expresses itself in charity and truth.

The new successor of Peter in the See of Rome, today makes a fervent, humble, and trusting prayer: Christ, make me become and remain the servant of your unique power, the servant of your sweet power, the servant of your power that knows no eventide. Make me be a servant. Indeed, the servant of your servants.

5.

Brothers and sisters, do not be afraid to welcome Christ and accept his power. Help the pope and all those who wish to serve Christ and with Christ's power to serve the human person and the whole of mankind. Do not be afraid. Open wide the doors for Christ. To his saving power open the boundaries of states, economic and political systems, the vast fields of culture, civilization and development. Do not be afraid. Christ knows "what is in man". He alone knows it.

So often today man does not know what is within him, in the depths of his mind and heart. So often he is uncertain about the meaning of his life on this earth. He is assailed by doubt, a doubt which turns into despair. We ask you therefore, we beg you with humility and trust, let Christ speak to man. He alone has words of life, yes, of eternal life.

Precisely today the whole Church is celebrating "World Mission Day"; that is, she is praying, meditating and acting in order that Christ's words of life may reach all people and be received by them as a message of hope, salvation, and total liberation.

6.

I thank all of you here present who have wished to participate in this solemn inauguration of the ministry of the new successor of Peter.

I heartily thank the heads of state, the representatives of the authorities, and the government delegations for so honoring me with their presence.

Thank you, eminent Cardinals of the Holy Roman Church.

I thank you, my beloved brothers in the episcopate.

Thank you, priests.

To you, sisters and brothers, religious of the orders and congregations, I give my thanks.

Thank you, people of Rome.

Thanks to the pilgrims who have come here from all over the world.

Thanks to all of you who are linked with this sacred ceremony by radio and television.

7.

I speak to you, my dear fellow-countrymen, pilgrims from Poland, brother bishops with your magnificent primate at your head, priests, sisters and brothers of the Polish religious congregations—to you representatives of Poland from all over the world.

What shall I say to you who have come from my Krakow, from the see of Saint Stanislaus of whom I was the unworthy successor for fourteen years? What shall I say? Everything that I could say would fade into insignificance compared with what my heart feels, and your hearts feel, at this moment.

So let us leave aside words. Let there remain just great silence before God, the silence that becomes prayer. I ask you: be with me! At Jasna Gora and everywhere. Do not cease to be with the pope who today prays with the words of the poet: "Mother of God, you who defend Bright Czestochowa and shine at Ostrabrama." And these same words I address to you at this particular moment.

8.

That was an appeal and a call to prayer for the new pope, an appeal expressed in the Polish language. I make the same appeal to all the sons and daughters of the Catholic Church. Remember me today and always in your prayers!

To the Catholics of French-speaking lands, I express my complete affection and devotedness. I presume to count upon your unreserved filial assistance. May you advance in the faith! To those who do not share this faith, I also address my respectful and cordial greetings. I trust that their sentiments of goodwill may facilitate the spiritual mission that lies upon me, and which does not lack repercussions for the happiness and peace of the world.

To all of you who speak English I offer in the name of Christ a cordial greeting. I count on the support of your prayers and your goodwill in carrying out my mission of service to the Church and mankind. May Christ give you his grace and his peace, overturning the barriers of division and making all things one in him.

[The Holy Father spoke in similar terms in German, Spanish, Portuguese, Czechoslovakian, Russian, Ukrainian, and Lithuanian].

I open my heart to all my brothers of the Christian Churches and Communities, and I greet in particular you who are here present, in anticipation of our coming personal meeting; but for the moment I express to you my sincere appreciation for your having wished to attend this solemn ceremony.

And I also appeal to all men—to every man (and with what veneration the apostle of Christ must utter this word: "man"!)

— pray for me!

— help me to be able to serve you! Amen.[1]

Questions for Reflection

• *This is an eminently Christocentric homily. With theological depth but concise expression, St. John Paul II pointed out to Christ, highlighting Peter's confession of faith: You are the Christ.*

• *A particularly significant emphasis is that of the absolute and sweet power of Christ. Why is the stress on Christ's power important in the ecclesial and political context of 1978?*

• *This is also a deeply anthropological homily: only in Christ do we know who we are. Do you see the connection with the Second Vatican Council?*

• *"Do not be afraid." This is an excellent example of the memorable power of a few words said in the right way at the right time.*

---

1 John Paul II, "Inaugural Homily of His Pontificate" (St. Peter's Square, Vatican City, October 22, 1978). Available at: http://www.vatican.va/content/john-paul-ii/en/homilies/1978/documents/hf_jp-ii_hom_19781022_inizio-pontificato.html

22

Joseph Cardinal Ratzinger— Benedict XVI (b. 1927)

Homily at the Mass "Pro Eligendo Romano Pontifice"

After the great St. John Paul II passed away, it was hard to think of anyone who could succeed him. One of his closest collaborators was the one chosen for such a heavy task: Joseph Ratzinger. Although many great minds have exercised the office of Peter, few have come to the pontificate with the theological experience of Benedict XVI. This homily preached at the conclave was his last one before his election. Pay attention to his way of illuminating such a decisive occasion with God's Word.

At this moment of great responsibility, let us listen with special attention to what the Lord says to us in his own words. I would like to examine just a few passages from the three readings that concern us directly at this time.

The first one offers us a prophetic portrait of the person of the Messiah—a portrait that receives its full meaning from the moment when Jesus reads the text in the synagogue at Nazareth and says, "Today this Scripture passage is fulfilled in your hearing" (Lk 4:21).

At the core of the prophetic text we find a word which seems contradictory, at least at first sight. The Messiah, speaking of himself, says that he was sent "to announce a year of favor from the Lord and a day of vindication by our God" (Is 61:2). We hear with joy the news of a year of favor: divine mercy puts a limit on evil, as the Holy

Father told us. Jesus Christ is divine mercy in person: encountering Christ means encountering God's mercy.

Christ's mandate has become our mandate through the priestly anointing. We are called to proclaim, not only with our words but also with our lives and with the valuable signs of the sacraments, "the year of favor from the Lord."

But what does the prophet Isaiah mean when he announces "the day of vindication by our God"? At Nazareth, Jesus omitted these words in his reading of the prophet's text; he concluded by announcing the year of favor. Might this have been the reason for the outburst of scandal after his preaching? We do not know.

In any case, the Lord offered a genuine commentary on these words by being put to death on the Cross. St. Peter says: "In his own body he brought your sins to the cross" (1 Pt 2:24). And St. Paul writes in his Letter to the Galatians: "Christ has delivered us from the power of the law's curse by himself becoming a curse for us, as it is written, 'Accursed is anyone who is hanged on a tree.' This happened so that through Christ Jesus the blessing bestowed on Abraham might descend on the Gentiles in Christ Jesus, thereby making it possible for us to receive the promised Spirit through faith" (Gal 3:13–14).

Christ's mercy is not a grace that comes cheap, nor does it imply the trivialization of evil. Christ carries the full weight of evil and all its destructive force in his body and in his soul. He burns and transforms evil in suffering, in the fire of his suffering love. The day of vindication and the year of favor converge in the Paschal Mystery, in the dead and Risen Christ. This is the vengeance of God: he himself suffers for us, in the person of his Son. The more deeply stirred we are by the Lord's mercy, the greater the solidarity we feel with his suffering—and we become willing to complete in our own flesh "what is lacking in the afflictions of Christ" (Col 1:24).

Let us move on to the second reading, the letter to the Ephesians. Here we see essentially three aspects: first of all, the ministries and charisms in the Church as gifts of the Lord who rose and ascended into heaven; then, the maturing of faith and the knowledge of the Son of God as the condition and content of unity in the Body of Christ; and lastly, our common participation in the growth of the Body of Christ, that is, the transformation of the world into communion with the Lord.

Let us dwell on only two points. The first is the journey towards "the maturity of Christ," as the Italian text says, simplifying it slightly. More precisely, in accordance with the Greek text, we should speak of the "measure of

JOSEPH CARDINAL RATZINGER—BENEDICT XVI

the fullness of Christ" that we are called to attain if we are to be true adults in the faith. We must not remain children in faith, in the condition of minors. And what does it mean to be children in faith? St. Paul answers: it means being "tossed here and there, carried about by every wind of doctrine" (Eph 4:14). This description is very timely!

How many winds of doctrine have we known in recent decades, how many ideological currents, how many ways of thinking. The small boat of the thought of many Christians has often been tossed about by these waves—flung from one extreme to another: from Marxism to liberalism, even to libertinism; from collectivism to radical individualism; from atheism to a vague religious mysticism; from agnosticism to syncretism and so forth. Every day new sects spring up, and what St. Paul says about human deception and the trickery that strives to entice people into error (cf. Eph 4:14) comes true.

Today, having a clear faith based on the creed of the Church is often labeled as fundamentalism. Whereas relativism, that is, letting oneself be "tossed here and there, carried about by every wind of doctrine," seems the only attitude that can cope with modern times. We are building a dictatorship of relativism that does not recognize anything as definitive and whose ultimate goal consists solely of one's own ego and desires.

We, however, have a different goal: the Son of God, the true man. He is the measure of true humanism. An "adult" faith is not a faith that follows the trends of fashion and the latest novelty; a mature adult faith is deeply rooted in friendship with Christ. It is this friendship that opens us up to all that is good and gives us a criterion by which to distinguish the true from the false, and deceit from truth.

We must develop this adult faith; we must guide the flock of Christ to this faith. And it is this faith—only faith—that creates unity and is fulfilled in love. On this theme, St. Paul offers us as a fundamental formula for Christian existence some beautiful words, in contrast to the continual vicissitudes of those who, like children, are tossed about by the waves: make truth in love. Truth and love coincide in Christ. To the extent that we draw close to Christ, in our own lives too, truth and love are blended. Love without truth would be blind; truth without love would be like "a clanging cymbal" (1 Cor 13:1).

Let us now look at the Gospel, from whose riches I would like to draw only two small observations. The Lord addresses these wonderful words to us: "I no longer speak of you as slaves.... Instead, I call you friends" (Jn 15:15). We so often feel, and it is true, that we are only useless servants (cf. Lk 17:10).

Yet, in spite of this, the Lord calls us friends, he makes us his friends, he gives us his friendship. The Lord gives friendship a dual definition. There are no secrets between friends: Christ tells us all that he hears from the Father; he gives us his full trust and with trust, also knowledge. He reveals his face and his heart to us. He shows us the tenderness he feels for us, his passionate love that goes even as far as the folly of the Cross. He entrusts himself to us, he gives us the power to speak in his name: "this is my body…", "I forgive you…." He entrusts his body, the Church, to us.

To our weak minds, to our weak hands, he entrusts his truth—the mystery of God the Father, the Son and the Holy Spirit; the mystery of God who "so loved the world that he gave his only Son" (Jn 3:16). He made us his friends—and how do we respond?

The second element Jesus uses to define friendship is the communion of wills. For the Romans *"Idem velle—idem nolle"* [same desires, same dislikes] was also the definition of friendship. "You are my friends if you do what I command you." (Jn 15:14) Friendship with Christ coincides with the third request of the *Our Father:* "Thy will be done on earth as it is in heaven." At his hour in the Garden of Gethsemane, Jesus transformed our rebellious human will into a will conformed and united with the divine will. He suffered the whole drama of our autonomy—and precisely by placing our will in God's hands, he gives us true freedom: "Not as I will, but as you will" (Mt 26:39).

Our redemption is brought about in this communion of wills: being friends of Jesus, to become friends of God. The more we love Jesus, the more we know him, the more our true freedom develops and our joy in being redeemed flourishes. Thank you, Jesus, for your friendship!

The other element of the Gospel to which I wanted to refer is Jesus's teaching on bearing fruit: "It was I who chose you to go forth and bear fruit. Your fruit must endure" (Jn 15:16).

It is here that appears the dynamism of the life of a Christian, an apostle: *I chose you to go forth.* We must be enlivened by a holy restlessness: a restlessness to bring to everyone the gift of faith, of friendship with Christ. Truly, the love and friendship of God was given to us so that it might also be shared with others. We have received the faith to give it to others—we are priests in order to serve others. And we must bear fruit that will endure.

All people desire to leave a lasting mark. But what endures? Money does not. Even buildings do not, nor books. After a certain time, longer or shorter, all these things disappear. The only thing that lasts forever is the human soul, the human person created by God for eternity.

The fruit that endures is therefore all that we have sown in human souls: love, knowledge, a gesture capable of touching hearts, words that open the soul to joy in the Lord. So let us go and pray to the Lord to help us bear fruit that endures. Only in this way will the earth be changed from a valley of tears to a garden of God.

To conclude, let us return once again to the Letter to the Ephesians. The Letter says, with words from Psalm 68, that Christ, ascending into heaven, "gave gifts to men" (Eph 4:8). The victor offers gifts. And these gifts are apostles, prophets, evangelists, pastors and teachers. Our ministry is a gift of Christ to humankind, to build up his body—the new world. We live out our ministry in this way, as a gift of Christ to humanity!

At this time, however, let us above all pray insistently to the Lord that after his great gift of Pope John Paul II, he will once again give us a pastor according to his own heart, a pastor who will guide us to knowledge of Christ, to his love and to true joy. Amen.[1]

Questions for Reflection

• *Here we find yet another way of preparing a homily: a brief meditation on each reading.*

• *In the face of such a momentous decision, then-Cardinal Ratzinger did not speak about political or practical urgencies; he led the cardinal electors into a journey through God's words. Why is this significant?*

• *There are many beautiful spiritual insights in this homily, such as the reflections on friendship with Christ. Are there any other reflections that struck you?*

• *A phrase has been frequently quoted by many: the "dictatorship of relativism." Are there any other quotable phrases in this homily?*

1   Joseph Ratzinger, "Homily at the *Missa Pro Eligendo Pontifice*" (Vatican Basilica, Vatican City, April 18, 2005). Available at: http://www.vatican.va/gpII/documents/homily-pro-eligendo-pontifice_20050418_en.html

23

Pope Francis
(b. 1936)

Homily at the "Missa Pro Ecclesia"
with the Cardinal Electors

Right after the conclave that elected Jorge Mario Bergoglio as the new successor of Peter, the Holy Father offered a Mass for the Church with the cardinals who participated in the election. Needless to say, it was a memorable and important occasion: the first words of the new pope to a small assembly, the cardinal-electors. In this context, Pope Francis spoke brief and powerful words.

In these three readings, I see a common element: that of movement. In the first reading, it is the movement of a journey; in the second reading, the movement of building the Church; in the third, in the Gospel, the movement involved in professing the faith. Journeying, building, professing.

Journeying. "O house of Jacob, come, let us walk in the light of the Lord" (Is 2:5). This is the first thing that God said to Abraham: Walk in my presence and live blamelessly. Journeying: our life is a journey, and when we stop moving, things go wrong. Always journeying, in the presence of the Lord, in the light of the Lord, seeking to live with the blamelessness that God asked of Abraham in his promise.

Building. Building the Church. We speak of stones: stones are solid; but living stones, stones anointed by the Holy Spirit. Building the Church, the Bride of Christ, on the cornerstone that is the Lord himself. This is another kind of movement in our lives: building.

Thirdly, professing. We can walk as much as we want, we can build many things, but if we do not profess Jesus Christ, things go wrong. We may become a charitable NGO, but not the Church, the Bride of the Lord. When we are not walking, we stop moving. When we are not building on the stones, what happens? The same thing that happens to children on the beach when they build sandcastles: everything is swept away, there is no solidity. When we do not profess Jesus Christ, the saying of Léon Bloy comes to mind: "Anyone who does not pray to the Lord prays to the devil." When we do not profess Jesus Christ, we profess the worldliness of the devil, a demonic worldliness.

Journeying, building, professing. But things are not so straightforward, because in journeying, building, professing, there can sometimes be jolts, movements that are not properly part of the journey: movements that pull us back.

This Gospel continues with a situation of a particular kind. The same Peter who professed Jesus Christ now says to him: You are the Christ, the Son of the living God. I will follow you, but let us not speak of the Cross. That has nothing to do with it. I will follow you on other terms, but without the Cross. When we journey without the Cross, when we build without the Cross, when we profess Christ without the Cross, we are not disciples of the Lord, we are worldly: we may be bishops, priests, cardinals, popes, but not disciples of the Lord.

My wish is that all of us, after these days of grace, will have the courage, yes, the courage, to walk in the presence of the Lord, with the Lord's Cross; to build the Church on the Lord's blood which was poured out on the Cross; and to profess the one glory: Christ crucified. And in this way, the Church will go forward.

My prayer for all of us is that the Holy Spirit, through the intercession of the Blessed Virgin Mary, our Mother, will grant us this grace: to walk, to build, to profess Jesus Christ crucified. Amen.[1]

---

1 Francis, "Homily at the 'Missa Pro Ecclesia' with the Cardinal Electors" (Sistine Chapel, Vatican City, March 14, 2013). Available at: http://www.vatican.va/content/francesco/en/homilies/2013/documents/papa-francesco_20130314_omelia-cardinali.html

Questions for Reflection

• *This is a short homily, built on three verbs: journeying, building, and professing. The Holy Father took one idea in each reading and used that as the structure for his speech. Here we find yet another way of composing a homily: a few brief points explained with simple eloquence.*

• *It is a challenging, simple, and deep homily. What do you think about the fact that the audience was the cardinal electors? What can we learn from this?*

Bibliography

Anderson, C. Colt. *Christian Eloquence: Contemporary Doctrinal Preaching*. Chicago: Hillenbrand Books, 2005.

Anderson, Chris. *TED Talks: The Official TED Guide to Public Speaking*. Boston: Mariner Books, 2016.

Augustine. *The City of God* [De Civitate Dei]. XI-XXII. Translated by William Babcock. The Works of Saint Augustine: A Translation for the 21st Century, part 1, vol. 7. Hyde Park, N.Y.: New City Press, 1993.

_____. *Confessions*. Translated by Maria Boulding, OSB. The Works of Saint Augustine, part 1, vol. 1. Hyde Park, N.Y.: New City Press, 2016.

_____. *Confessions*. Translated by Henry Chadwick. Oxford: Oxford University Press, 2008.

_____. *Instructing Beginners in Faith* [De Catechizandis Rudibus]. Translated by Raymond Canning. The Works of Saint Augustine, part 1, vol. 10. New York: New City Press, 2006.

_____. *Teaching Christianity* [De Doctrina Christiana]. Translated by Edmund Hill, OP. The Works of Saint Augustine, part 1, vol. 11. Hyde Park, N.Y.: New City Press, 1996.

_____. *Saint Augustine: Letters II/1 (1–99)*. Translated by Roland Teske, SJ. The Works of Saint Augustine, part 2, vol. 1. Hyde Park, N.Y.: New City Press, 2001.

_____. *Expositions on the Psalms*. Translated by Maria Boulding, OSB. 6 vols. The Works of Saint Augustine, part 3, vols. 15–21. Brooklyn, N.Y.: New City Press, 2000–2004.

_____. *Homilies on the First Epistle of St. John*. Translated by Boniface Ramsey. The Works of Saint Augustine, part 3, vol. 14. Hyde Park, N.Y.: New City Press, 2008.

_____. *Sermons*. Translated by Edmund Hill, OP. 11 vols. The Works of Saint Augustine, part 3, vols. 1–11. Brooklyn, N.Y.: New City Press, 1990–1997.

_____. *Tractates on the Gospel of John*. Translated by John W. Rettig. 5 vols. Fathers of the Church 78, 79, 88, 90, 92. Washington, D.C.: The Catholic University of America Press, 1988–1995.

Balz, Horst, and Gerhard Schneider, eds. *Exegetical Dictionary of the New Testament*. Grand Rapids, Mich.: Eerdmans Publishing, 1990.

Bass, Alden. "Preaching in the Early Church." In *A Handbook for Catholic Preaching*, edited by Edward Foley, 51–61. Collegeville, Minn.: Liturgical Press, 2016.

Bellinger, Karla J. *Connecting Pulpit and Pew: Breaking Open the Conversation about Catholic Preaching*. Collegeville, Minn.: Liturgical Press, 2014.

Benedict XVI. *Homily at the Easter Vigil of 2006*. April 15, 2006. https://w2.vatican.va/content/benedict-xvi/en/homilies/2006/documents/hf_ben-xvi_hom_20060415_veglia-pasquale.html

_____. Post-Synodal Apostolic Exhortation *Sacramentum Caritatis* [Sacrament of Charity]. February 22, 2007.

_____. *Homily at the Easter Vigil of 2007*. April 7, 2007. https://w2.vatican.va/content/benedict-xvi/en/homilies/2007/documents/hf_ben-xvi_hom_20070407_veglia-pasquale.html

_____. *Jesus of Nazareth: From the Baptism in the Jordan to the Transfiguration*. New York: Doubleday, 2007.

_____. *Homily at the Easter Vigil of 2008*. March 22, 2008. http://www.vatican.va/content/benedict-xvi/en/homilies/2008/documents/hf_ben-xvi_hom_20080322_veglia-pasquale.html

_____. *Homily at the Easter Vigil of 2009*. April 11, 2009. http://www.vatican.va/content/benedict-xvi/en/homilies/2009/documents/hf_ben-xvi_hom_20090411_veglia-pasquale.html

_____. *Homily at the Easter Vigil of 2010*. April 3, 2010. https://w2.vatican.va/content/benedict-xvi/en/homilies/2010/documents/hf_ben-xvi_hom_20100403_veglia-pasquale.html

_____. Post-Synodal Apostolic Exhortation *Verbum Domini* [Word of the Lord]. September 30, 2010.

_____. *Homily at the Easter Vigil of 2012*. April 7, 2012. https://w2.vatican.va/content/benedict-xvi/en/homilies/2012/documents/hf_ben-xvi_hom_20120407_veglia-pasquale.html

Bernanos, Georges. *The Diary of a Country Priest*. New York: Caroll & Graf Publishers, 2002.

Bizzell, Patricia, Bruce Herzberg, and Robin Reames. *The Rhetorical Tradition: Readings from Classical Times to the Present*. Boston: Bedford Books, 2020.

Bossuet, Jacques-Bénigne. *Ouevres complètes de Bossuet*. Vol. 9. Edited by *François* Lachat. Paris: Vives, 1862.

Bouchard, OP, Charles. "How to Listen to the Sunday Homily." *Scripture in Church* 46, no. 183 (2016): 117–23.

Bouyer, Louis, and Charles Underhill Quinn. *Dictionary of Theology*. New York: Desclée, 1966.

Brown, Peter. *Augustine of Hippo: A Biography. A New Edition with an Epilogue*. Berkeley: University of California Press, 2000.

_____. *The Cult of the Saints: Its Rise and Function in Latin Christianity*. Chicago: University of Chicago Press, 2015.

Bullivant, Stephen. *Mass Exodus: Catholic Disaffiliation in Britain and America since Vatican II*. Oxford: Oxford University Press, 2019.

Burghardt, Walter J., SJ. *Preaching: The Art and the Craft*. New York: Paulist Press, 1987.

Cameron, Michael. *Christ Meets Me Everywhere: Augustine's Early Figurative Exegesis*. Oxford: Oxford University Press, 2012.

Cameron, Peter, OP. *Why Preach: Encountering Christ in God's Word*. San Francisco: Ignatius Press, 2009.

Cano, Melchor. *De Locis Theologicis*. Salamanca: Mathias Gastius, 1563.

Cantalamessa, Raniero. *First Sermon of Advent to the Roman Curia*. December 4, 2020. http://www.cantalamessa.org/?p=3890&lang=en

Canons and Decrees of the Council of Trent. Translated by Theodore Alois Buckley. London: George Routledge, 1851.

Cardó, Daniel. *The Cross and the Eucharist in Early Christianity: A Theological and Liturgical Investigation*. Cambridge: Cambridge University Press, 2019.

_____. *What Does It Mean to Believe? Faith in the Thought of Joseph Ratzinger*. Steubenville, Ohio: Emmaus Academic, 2020.

Catholic Church. *Code of Canon Law*. Washington, D.C.: Canon Law Society of America, 1983.

Chadwick, Henry. *Augustine of Hippo: A Life*. Oxford: Oxford University Press, 2009.

Chapell, Bryan. *Christ-Centered Preaching: Redeeming the Expository Sermon*, 3rd ed. Grand Rapids, Mich.: Baker Academic, 2018.

Chesterton, G. K. *What's Wrong with the World*. San Francisco: Ignatius Press, 1994.

Cicero. *Brutus*. Translated by G. L. Hendrickson. Loeb Classical Library 342. Cambridge, Mass.: Harvard University Press, 1952.

Congar, Yves M. J., OP. "Théologie." In *Dictionnaire de Théologie Catholique*. Vol. 15. Paris: Librairie Letouzey et Ané, 1929.

Congregation for Divine Worship and the Discipline of the Sacraments. Instruction *Redemptionis Sacramentum*. Washington, D.C.: USCCB, 2004.

_____. *Homiletic Directory*. Washington, D.C.: USCCB, 2015.

Conley, Thomas M. *Rhetoric in the European Tradition*. Chicago: University of Chicago Press, 1990.

Connors, Michael E., CSC, ed. *Effective Preaching: Bringing People into an Encounter with God*. Chicago: Liturgy Training Publications, 2018.

Corbon, Jean. *The Wellspring of Worship*. San Francisco: Ignatius Press, 2005.

Dalla Costa, Claudio. *Avete Finito di Farci la Predica? Riflessioni Laicali Sulle Omelie*. Cantalupa: Effatà Editrice, 2011.

Dei Verbum [Dogmatic Constitution on Divine Revelation]. November 18, 1965. In *The Sixteen Documents of Vatican II,* edited by Marianne Lorraine Trouve. Boston: Pauline Books and Media, 1999.

DeLeers, Stephen Vincent. *Written Text Becomes Living Word: The Vision and Practice of Sunday Preaching*. Collegeville, Minn.: Liturgical Press, 2004.

Dillon, Michele. *Postsecular Catholicism: Relevance and Renewal*. Oxford: Oxford University Press, 2018.

DuPont, Anthony. *Preaching in the Patristic Era: Sermons, Preachers, and Audiences in the Latin West.* Leiden: Brill, 2018.

Edwards, O. C., Jr. *Elements of Homiletic: A Method for Preparing to Preach.* Collegeville, Minn.: Liturgical Press, 1990.

_____. *A History of Preaching.* Nashville, Tenn.: Abingdon Press, 2004.

Eudes, John. *The Priest: His Dignity and Obligations.* Translated by W. Leo Murphy. Fitzwilliam, N.H.: Loreto Publications, 2008.

Exegetical Dictionary of the New Testament. Edited by Horst Balz and Gerhard Schneider. Grand Rapids, Mich.: Eerdmans Publishing, 1990.

Foley, Edward, ed. *A Handbook for Catholic Preaching.* Collegeville, Minn.: Liturgical Press, 2016.

Francis. Apostolic Exhortation *Evangelii Gaudium* [The Joy of the Gospel]. November 24, 2013.

Gardeil, Ambroise. "Lieux Théologiques." In *Dictionnaire de Théologie Catholique.* 9:712–42. Paris: Librairie Letouzey et Ané, 1929.

Gaudium et Spes [Pastoral Constitution on the Church in the Modern World]. December 7, 1965. In *The Sixteen Documents of Vatican II,* edited by Marianne Lorraine Trouve.

Gil, Alberto. *Cómo Convencer Eficazmente: Hacia una Retórica Anclada en la Personalidad y en los Valores.* Madrid: Palabra, 2014.

Glover, Dennis. *The Art of Great Speeches and Why We Remember Them.* Cambridge: Cambridge University Press, 2011.

Grasso, Domenico, SJ. *Proclaiming God's Message: A Study in the Theology of Preaching.* Notre Dame, Ind.: University of Notre Dame Press, 1965.

Gregory I. *Pastoral Care.* Translated by Henry Davis, SJ. Ancient Christian Writers 11. Westminster, Md.: Newman Press, 1950.

_____. *Forty Gospel Homilies.* Translated by David Hurst, OSB. Cistercian Studies 123. Kalamazoo, Mich.: Cistercian Publications, 1990.

Harmless, William. *Augustine in His Own Words.* Washington, D.C.: The Catholic University of America Press, 2010.

_____. "A Love Supreme: Augustine's 'Jazz' of Theology." *Augustinian Studies* 43 (2012): 149–77.

_____. *Augustine and the Catechumenate.* Collegeville, Minn.: Liturgical Press, 2014.

Harris, Daniel E. *We Speak the Word of the Lord: A Practical Plan for More Effective Preaching.* Chicago: ACTA Publications, 2001.

Harrison, Carol. *The Art of Listening in the Early Church.* Oxford: Oxford University Press, 2013.

Hunter, David G., ed. *Preaching in the Patristic Age: Studies in Honor of Walter J. Burghardt, S.J.* New York: Paulist Press, 1989.

Ignatius of Antioch. *Letters.* In *1 Clement, II Clement, Ignatius, Polycarp, Didache..* Vol. 1 of *The Apostolic Fathers.* Translated by Bart D. Ehrman. Loeb Classical Library 24. Cambridge, Mass.: Harvard University Press, 2003.

International Committee on English in the Liturgy. *General Instruction of the Roman Missal*. Washington, D.C.: USCCB, 2003.

Irenaeus of Lyon. *Against the Heresies Book 1*. Translated and annotated by Dominic J. Unger, OFM Cap. Ancient Christian Writers 55. New York: Paulist Press, 1992.

_____. *Against the Heresies Book 3.*. Translated and annotated by Dominic J. Unger, OFM Cap. Ancient Christian Writers 64. Mahwah, N.J.: Newman Press, 2012.

John Chrysostom. *On the Priesthood*. In *Saint Chrysostom: On the Priesthood, Ascetic Treatises, Select Homilies and Letters, Homilies on the Statues*. Translated by William R. W. Stephens. Vol. 9 of *A Select Library of the Nicene and Post Nicene Fathers of the Christian Church, First Series*. Edited by Philip Schaff. New York: Christian Literature, 1889.

John Paul II. Apostolic Exhortation *Pastores Dabo Vobis* [I Shall Give You Shepherds]. March 15, 1992.

Jungmann, Joseph A. *The Mass of the Roman Rite: Its Origins and Development*. Vol. 2. Notre Dame, Ind.: Christian Classics, 2012.

Justin Martyr. "First Apology." In *Writings of Saint Justin Martyr*. Translated by Thomas B. Falls. New York: Christian Heritage, 1948.

_____. "Second Apology." In *Writings of Saint Justin Martyr*. Translated by Thomas B. Falls. New York: Christian Heritage, 1948.

Kennedy, George. *A New History of Classical Rhetoric*. Princeton, N.J.: Princeton University Press, 1994.

Lausberg, Heinrich, George Alexander Kennedy, Matthew T. Bliss, and David E. Orton, eds. *Handbook of Literary Rhetoric: A Foundation for Literary Study*. Leiden: Brill, 1998.

Lawless, George, OSA. "Preaching." In *Augustine through the Ages: An Encyclopedia*, edited by Allan D. Fitzgerald, 675–77. Grand Rapids, Mich.: Eerdmans, 1999.

Leith, Sam. *Words Like Loaded Pistols: Rhetoric from Aristotle to Obama*. New York: Basic Books, 2012.

Leiva-Merikakis, Erasmo. *Fire of Mercy, Heart of the Word: Meditations on the Gospel According to St. Matthew*. Vol. 1. San Francisco: Ignatius Press, 1996.

Lewis, C. S. *Mere Christianity*. New York: HarperOne, 2000.

"Life of Adam and Eve" [Latin]. In *The Old Testament Pseudepigrapha*. Edited and translated by James Charlesworth. Vol. 2. New York: Doubleday, 1985.

Liftin, Duane. *St. Paul's Theology of Proclamation: 1 Corinthians 1–4 and Greco-Roman Rhetoric*. Cambridge: Cambridge University Press, 1994.

Lischer, Richard, ed. *The Company of Preachers: Wisdom on Preaching, Augustine to the Present*. Grand Rapids, Mich.: Eerdmans Publishing, 2002.

Liske, Thomas V. *Effective Preaching*. New York: The Macmillan Company, 1951.

Lubac, Henri de, SJ. *Medieval Exegesis: The Four Senses of Scripture*. Vol. 1. Edinburgh: T&T Clark, 1998.

Lumen Gentium [Dogmatic Constitution on the Church]. November 21, 1964. In *The Sixteen Documents of Vatican II*, edited by Marianne Lorraine Trouve.

Mayer, Wendy. "Homiletics." In *The Oxford Handbook of Early Christian Studies*, edited by Susan Ashbrook Harvey and David G. Hunter, 565–83. Oxford: Oxford University Press, 2011.

McBride, Alfred. *How to Make Homilies Better, Briefer, and Bolder: Tips from a Master Homilist.* Huntington, Ind.: Our Sunday Visitor, 2007.

National Conference of Catholic Bishops. Bishops' Committee on Priestly Life and Ministry. *Fulfilled in Your Hearing: The Homily in the Sunday Assembly.* Washington, D.C.: United States Catholic Conference, 1982.

Newman, John Henry. "Sermon 15. The Theory of Developments in Religious Doctrine." In *Fifteen Sermons Preached before the University of Oxford.* Edited by James David Earnest and Gerard Tracey. Oxford: Oxford University Press, 2006.

———. *The Idea of a University.* Notre Dame, Ind.: University of Notre Dame Press, 1982.

Ong, Walter J. *Orality and Literacy: The Technologizing of the Word.* London: Methuen, 1982.

Origen. *Homilies on Leviticus.* Translated by Gary Wayne Barkley. Washington, D.C.: The Catholic University of America Press, 1990.

Pascal, Blaise. *Pensées.* In *Blaise Pascal: Pensées and Other Writings.* Translated by Honor Levi. Oxford: Oxford University Press, 1995.

Pasquarello III, Michael. *We Speak Because We Have First Been Spoken: A Grammar of the Preaching Life.* Grand Rapids, Mich.: Eerdmans Publishing, 2009.

Paul VI. Encyclical Letter *Mysterium Fidei* [Mystery of Faith]. September 3, 1965.

Pellegrino, Michele. General Introduction to *Augustine: Sermons I (1–19)*, 13–136. Edited by John E. Rotelle, OSA, and translated by Edmund Hill, OP. Vol. 1 of *Augustine: Sermons.* The Works of Saint Augustine, part 3, vol. 1. Brooklyn, N.Y.: New City Press, 1990.

Quintilian. *Institutio Oratoria.* Translated by Harold E. Butler. Vol. 1. Loeb Classical Library 124. Cambridge, Mass.: Harvard University Press, 1953.

Rahner, Hugo, SJ. *A Theology of Proclamation.* New York: Herder and Herder, 1968.

Ratzinger, Joseph. *Introduction to Christianity.* Translated by J. R. Foster and Michael J. Miller. San Francisco: Ignatius Press, 2004.

———. *Called to Communion: Understanding the Church Today.* Translated by Adrian Walker. San Francisco: Ignatius Press, 1991.

———. *Storia e Dogma.* Milan: Jaca Book, 1993.

———. *The Nature and Mission of Theology: Approaches to Understanding its Role in the Light of Present Controversy.* San Francisco: Ignatius Press, 1995.

———. *Gospel, Catechesis, Catechism: Sidelights on the Catechism of the Catholic Church.* San Francisco: Ignatius Press, 1995.

———. *Intervento del Cardinale Joseph Ratzinger Durante il Convegno dei Catechisti e dei Docenti di Religione.* Address delivered for the Jubilee of Catechists. December 10, 2000.

———. *The God of Jesus Christ: Meditations on the Triune God.* San Francisco: Ignatius Press, 2008.

_____. *Dogma and Preaching: Applying Christian Doctrine to Christian Life.* Translated by Michael J. Miller and Matthew J. O'Connell. San Francisco: Ignatius Press, 2011.

Sacrosanctum Concilium [Constitution on the Sacred Liturgy]. December 4, 1963. In *The Sixteen Documents of Vatican II,* edited by Marianne Lorraine Trouve.

Sanlon, Peter T. *Augustine's Theology of Preaching.* Minneapolis: Fortress Press, 2014.

Sarah, Robert. *The Power of Silence: Against the Dictatorship of Noise.* San Francisco: Ignatius Press, 2017.

Semmelroth, Otto, SJ. *The Preaching Word: On the Theology of Proclamation.* New York: Herder and Herder, 1965.

Sertillanges, A. D., OP. *L'Orateur Chrétien: Traité de Prédication.* Juvisy: Les Éditions du Cerf, 1930.

Smith, Christian, and Melinda Lundquist. *Soul Searching: The Religious and Spiritual Lives of American Teenagers.* Oxford: Oxford University Press, 2011.

Soames, Nicholas. "Sweat and Tears Made Winston Churchill's Name." *The Telegraph.* May 4, 2011. https://winstonchurchill.org/resources/in-the-media/churchill-in-the-news/sweat-and-tears-made-winston-churchills-name/

Söhngen, Gottlieb. *Symbol und Wirklichkeit im Kultmysterium.* Bonn: Hanstein, 1937.

Stewart-Sykes, Alistair. *From Prophecy to Preaching: A Search for the Origins of the Christian Homily.* Leiden: Brill, 2001.

Stravinskas, Peter M. J. *Our Sunday Visitor's Catholic Encyclopedia.* Huntington, Ind.: Our Sunday Visitor, 1991.

Theological Dictionary of the New Testament. Edited by Gerhard Kittel, Geoffrey W. Bromiley, and Gerhard Friedrich. Grand Rapids, Mich.: Eerdmans, 1964–1976.

Thomas Aquinas. *The Academic Sermons.* Translated by Mark Robin Hoogland, CP. Fathers of the Church Medieval Continuation 11. Washington, D.C.: The Catholic University of America Press, 2010.

Topping, Ryan N. S. *The Elements of Rhetoric: How to Write and Speak Clearly & Persuasively—A Guide for Students, Teachers, Politicians & Preachers.* Kettering, Ohio: Angelico Press, 2016.

Trouve, Marianne Lorraine, ed. *The Sixteen Documents of Vatican II.* Boston: Pauline Books & Media, 1999.

United States Conference of Catholic Bishops. *Preaching the Mystery of the Faith: The Sunday Homily* Washington, D.C.: USCCB, 2012.

Van der Meer, Frederik. *Augustine the Bishop: Church and Society at the Dawn of the Middle Ages.* Translated by Brian Battershaw and G. R. Lamb. New York: Harper & Row, 1961.

Waznak, Robert P., SS. *An Introduction to the Homily.* Collegeville, Minn.: Liturgical Press, 1998.

Whitfield, Joshua J. *The Crisis of Bad Preaching: Redeeming the Heart and Way of the Catholic Preacher.* Notre Dame, Ind.: Ave Maria Press, 2019.

Williams, Rowan. *On Augustine.* London: Bloomsbury, 2016.

Wilson, Paul Scott, ed. *The New Interpreter's Handbook of Preaching*. Nashville, Tenn.: Abingdon Press, 2008.

SOURCES FOR THE HOMILETIC READER (IN ORDER OF APPEARANCE)

Gregory of Nazianzus. "Oration 38—On the Nativity of Christ." In *S. Cyril of Jerusalem, S. Gregory Nazianzen*. Translated by Charles Gordon Browne and James Edward Swallow, 350–351. Vol. 7 of *A Select Library of the Nicene and Post-Nicene Fathers of the Christian Church, Second Series*, edited by Philip Schaff and Henry Wace. New York: Christian Literature Company, 1894.

Ambrose of Milan. "On the Death of his Brother Satyrus." In *St. Ambrose: Select Works and Letters*. Translated by Henry de Romestin, Eugene de Romestin, and Henry T. F. Duckworth, 159–162. Vol. 10 of *Nicene and Post-Nicene Fathers, Second Series*, edited by Schaff and Wace. 1896.

John Chrysostom. "First Homily on Eutropius, the Eunuch, Patrician and Consul." In *Saint Chrysostom: On the Priesthood, Ascetic Treatises, Select Homilies and Letters, Homilies on the Statues*. Translated by William R. W. Stephens, 249–252. Vol. 9 of *A Select Library of the Nicene and Post-Nicene Fathers of the Christian Church, First Series*, edited by Philip Schaff. New York: Christian Literature Company, 1889.

Leo the Great. "Sermon 74—On the Ascension." In *St. Leo the Great Sermons*. Translated by Jane Patricia Freeland, CSJB and Agnes Josephine Conway, SSJ, 325–29. Fathers of the Church 93. Washington, D.C.: The Catholic University of America Press, 1996. Bernard of Clairvaux, *Sermons on the Canticle of Canticles*. Translated from the Original Latin by a priest of Mount Melleray. Vol. II (Dublin, Belfast, Cork, Waterford: Browne and Nolan, 1920), 196–200.

Thomas Aquinas. "Sermon 6—Celum et Terra Transibunt." In *The Academic Sermons*. Translated by Mark-Robin Hoogland, CP. Fathers of the Church Medieval Continuation 11. Washington, D.C.: The Catholic University of America Press, 2010.

Borromeo, Charles. "On Praying." In *Saint Charles Borromeo (Acta Ecclesiae Mediolanensis, Mediolani 1599, 1177–1178)*. *Taken from the Office of Readings for the Memorial of St. Charles Borromeo on November 4*.

Bossuet, Jean-Bénigne. "Sermon on Death." In *Oeuvres Oratoires*, édition critique de l'abbé Joseph Lebarq, revue et augmentée par Charles Urbain et Eugène Levesque (Paris: Desclée, 1926), 4, 262–81. Translated by Christopher O. Blum. Used with permission.

Newman, John Henry. "On the Mental Sufferings of Our Lord in His Passion." In *Discourses Addressed to Mixed Congregations*. New Impression. New York: Longmans, Green, and Co., 1906.

Knox, Ronald Arbuthnott. "Homily on the Sacred Heart of Jesus." University and Anglican Sermons of Ronald A. Knox Together with Sermons Preached on Various Occasions. Edited by Philip Caraman, 342–45. New York: Sheed and Ward, 1963.

Paul VI. "Homily at the Mass at the 'Quezon Circle' in Manila." November 29, 1970. http://www.vatican.va/content/paul-vi/en/homilies/1970/documents/hf_p-vi_hom_19701129.html

John Paul II. "Inaugural Homily of His Pontificate." October 22, 1978. http://www.vatican.
     va/content/john-paul-ii/en/homilies/1978/documents/hf_jp-ii_hom_19781022_
     inizio-pontificato.html

Ratzinger, Joseph Cardinal (Benedict XVI). "Homily at the Mass 'Pro Eligendo
     Romano Pontifice'," April 18, 2005. http://www.vatican.va/gpII/documents/
     homily-pro-eligendo-pontifice_20050418_en.html

Francis. "Homily at the 'Missa Pro Ecclesia' with the Cardinal Electors." March 14, 2013.
     http://www.vatican.va/content/francesco/en/homilies/2013/documents/papa-
     francesco_20130314_omelia-cardinali.html

Index